I0778282

The Humane
Particulars

Studies in Rhetoric/Communication
Thomas W. Benson, Series Editor

The Humane Particulars

The Collected Letters of William Carlos Williams and Kenneth Burke

Edited by James H. East

University of South Carolina Press

Published in Columbia, South Carolina, by the
University of South Carolina Press

Manufactured in the United States of America

23 22 21 20 19   6 5 4 3 2

Library of Congress Cataloging-in-Publication Data

Williams, William Carlos, 1883–1963.
   The humane particulars : the collected letters of William Carlos Williams and Kenneth Burke / edited by James H. East.
      p. cm. — (Studies in rhetoric/communication)
   Includes bibliographical references and index.
   ISBN 1-57003-507-5 (cloth : alk. paper)
   1. Williams, William Carlos, 1883–1963—Correspondence. 2. Poets, American—20th century—Correspondence. 3. Burke, Kenneth, 1897– —Correspondence. 4. Critics—United States—Correspondence. I. Burke, Kenneth, 1897– II. East, James H., 1951–
III. Title. IV. Series.
PS3545.I544 Z497 2003
811'.52—dc21   2003005003

Boon, Teach, Uncle Jim, and The Phene

Lovers, Mentors, Projectors, Boatswain, Bacon Hogs, indeed!

Contents

Series Editor's Preface

In *The Humane Particulars*, editor James East brings together the collected letters of two major figures of American modernism, William Carlos Williams (1883–1963) and Kenneth Burke (1897–1993). The long personal and literary friendship between the two men began in 1921 and is documented here with almost two hundred and sixty letters, ending with a 1963 letter from Burke to Williams's wife Florence, written from Florida, where he had heard on the radio the news of Williams's death. Burke wrote that "Bill's work is eternally fresh. And he is written into the very constitution of our country." The men's self consciousness of their relationship as a both a literary and a personal friendship, and of their place in American cultural history, had been established in the very first letter, by Williams, writing from Rutherford, New Jersey, in January 1921: "I met that Russian, Gilbert Seldes, ten days ago for the first time. He told me that *The Dial* was preparing to use your essay on my place in our America. He did not, most positively, say that you would put me in my place. They are also printing two new poems of mine. Damn you, if your article slams me my poems will show you up, so there!"

Williams and Burke at once proclaimed to each other that they had much in common, and this they celebrated across the decades. The two also sharply celebrated their differences, especially as Burke's work took him in theoretical and philosophical directions and as Williams insisted on his loyalty to particulars. Williams, who carried on his career as a poet while at the same time serving as a family doctor, wrote in his epic poem "Paterson": "No ideas but in things."

Early in the correspondence, Williams wrote to Burke that "I have long wanted to have a correspondence with someone very dissimilar to myself, the thing to be planned as a dialogue criticizing the universe (literature), which might be published later" (March 22, 1921). What followed was a correspondence richly embodying the dialogue Williams hoped for, and one that documents, as well, an abiding friendship. James East has done us all a great service in finally bringing to publication this dialogue criticizing the universe.

Thomas W. Benson

Acknowledgments

Many thanks to all those who have contributed time, information, facility, criticism, or financial support to this project: Stephanie East, Marjorie East, Tom Kirby-Smith and the graduate faculty of English at the University of North Carolina at Greensboro, Charles Davis, Michael Burke, William E. Williams, Robert A. Newton, the late Charles Mann (Pattee Library at Penn State), Jack Selzer (Penn State), Miriam Marty Clark (Auburn), David Blakesley (Purdue), Barry Blose (USC Press), the late Robert M. Crunden (Texas), the staffs of the libraries at Yale University, Pennsylvania State University, Wake Forest University, the University of North Carolina at Chapel Hill and Greensboro, the University of Maine at Orono, the University of Indiana at Bloomington, and Salem College. I should like to extend a special thanks and cover note to Herb Simons, Paul Mariani, Tilly Warnock, Paul Jay, William Irmscher, Wendell Harris, Robert Trapp, Sonja Foss, and Karen Foss, whose compositions were indispensable as an introduction to the works of Kenneth Burke. Any interpretations of Burke's work that may appear to have been discovered by the editor belong to the aforementioned; all other errors are mine.

Introduction

The first encounter between William Carlos Williams and Kenneth Burke occurred on January 2, 1921. We have the circumstances and much of the content of their conversation preserved for us in Matthew Josephson's *Life Among the Surrealists*.[1] They, with Josephson and Robert McAlmon, made their way through "the great swamp," where they saw the Hackensack River, eastward, winding through the meadowlands below; to the west, closely parallel to the roadway, the Passaic River headed toward its union with the Hackensack into Newark Bay. By contrast, in the foreground they witnessed "the mean streets of the industrial suburbs . . . dilapidated factories and warehouses, grimy railway yards, coal bunkers, and mountains of rubble and tin cans; in short, one of the ugliest and most blighted areas in all America."[2] As early as 1918, Burke had heard of Williams through a correspondence with his lifelong friend, Malcolm Cowley, where in a note sent from Harvard in March of that year Cowley wrote: "And, oh God, read Al Que Quiere! (Williams). It is the framework and the suggestion of much good poetry, much excellent, super excellent poetry."[3] Apparently the enthusiasm spread; a couple of years later he wrote to Cowley: "I am thinking of hatching up some sort of a club-article on Eliot, Williams, and Masters."[4] Instead, his interest blossomed into a full-fledged manifesto: "Our school is INTEGRALISM," he wrote in September 1920, "the emphasis of the unit, the vision of art as a succession of units or integers. . . . Willy-Nilly, W.C.W., is our first Integralist and we should write and tell him so."[5]

Of the many topics they covered that day Josephson remembered "contact" was central to their talk. "Above all [Williams] desired to 'contact' nature and life as swiftly and as directly as possible, without much rationalizing or analyzing, and to give evidence of such contact in racy native speech."[6] Though we have only this excerpt as a record of what transpired on their first meeting, McAlmon's letter to Williams near the end of 1921 preserves, in content and tone, what must surely be a significant remnant of the interchange.

The idea of contact simply means that when one writes they write about something, and not to write "literature" because it is a day of publications, and publishing houses. Burke wanting a manifesto—hasn't he, or anybody else, copulated, desired, thought, detested, been abused, enough by actual experience, to say something about existence that has a quality that is his own . . . it isn't lack of contact that condemns most writing. . . . It's lack of an individual quality that makes the stuff worth reading, and presence of too much desire to be a "literary figure." And when people justify "conscious art" and an eternal talk about "form" and technique, by mentioning the painstaking Flaubert, they overlook the fact that Flaubert's bigness rests a great deal more upon the fact that he created his characters, understood the psychology of people, and got the drama of his drab situations. . . . Burke would say that was howling about the great throb drama of humanity. . . . But the situation is made art by the understanding and ability to note how the characters spoken of react emotionally. Flaubert was simply able to be both a formalist—which means a good deal pedantic regarding "style"—and an observing psychologist and intelligence.[7]

Unaffected by McAlmon's dismissal, Williams's enthusiastic reception of Burke, as best we might conjecture, still echoed in a letter he sent Burke complimenting an essay he had recently placed:

Laforgue is a new Laforgue in America. Our appreciation of him creates him for us and this I feel in your work. You have taken what you want from the master in order to satisfy your needs and your needs are the product of your environment. (I wish to God I dared print this note somewhere in the next issue where your paper will be used. What do you say?) You fairly illustrate what Bob and I mean by contact.[8]

As evening approached, they stopped at a tavern and drank bootleg beer. The practicing physician avoided drinking, but he continued to tell them tales of his medical practice in Rutherford, peopling them with the same figures who would later appear in his modern epic, *Paterson.* Josephson remembered that toward the end of this first meeting, the conversation sputtered; they had all grown tired of "tramping for hours amid the dun winter scenery and pungent stench."[9] In any event, the meeting, there in the surroundings they all hoped to rejuvenate with their ambitious literary projects, had been a successful one. Indeed, until Williams's death forty-two years later, he and Burke remained close literary and personal friends who contributed a great deal to the shape and tenor of the modernist scene in America.

Before going on to outline the patterns of their relationship and the mutual lines of influence on aesthetic or creative matters disclosed in these letters, a word about the provenance and physical appearance of them may be helpful. The collection comprises nearly two hundred and sixty letters. As John C. Thirlwall noted in the introduction of his *Selected Letters of William Carlos Williams* (1957), Williams wrote more to Burke than to any other correspondent.[10] Williams's estate sold their lot, sixty-nine letters from Burke to Williams, to the Beinecke Rare Book and Manuscript Library at Yale sometime in the early sixties, but according to the curator of American Literature there, Patricia Willis, the exact details of the purchase were unavailable.[11] One hundred seventy-seven letters were sold to the Pattee Library of The Pennsylvania State University in 1969. Charles Mann, the late Chief of Special Collections, reported that their portion, from Williams to Burke, was purchased at the prompting of Burke's long-time friend at Penn State, Professor Henry Sams.[12] Nearly all from the Pattee Library still have envelopes with them, although many had become separated from their letters, a fact which made it difficult to sequence the ones without dated headings. Nevertheless, the envelopes were useful in determining points of origin and termination, a task made easier by the fact that they both had occupied essentially one household —either at Rutherford or Andover, New Jersey—their entire lives. Fortunately, a majority of the letters in both collections were typed on standard eight-and-one-half-by-eleven sheets; a few are handwritten and many of those are either on post cards or, as in Williams's case, prescription pad paper. One errant letter, November 21, 1955, was discovered by Michael Burke while he was closing the affairs of his father in Andover.[13] Another, March 5, 1963, Burke's note to Florence Williams upon the death of her husband, was in the Williams manuscripts housed at The Lilly Library at Indiana University.[14]

Interesting patterns of proportion and frequency occur throughout their forty-two-year correspondence as well as recurrent motifs. Williams's share of the exchange comprises more than twice that of Burke's, which leads us to conclude, since many of Williams's letters clearly are responses to missing queries, that either Burke had already made selections of valuable letters and discarded the rest, or that there are letters as yet unearthed. The patterns of frequency provoke curiosity as well: whereas in the nine years between 1921 and 1929, fifty-four letters were exchanged, in the next fourteen years, 1930 to 1943, only thirty-eight were exchanged, twelve of these occurring in one year, 1933. In the last eighteen years of their correspondence, 1945 to 1962, over 150 letters were exchanged. The contents of the letters in these periods suggest three general stages to their relationship, hence the editorial grouping of the collection. Although a close examination reveals occasions of distance between the two within every decade, *in toto* they show us that Williams and

Burke were fast friends during the experimental twenties, preoccupied by their individual and divergent projects and busy lives in the thirties and early forties, and reunited after World War II.

In an effort to explain the anomaly of the smallest block of letters, 1930–1943, we will discover that the contents in no way suggest that their relationship had undergone a rupture; rather, it seems that their domestic and professional lives, divergent aesthetic interests, and geopolitical circumstances simply got in the way. We have little evidence of their having visited each other much during those years. Even though the Burkes were living in the city during the winter and thus close enough to dispense with the necessity of writing, at least four of the letters were posted during winter months. Additionally, the tone in their correspondences during this period sounds remote: in answer to Burke's news about a house for sale near his Andover retreat, Williams writes (February 16, 1930) that he and his wife were no longer searching for a summer cottage; an April 1930 letter asks Ken "Watchadoin these days?" On November 11, 1935, the poet reports:

> There's no overpoweringly great news to pass on—no great victory won—just guerrilla warfare as usual—and common in an uncivilized and overgrown terrain. But the boys are in college and I have my garden all in order for spring. My best to—whoever remembers me.

The only reference to a visit during the thirties—others were canceled—comes in Williams's letter of November 16, 1936, in response to Burke's wish to interview the poet for the *New York Times Book Review*. This pattern continues into the early forties (May 5, 1940; April 21, 1941; July 12, 1943; July 30, 1943); each echoes the note that Burke sent in 1941 with his return of an unidentified document:

> Going through my sack, I came upon the enclosed, which you asked me to return. Here it is. I guess we mean well, you and me. And maybe we even really intend now and then to have a session together. But we just go along his or her individual way. It's too bad probably.[15]

For Williams's part, managing his family, exhausted with his doctoring across six townships, and plagued by the fear that his gift for poetry had abandoned him, the thirties must have seemed like his least productive decade in an artistic sense, his winning *Poetry* magazine's one-hundred-dollar Guarantor's prize notwithstanding (1931). In the twenties and earlier on he had posted some major successes: *Al Que Quiere!* (1917), *Kora in Hell* (1920), *Sour Grapes* (1921), *Spring and All* (1923), as well as his own little magazine, *Contact*

(1920–23). Williams continued to publish during the early- to mid-thirties—*The Knife of the Times* (1932), *Collected Poems, 1921–1931* (1934), a fleeting revival of *Contact* (1932), *Life Along the Passaic* (1937), and over twenty poems in various magazines (1935)—but the poetry in his *Collected Poems, 1921–1931* seemed to summarize his past work rather than to herald anything new, and recognition on a grand scale eluded him. He could find no steady publisher; even Burke had refused his works (January 26 and June 6, 1933); his opera project of three years had fizzled out; Robert McAlmon, unproductive and drunk, was back in New York after the inevitable failure of his marriage; Ezra Pound, from various locations on earth, bellowed, *basso continuo*, that Williams was wasting his life in America, and at home he had two growing boys and the added burden of two aging mothers needing care.[16] Even his brief forays into political compositions proved fruitless and often left him and his objectivist poetry open to attack from, among others, the leftists of the *Partisan Review*.[17] But in the late thirties, after he had withdrawn from manifestoing altogether, some important reversals occurred: the popular reception of his *The White Mule* (1937) and an influential exchange with the Russian surrealist Pavel Tchelitchew, whose *Phenomena* had a rejuvenating effect on the poet, one that rekindled his quest for an American idiom in poetry.[18] He had already started by clearing the field, so to say, taking his battle to the obstructionists: the universities, where in the mid-thirties, he spoke at such venues as Barnard, Vassar, Brooklyn Institute of Arts and Letters, and the Bread Loaf Writers' Conference, directing his charges against antiquated poetic modes and claiming that the American language as yet had not been "broken to poetic form," even as T. S. Eliot was urging a return to the forms of Milton.[19] Despite this resurgence, in his August 14, 1943 letter to Burke, the tone reminds us of the distance that had come between the two during this period, and its contents point to further cause: "But the work is very hard and will get much harder in the coming winter with more of the men in the profession [medicine] going into the armed forces. . . . I have to a great extent succeeded in keeping my body at a sort of ease even when I am harassed to the point of complete exhaustion."

The thirties and early forties were a mixed blessing for Burke as well. He had early published *Counter-Statement* (1931), which comprised most of his theoretical output from 1920 to 1931, and his novel *Towards a Better Life* (1932); however, the novel's lackluster reception, *The Dial*'s demise, a failing marriage, and the subsequent indecision over his life's work—fiction or theory —was taking its toll on him. As early as 1927, he sensed that an "aesthetic paralysis" had begun to spread over all of his writing.[20] In October 1931, he wrote Williams cynically that he felt an eagerness "to spend a couple of months on a long political tirade, but who would want it?" And whether it was symptomatic or causal, his relationship with his wife Lily ended with divorce in 1933; shortly thereafter he married her younger sister, Libbie.[21] Much like Williams, Burke during the mid-thirties turned his compositional powers to politics, specifically toward communism. Again like Williams, he adopted an esoteric approach that infuriated the orthodox Marxists like Matthew Josephson who wanted him to employ his pen for the cause in a purer fashion.[22] Yet, Burke held firm to his convictions, confiding to Cowley that his work *Permanence and Change* (1935), which first introduced his notion of "perspective by incongruity," had "communist objectives," but the "approach was his."[23] Nevertheless, though he disapproved of communist orthodoxy and their propagandistic strategies in his "Revolutionary Symbolism in America," he was elected to the executive committee of the League of American Writers in 1935 and on two subsequent occasions.[24] After the many disappointments of the revolution, however, Burke turned to a more conventional existence in the academic community, a shift that may have permitted more time for his theorizing in that it allowed him to develop his theories and, as he put it, it provided a forum in which to "try it out on the dog" with his students.[25] So, the mid- to late-thirties must have seemed a relief for Burke in many ways: he was a music critic for *The Nation* (1933–36), he was awarded a Guggenheim Fellowship (1935), and he started to lecture at the New School for Social Research (1937); at the same time, he published over fifty articles and reviews in various periodicals as well as three books that would signal his final shift from fiction and literary criticism to rhetorical theory: *Permanence and Change* (1935), his first theoretical work that examined the function of ideology in the interpretation of reality or experience; *Attitudes toward History* (1937), a critical theory of historical change and human motivation, and *The Philosophy of Literary Form* (1941), a work that extended the definition of literary form first set down in *Counter-Statement* (1931) and linked it to a method, dramatism, for analyzing all discursive forms of writing.

Although the early essays of *The Philosophy of Literary Form* (1941) sparked a renewed interest in Williams as early as May 5, 1940, the correspondence suggests that it was the close of the World War II as well as other needs—both medical and artistic—that contributed to a rehabilitation of their relationship. As if in celebration of the war's conclusion, their correspondence increases dramatically after October 1945, representing over sixty percent of the collection. "Damn it, I must run up to see you now the war is over and gas is free-er,"

Williams wrote on October 15, 1945, suggesting that his visits would soon be renewed. The mood and frequency of the letters in these years seem in accord with this assertion, and with the exception of a few months of separation interspersed among the remaining years of their friendship, they maintained a fairly constant and congenial interchange until the last. Surely, the injunction in the closing passage of Williams's 1945 poem "At Kenneth Burke's Place," addressing itself to a basket of apples on Burke's porch, reflects the poet's conscious celebration of this fact:

> . . . Take up one
> and bite into it. It is still good
> even unusual compared with the usual,
> as if a taste long lost and regretted
> had in the end, finally,
> been brought to life again.[26]

When the letters disclose evidence of their having made fifteen visits during this period (1945–62), mostly to Andover, we may assume that there were many more besides. Most of the gatherings occurred at the Burkes on Sundays, an obvious arrangement when we recall that Williams lived and practiced medicine in the same house, and that even though he was officially closed to business on Sundays, many letters refer to the constant interruptions he suffered as a result of his proximity to the crowded apartments of his importunate indigents. Moreover, Burke's house had already been established as the central meeting spot, or salon, for many of the New York crowd. Before the literary disputes or shared readings, they would often play a game of tennis, or Burke would lead the gathering on a trek through the woods.[27] Williams, in 1948, revealed the power these gatherings held for him:

> The life he has led on his old abandoned farm in Andover has always fascinated me. I approve of it. I admire the mind that conceived and carried out such a life. We'd meet there Peggy Cowley who'd be bitten by a rattlesnake and yell for me before she'd be taken to the hospital to be cured, Mattie Josephson, Malcolm Cowley, Gorham Munson, in striped pants and carrying a cane in that country place. All afternoon would be spent in argument, we hugging our glasses of applejack. Reactivated, I'd go home to the eternally rewarding game of scribbling. Thought was never an isolated thing with me; it was a game of tests and balances, to be proven by the written word.[28]

More often than not, before they had entered the door and had time to warm themselves with the Burkes' homemade rice wine, even before they had disembarked from their cars, Burke would deliver his first lecture, which he had ready as if impatient for listeners after having been long isolated. During one meeting, "he spoke with so much verve and at such great length that afterward, as he said, he had neither strength nor will to write down the big ideas he had talked out."[29] In these visits, Williams was both audience as well as performer. Many passages in these letters refer to essays or poems packed along with wine and steaks. In Burke's June 6, 1948 letter, we find evidence that Williams had been rehearsing his "variable foot" on his favorite philosopher; Burke had delayed his response until the poet returned home: "Your essay sounded like a good act. I could even see where you cunningly laid plans for some of your most winsome spontaneous boyish effects. (Spontaneous! You old whore!)."[30] In what was a typical scene on Sunday evenings, Michael Burke remembers how the far end of the living room in their house at Andover became a stage when friends visited; there Malcolm Cowley would sing bawdy songs, or Ralph Ellison would read a chapter from *Invisible Man*.

> Williams read "A Sort of a Song" on one of his visits. . . . And as I had come to expect when my father's friends arrived, there was laughing, drinking, and eventually a big meal. The party began at the door of their car, with so much animated conversation that it took an hour to get from the car through the yard and into the house. . . . KB would take the group on the "Grand Tour," a trail he had cleared through the woods, along the rock walls, and the fallen barbed wire fence, by the little house on the hill where he courted my mother, and back across the field to our back porch. Everyone would gather in the kitchen, and as the evening arrived gravitate into the dining room for the evening meal. Upon arriving for one of these visits, Bill announced that he had a new poem to read, and it was postponed until after dinner, when everyone moved towards the far end of the living room, where Butchie and I were moved out of the best chairs to make room for the grown-ups.[31]

Seated on an old straight back chair, with the caning just beginning to unravel, Bill Williams recited his new poem. A few false starts were necessary till everyone reasonably quieted down. No-one ever managed to get through a poem, or piano piece, or story without everyone in the room adding a little something along the way, and several attempts were usually necessary. He bent forward to read from his notes, and with a high and melodic voice, read with a meter that was part song and part story telling. He began a poem about a snake and a rock.

Bill described the rock, shaping it with his hands, and repeated the last line. His gestures were precise, and I can still see the large gray boulder, with tiny blossoms peeking out of the cracks, sitting on the wooden floor next to the front hall post. "No ideas but in things,". . . I remember the thing so well it still sits in my memory in the corner of the living room.[32]

Even when such an evening was complete and Williams had returned to the hospital or yet another expectant mother, his weekend excursion to Burke's would still be churning in him: ". . . if the fit was on me—if something Stieglitz or Kenneth had said was burning inside me, having bred their overnight demanding outlet—I would be like a woman at term; no matter what else was up, that demand had to be met."[33] Another interesting feature revealed by the record of their visits derives from an incipient darkness that made its way into Williams's comments in the late fifties: in a September 8, 1955 note we sense the poet's slipping into the weariness of old age:

> It was a good afternoon, I wish it could be repeated. I wish for impossible things: that we could communicate in ways that would surpass ordinary communication. That is where I feel my inadequacy: I'm not up to it any more—if I was ever up to it.

Although the weariness evidenced here (see also September 26, 1956) ought to be expected, the poet's continued decline in health caused by a series of strokes must have been responsible for such sad notes. It is important to observe, however, that many of the later visits referred to in the letters suggest that such tendencies toward the morose were exceptional; even in the late fifties, their correspondences contain references to enjoyable picnics and swims that still had the power, for Williams, of provoking a poetic response such as that, for instance, recorded in this July 2, 1957 acknowledgment to Libbie with which he had enclosed a new poem, "The Birth": "We had a good quiet time, I enjoyed it including the drinks and the dinner, which was delicious. The thunder shower and the scamper with you under the towel to shelter left me breathless but I enjoyed it." Although we do not know the last time Williams was able to visit Andover—in the later years young Dr. Bill Williams, who had gradually taken over his father's practice on Ridge Road, would often drive his parents over—we do know that in the winter of 1960 both the Williamses and the Burkes rented places together in Englewood, Florida (December 1961).[34] An incident that occurred on one of their many walks there provided Burke with the crystallizing image of his eulogy for the poet. His having watched the poet-doctor minister to a limping dog, who had picked up a sand spur, offered a convenient image on which to build his closing impression of the "imaginative physician and . . . nosological poet": "And here I've learned one more thing about Williams's doctrine of 'contact,'" he would write.[35]

Amusingly, Burke's preoccupation with Williams's double life as "poet and physician" may have been more revealing than the philosopher expected. For Burke's physical ailments make up another noteworthy portion of the letters' contents. Indeed, on August 24, 1950, one of the letters offers this quid pro quo: "Every once in a while (as regards the ailments), I discover that I'm a breath behind. If WCW the doctor can keep Ignatius Burpius alive, Ignatius Burpius will in his ignatian-burpian way sing of WCW the poet." Although it would seem reasonable to direct one's medical questions to a doctor friend, it remains, nevertheless, remarkable that nearly thirty pieces of their correspondence have to do with the medical ailments of Kenneth Burke and family, some of the exchanges more comical than others. "You're a damned irascible Irishman," Williams started his note on February 24, 1921, "with more sense than you deserve to have. Of course you have Typhus; couldn't anyone tell it by the smell of your letter? Meanwhile—am awaiting death—I'm damned sorry for your eyes & your headaches." Less than three months later (May 12, 1921), Williams responded to a question about the source of lockjaw:

> No, dearest anal—assist . . . lockjaw does not come from skin wounds, barking of the knuckles, splinters in the glands or any such light affair. . . . It delights in deep wounds the external opening of which has closed up leaving a focus of infection deep in. This is the reason that one is annoyed when a four inch spike penetrates the shoe and the foot carrying the manure, etc., deeply in there to lodge and do harm. If you are thus wounded put your foot in your mouth and yell for help. Meanwhile suck the foot as hard as you can . . . continuing in this way till you are unconscious from loss of blood.

The letter continues to address another ailment, rheumatism, as if Burke had passed Williams a catalog of symptoms; finally, the doctor concluded with a disarming prescription: "Shift your cud, you have a cold." Williams's opening with "dearest anal—assist" as well as comments that occur elsewhere certainly attests to the doctor's consciousness of Burke's preoccupation with his health as we see, again, in this November 1935 note:

> It sounded as though you really had something this time but I suppose the bugs got mixed up trying to get through the intricate maze of your psychologic entity and just lay down and died of starvation without reaching the spot where they could piss on your essential fires.

Indeed, we may, while pondering the cause of their 1940s reunion, owe more to Burke's hypochondria than we do to the conclusion of World War II: of the twenty letters that exchanged hands in 1945, eleven concern themselves with Burke's physical ailments. In all fairness to the philosopher, he was in on the joke from the outset; most of his complaints are accompanied by self-disparaging comments, such as his having been the first to discover the "migratory symptom" (August 26, 1959), or "this is a hell of a way to pipe up," he writes on June 30, 1950, "I seem to turn up thus, every once in a while, with a burden which I would plague you with."[36] On October 12, 1945, in a humorous description of his latest ailment—a lump on the roof of his mouth—he first launched an elaborate analysis of possible causes—one that reached all the way to his nursery—and concluded with the source of a genuine "hypochondriac's incentive": "I'm finding it more and more difficult to give priority rating to my other worries. So, if you had someone to suggest? Particularly some thoughtful soul like me who might be more prone to diagnosis than action." What should not escape our attention from this group of letters is their disclosure of the humanitarian side of Williams. Throughout the years, the poet ministered to the protuberances on Burke's mouth, his eustachian tubes, his son's hernia, his mother's hemorrhages, plugged ears, and cancerous cysts with selfless promptitude: hence, the central image for Burke's eulogy.

The full article Burke had promised with his quid pro quo of August 1950, represents another leitmotif of *The Collected Letters*, his review of *Sour Grapes* (1922) and a short essay on his methods (1927) notwithstanding.[37] It had started as a pledge and become a regular feature of their letters for forty years. "Bill I am still resolved, by the way, that I shall some day do that essay on you . . . using the cluster business," he promised in October 1935. An escalation of such promises occurred in the mid-forties where in October 1945 he wrote: "Bill would it be correct to say that you have learned how to make a poem out of notes for a poem? . . . I hope that, some time before I'm through, I'll be able to carry out my plans to do one of my studies of 'equations' in your work." Clearly, the poet's evasions and uncharitable outlook on Burke's theorizing served as an impediment to the philosopher's researches. Even so, when his direct questions on "clusters" and "equations" had failed to elicit any response from Williams, he adopted other contrivances such as the one we see in June 1948: "I wish you'd try writing a poem, as fast as you can, on Rhythm and the Foot. Or the New Rhythm, the New Foot, etc. Including your doctrine of the stress upon Change.[38] Knock it off at top speed. . . . (For I still hope to do a really thorough analysis of your work, from the standpoint of my lucubrations on Motives)."[39] A few years later, after a gap in the letters that suggests Burke had tabled the project, in October 1951, he adopted the maneuver of composing a poem along the lines he felt that Williams would have chosen and presented it to him for *his* analysis: "If, on looking over that poem, you have any notions (spontaneously) as to where in your opinion it's not in your groove, and how you would tinker with it, to make it more along your lines, bejeez I could I'm sure get some angles by your saying so." With only slight variations, many such dodges and lures—perhaps fueled by an urgency brought on by Williams's frequent strokes—were offered the poet into the sixties; however, we have no sign to suggest that Williams took up the gambit. Finally, near the end of the poet's life, the story of Burke's recurrent project climaxes in this plaintive note on January 14, 1962: "Have just read the article by Robert Lowell on you in the current *Hudson Rev.*[40] . . . I have not written it because I'd love to have done a long piece having exactly the quality of those . . . pages by Lowell. . . . Mea culpa, mea maxima culpa. Forgive, Bill."

Regardless of their failing to yield an article, the exchanges that record Burke's attempt to draw Williams out, as well as some others that make reference to the direct borrowing of ideas, certainly guide us, albeit inconclusively, to the lines of their relationship in terms of artistic or philosophical influence despite the early conflict they evidence. Unquestionably, in the early going, the two of them intended to conduct a collaboration on artistic and philosophical grounds; even so, while their mutual enthusiasm for certain aspects of the project drew them constantly together, their approaches would prove to be diametrically opposed, particularly as Burke's interests turned to theory. Less than two months after their first meeting, Williams went so far as to characterize the nature of it: "I have long wanted to have a correspondence with someone very dissimilar to myself, the thing to be planned as a dialogue criticizing the universe (literature), which might be published later . . . though I feel, . . . that I'll be the gainer rather than you" (March 22, 1921). Paradoxically, in the same correspondence, after defending McAlmon's position that must have set him at odds with Burke, Williams withdrew his offer and stated that: "We are too far apart yet to indulge in talk profitably. Perhaps someday we'll get some sense out of each other." As the rest of the correspondence verifies, these lines prophetically herald the combative nature of their forty-two-year relationship: a necessary and emphatic opposition, "a game of tests and balances" all done congenially, of course.[41]

What Williams opposed in Burke was his theorizing, specifically, as the years went by, the philosopher's drift toward a calculus of "clusters and equations" as if cooking up recipes for poetry. Thus, with few exceptions the poet's comments tended to subordinate the disciplines of science and philosophy, or "s and p.," to poetry. Just as Williams cavalierly classified Burke as a philosopher, it seems he lumped science and philosophy into a single camp, one opposed to poetry. "From a man partially informed," the poet wrote before refusing to send his compositional notes to Burke, "that is, not yet an artist, springs now science, a detached mass of pseudo-knowledge, now philosophy, frightened acts of half realization. Poetry, however, is the flower of action and presents a different kind of knowledge from that of S. and P. . . . hence my reluctance to show anyone my notes save as 'my mode of procedure'" (January 26, 1933). We have Burke's response to such dismissals in a note he wrote to Cowley in the summer after their inaugural meeting wherein he complains of the poet's evasions: "for a whole summer, Malcolm, I patiently poured my most valuable discoveries into the sewer."[42] Burke's own words, however, attest to a similar symbiotic bond when he writes in December, again to Cowley, after Williams had responded to a series of questions from the philosopher by gnomically quoting from his poem "The Great Figure Five": "I see now just why I am interested in Williams: because he has frequently done to perfection just the sort of thing I do not want to do. In other words, in him I find a superb adversary, thus making one less likely to grow lax in his own productions" (December 23, 1921).[43] Inauspicious as these early communications may appear, Williams repeatedly paid homage to the necessity of their relationship in a spirit of joint enterprise. "We each of us do what we can," he wrote before refusing Burke's proffered formulaic solution for the structural problem of *Paterson*, "My approach, as a poet, is just as valid as your approach as a philosopher to whatever mass of material is presented to us to work with."[44] He extended this sentiment to the following letter: "We, you and I, have nothing to quarrel about once we get by the simple beginnings (the universal activity of the mind—analysis is merely an adjunct to that). At that point we may begin to use each other at will . . . keep separate in order to be of as much use to each other as possible" (February 25, 1947).

In addition to the conciliatory spirit that pervades the correspondence of the later years, details of mutual interest begin to emerge and take on greater definition. After a spirited exchange over a work that neither had read in full, Williams was awakened to what the two held in common by Burke's analysis of the key terms of W. S. Reich's work *The Function of the Orgasm*; as he said of Burke's letter: "It seems to state . . . what seems to be the basic reason for . . . our sustained interest in each other which has never been explicit—a desire on both our parts to find some basis for avoiding the tyranny of the symbolic without sacrificing fullness of imagery."[45] In the letter that solemnized their reunion in 1945, Williams brought to light another key term that had been a part of their conversations twenty-six years earlier. After the "nosological poet" had scheduled a treatment for a physical ailment of Burke's, he went on to thank him for the visit and their walk together:

> I saw the beginnings of many valuable conversations between us striking their heads up as we passed them by yesterday—I particularly liked your manner of explanation when you lowered your voice and spoke quietly of the elementals that interest us both, the humane particulars of realization and communication. I woke in the night with a half-sentence on my metaphorical lips "the limitations of form." It seemed to mean something of importance and to have been connected with what we had been saying. (November 10, 1945)

"Literary form," and the "tyranny of the symbolic," in a general sense, represent the common ground these two occupied for over forty years, and though a case has been made for both of their having profited from one another's ideas, Williams, as he said himself, was the real "gainer," for it was Burke's salons and his own constant clarifications of language use—the definition and elaboration of literary form (1931), "perspective by incongruity" (1935), the use of fictional or poetic modes to examine historical change (1937), the nature of symbolic action (1941), the method for discovering motivation (1945), and the strategies used for persuasion (1950)—that surely, despite Williams's bluster and abnegation, supplied the material for many of his poetic utterances.[46]

Though the humbler task of this introduction will confine its closing remarks to a bare description of how the key terms uttered in Williams's acknowledgment might shed light on the disputes in the letters as well as outline some connections between their divergent projects, it is important to note first that, as well as the text of the letters themselves, the labors of many scholars have borne testimony to the fact of their mutual influence as we see in the works of Michael Weaver, Jack Selzer, David Blakesley, Paul Mariani, and Brian Bremen to mention a few. Each has made valuable contributions that range from a recognition of Williams's appreciation of Burke's altered names and designations for literary tropes (Weaver), to the initial union of the two under the influence of Williams's attempt to discover a distinctly American culture (Selzer), to Williams's causing Burke to "reformulate his approach . . . and conceptualization of rhetoric" (Blakesley), to Burke's serving as a consultant for the poet's crises over the form and direction of his epic poem and essays (Mariani), to the most extensive assessment of the impact of Burke's theories on the aesthetics of Williams (Bremen).[47] Clearly the letters support such declarations. Some of the more obvious connections are derived from the record they present of solicitations for one another's publications; at least a dozen letters make or respond to such requests: Williams's *Contact* (October 1925); Burke's *Manuscript Editions* (1933); Charles Reznikoff's *Testimony* (1933); the centennial edition of Walt Whitman's *Leaves of Grass* (1954).[48] More concretely, many references to the sharing of materials will be discovered here: poems, paragraphs, terms, ideas. As early as December 6, 1922, Williams wrote that he had used one of Burke's suggestions—one that is lost to us—to overcome a problem with the soliloquy in his operatic project, *The First President*.[49] In another such reference, July 12, 1943, Williams sent an appreciative note for one of Burke's articles: "I enjoyed the coolness of your developments in the *View* piece.[50] My piece was written before, during and after my reading of what you said there."[51] Yet again, Williams reported to Burke that he had used his ideas on the four tropes during a review of Parker Tyler's *The Granite Butterfly* (April 20, 1946).[52] Significantly—and perhaps the most probable reason for their post-war reunion—when Williams was in a quandary over the shape and direction of *Paterson,* he renewed their correspondence. Kenneth Burke, for his part, on several occasions requested permission to use Williams's poems in his classes or made mention of his having discussed the poet with his students (June 12, 1952; November 7, 1955; December 31, 1960). Additionally, the letters suggest that the poet modified the philosopher's ideas from time to time; we see this in Burke's August 24, 1951, note where he asked permission to lift one of Williams's paragraphs on "perfection" from his *Autobiography* to add to his own ideas on the chief attribute of one's drive toward hierarchy (August 25, 1951).[53] His understanding of "identification," the key motive of humans that unites us through property or substance, and so extended the scope of rhetoric to all modes of discourse, was also broadened by Williams's views.[54]

In very general terms, however, it was an interest in literary form that drew them both together as experimental authors of fiction in the first decade of their relationship especially as they shared the moderns' revolt against nineteenth-century aesthetics. In a heated harmony, they would continue the epistemological debate over the relative importance of things versus ideas until the end. In Burke's 1920 letter to Malcolm Cowley, which we have already had occasion to mention, the aspiring author of fiction detected the manifesto for a literary movement in Williams's *Improvisations*, and he went on in his letter to describe its features and challenges:

By striving for essences, by attempting to fix one entire facet of approach in a few sentences, we thus attain a unit, so distinct that it almost gains complete independence of the form as a whole. These units fall together exclusively by emotional laws. Between us, the one great difficulty to overcome in Integralism is the attainment of organism; and again between us, it is a difficulty which will never be overcome. . . . Integralists or Post-Late Victorians—we have our choice.[55]

The passage of Williams's *Improvisations* that elicited Burke's enthusiasm was the poet's description of his meaning of "contact":

By the brokenness of his composition the poet makes himself master of a certain weapon which he could possess himself of in no other way. The speed of the emotions is sometimes such that thrashing about in a thin exaltation or despair many matters are touched but not held, more often broken by contact.[56]

The stress both of them lay on "emotional laws," or "emotions," and avoidance of "organism," or a thing "touched but not held," as guiding principles echoed the modernists' increasing emphasis on the psychological and individual aspect of the creative act as well as a reluctance to pour their works into proscribed forms. Significantly, the terms they deployed then resemble the "realization" and "communication" that the poet would revert to years later. At the outset, however, what Williams and Burke meant by "form" would remain a murky affair. Burke himself would confess as much years later (November 19, 1945) while responding to Williams's account of a dream where the words "limitations of form" had come to his lips: ". . . the dream words doubtless went back to the old battles of you and McAlmon vs. Matty and me, which were always about "form," though God only knows what we meant by it." Still, in this ill-defined enterprise against the perceived straitjacket of the genteel tradition, they were united.

Williams, though, as a literary nationalist, imagist, and physician by trade, was motivated in his artistic quest for form by a rejection of all European precursors, and insisted upon the creation of a uniquely American culture through "contact"—the name he had adopted for his periodical—with things American: the local soil, the local experiences all in the present. "For past objects have about them past necessities," he wrote in his autobiography, "like the sonnet—which have conditioned them and from which, as a form itself, they cannot be freed."[57] His virulent attacks on T. S. Eliot and his rejection of Pound's subjects were, in part, motivated by his sense of their having abandoned the American experiment and been crippled by outmoded forms and traditions. By his own admission, the poet was incapable of articulating the exact features of this new form, save to say, "the poem, like every form of art, is an object, an object that in itself formally presents its case and its meaning by the very form it assumes."[58] It was this object-driven sense of form that often prompted Williams to alter the shape of poems after they were on the page-proofs to "look" more like the meaning.[59] The goal was to achieve the meaning without all of the interrupting screens of metaphor and analysis. "There is the eye," Burke described the method of Williams, "and there is the thing upon which that eye alights."[60] The besetting flaw of such descriptions, from the analyst's perspective at least, derives from the fact that one cannot codify the forms or break them down into genres without making a catalogue, all over the place, of every object worthy of poetic expression. But we can, as Paul Mariani has, when we examine the content and suggested meaning of passages of Williams's poetry, find examples of the formal quality—its shape, its rhythm on the page—of a poetic passage making its own moral claim.[61] Thus, for instance, in *Paterson II* that begins with stanzas fragmented on the page as if they were mist from the nearby water falls, the poet/doctor/city-figure of Paterson begins his walk in search for the gist, or language of beauty that has been locked away. But when he leaves the beaten path—that is, departs from the old poetic measures—he experiences, even in a field of "stubble and matted brambles":

> From before his feet, half ripping,
> Picking a way, there starts
> A flight of empurpled wings!
> —invisibly created (their
> jackets dust-grey) from the dust kindled
> to sudden ardor!

Where the verb "starts" is doubly arrested by the break in the stanza and the delayed terminal point, and the next line's indentation creates added pause before its flight, the form imparts its moral on the reader: the language of beauty rests within each of us wherever we may be, yet it takes one's going out with an active imagination ("invisibly created") and gaining an intimate knowledge of one's place, Paterson, to release it, and even then the achievement is only momentary.[62] This pattern that we witness on the minute, or molecular, level—that is, the departure from the old as requisite to the creation of new forms—exists on all levels of *Paterson*: a loosely structured design that predicates the release of new forms on the destruction of the library in Book III; the mixed modes of prose and poetry that at once capture the feel of water (poetry) flowing over and between the rocks (prose) of Paterson, as well as standing as a refutation to preconceived notions of verse forms.

Burke, on the other hand, who had studied the likes of Mann, Spengler, Baudelaire, de Gourmont, and Flaubert under Ludwig Lewisohn at Ohio State University and thus was spared such untenable positions as those held by Williams, was nevertheless motivated by the incompatibility of the artistic forms that were relics of the genteel tradition—represented, for example, by the sonnets of Elizabeth Barrett Browning—with the new atmosphere of Freudian psychology and the realities of the modern world, hence the alternative name for "Integralists" above: "Post-Late Victorians." Williams must have been delighted with Burke's account of his having dramatically exited a meeting of "The Boar's Head"—the literary club at Columbia—through a window, rather than the conventional door, after a public disagreement over this matter with the head of the English Department, John Erskine.[63] Yet, "Form," Burke would insist critically in his review of Williams's own *Sour Grapes*, "must always have its beginnings in ideas."[64] He was the first of the two to clarify and elaborate this term in the early essays of his *Counter-Statement* (1931), a work that presaged his shift away from the view of art as an isolated act of an individual to one that was more socially integrated through its symbols.[65] The "emotional laws" of his proposed manifesto to Cowley had been transformed there to a full-fledged definition of literary form as "an arousal and fulfillment of desires of the audience," a definition that began to yoke the creative work to the auditor's emotional or psychological state.[66] He argued further that the forms we witness in literature, such as crisis, rising action, and climax, are effective because they resonate with preexistent, transhistorical psychological states in the mind of the reader. And while Burke's belief in the existence of these *a priori* forms may have agitated the imagist poet of Rutherford, U.S.A., the essays of *Counter-Statement* (1931) at the same time made allowances for Williams's need for form derived from the "local" and present scene by granting the existence of particular kinds of expressions of the universal forms within the context of particular conditions. As Burke put it, "The cluster of conditions is fluctuant (from age to age, from class to class, from person to person) thus calling for changes of emphasis."[67] Moreover, in his essay "Program," of the same work, after arguing that applied science had become a menace, he stated that the "aesthetic becomes a means of reclamation," implying that the forms associated with the aesthetic must "serve as anti-mechanization" in order to engender an informed skepticism.[68] Such advocacy seems consonant with Williams's opposition to the economic or cultural forces that would imprison the various representatives of beauty in *Paterson*: the mink and Kora.[69] And whether it was a genuine interest in Burke's essays or a desperate reach for help with his new project, Williams had expressed (May 5, 1940) an appreciation for the early pieces he had read in *The Philosophy of Literary Form* (1941), a work wherein Burke linked the function of form first set down in *Counter-Statement* (1931) to other discursive forms, and went on to trace the way in which the internal components of a work might be used to interpret its symbols—here, he refers to a symbol as unique to a work, measured "by the company it keeps," not its older nineteenth-century sense.[70] And later, he would link these ideas to the Aristotelian notion of catharsis in as much as a work of art, closely studied thus, may reveal the artist's maladjustment and how his composition both explicates the ailment and at the same time discharges it—"as we may even relieve ourselves of private burdens by befouling the public medium"—through his "symbolic action" whereby he "socializes his position" and achieves a "ritual catharsis" for both himself and his auditor.[71] Here, although Williams continued to rebuff Burke's exploration of the internal alignments in his works—"Of course I'm sorry you wouldn't play my game," Burke wrote the poet (May 31, 1960)—the subtle interplay of the relationships of author, symbols, and readers must have been, in part, what drew Williams to *The Philosophy of Literary Form*, and so back to Andover, at the very moment he had been contemplating the creation of his own symbolic act, or as he phrased it when he wrote McAlmon in August 1943, "an account psychologicsocial panorama of a city treated as if it were a man."[72]

So, it is this continual wrangling over the origin and nature of literary form that enlightens the many quarrels at the core of the conversations recorded in these letters. Williams's refusal to engage in any literary conversation under the headings of "equations or clusters" (October 31, 1945), and his rejection of Burke's suggested classical model of the *Aeneid* (February 14, 1947) as a possible solution for the uncertain shape and direction of his own epic poem are all animated, sometimes perversely, by his stance against premeditated form. Even after Burke would point up the contradictions from the poet's own works in all of their discursive forms, such as his revealing observation about Williams and Thirlwall's suspicious "selectivities" for *The Selected Letters of William Carlos Williams* (August 19, 1957), or the "spontaneous boyish effects" the poet had set in marginal notes of a lecture to manipulate his audience during one of his speeches and neglected to erase before handing them to Burke for review—"Spontaneous! You old whore!" (June 9, 1948)—Williams would turn back such reasoned observations with yet another of his paradoxical dismissals: "It is impossible for me to contradict myself—except logically which means nothing" (January 31, 1947). Yet, again, after a three-paragraph rejection of materials that Burke had forwarded to him in order to help him through a structural impasse on his poem, he was capable of such seemingly illogical reversals that must have delighted and puzzled his reader: "Many thanks, really, for the bit you copied out for me. I may use it in the part of *Paterson* I am working on now" (February 25, 1947). It is tempting to point out at this juncture, that as often as Williams deploys, in his conversations, the term "logic" synonymously with the idea of things academic and therefore opposed to his poetics, Burke's eulogy of the "nosological poet" may have meant to convey a mischievous reading for us.

In any event, the original enterprise that fueled their relationship in the early going—its reliance on emotions and the avoidance of "organism"—must surely have been in Williams's thoughts when he spoke to Burke of the "humane particulars of realization and communication," as well as the related interest contained in his phrase, "the tyranny of the symbolic." This, too, they held in common throughout their career together. Contrary to the attacks on Williams and Burke by the partisans for their failure to toe the ideological lines in their works during the thirties, neither of these men intended to retreat from the world into the comforts of their individual projects. What had been at the center of their compositions, early and late, was a very public interest in releasing the individual from the tyranny of symbols in one form or another. As early as 1920, the poet had staked his claim against the human habit of creating fixed values for the images one has gathered around oneself. The poet stated in his "Prologue to *Kora in Hell*" that his goal was to capture the "true value which gives an object a character by itself," a disability he attributed to a lack of imagination or "an easy lateral sliding" whereby an individual fell into the habit of assigning a fixed value—what he called its "sentimental value"—to an image or word regardless of its context.[73] Only words could unlock the line, "new combinations of words, as free as possible of their old associational weights."[74] The central thrust of *Paterson*, a work that dominated the forties for Williams, undertook, as its prefatory lines announced, to find out again the "rigour of beauty" and how to spring it out of the individual's mind "locked . . . past all remonstrance."[75]

For Burke's part, although his next projects—*A Grammar of Motives* (1945) and *A Rhetoric of Motives* (1950)—would seek to measure motivation by examining procedures of formal art and to disclose rhetorical motives formerly hidden, his entire life's project was devoted, in a sense, to the "tyranny of the symbol." In *Counter-Statement* (1931) when he first linked up ideology and form, he realized that a writer drew on a "vocabulary of belief" to manipulate one's attitude; thus, his essay "Program" advocates a "process of disintegration" to undercut the influence of such propaganda; in his adoption of "inefficiency" as one of the blazons for his program, he would symbolically subvert the tyranny of "efficiency" and "the practical" inasmuch as they are forces that imprison us in a mechanized world.[76] He realized, further, in *Permanence and Change* (1935), while arguing first that there are no absolute meanings in experience, only interpretations, that ideologies dictated those interpretations and thus our motives were not natural; instead, they were animated by that interpretative framework.[77] One corrective for such tyranny was a "planned incongruity" that would tear apart the "molecular compositions of noun and verb," much like Williams's attack on the "easy lateral sliding."[78] And though Burke would go on to examine symbols in many other contexts and permutations, under this heading, at least, he and Williams occupied an undivided field.

Fittingly, Williams's ultimate point of attack was at the elemental level of the poem—its word and foot—just as Burke's close examination of rhetoric drove at the psychosocial motives beneath our symbolic actions. In a very real sense, they had achieved what Williams had hoped for when he asked that they remain, "separate in order to be of as much use to each other as possible— to penetrate separately into the jungle, each by his own modes, calling back and forth as we can in order to keep in touch for better uniting of our forces" (February 25, 1947). Few would challenge, now, the claim that both of these men, "each by his own modes," had and continue to have a significant impact on their respective fields. Their acknowledgment of one another's achievements, in the final years, seemed to reflect their awareness of the fact in unqualified terms, terms that will aptly serve both as emblems and conclusion to this introduction. In response to Burke's article on Roethke (January 24, 1951), Williams again struck up the spirit of their joint enterprise:

> You show us how to think, I want to supply the material to think *with*. It isn't ever the terms, the terms can be ambiguous as there may be two kinds of terms, it is the shape, the context of the terms that engages me not their "meaning" as such. After all you ARE able to differentiate such things and you are willing, generous, toward their study. You WANT to join with another to elucidate such interests. (June 23, 1951)

In like fashion, Burke acknowledged the success of Williams's approach as we see in his response to the reception of an autographed copy of what would prove to be the poet's final book:

> Us critics and the John Birch Societies have got the dope on you. You could go down a filthy city street, and find there a poem as lovely as a babbling brook in June. And again and again you proved your point: The

poem "was there to be written." And that's subversive. . . . And thank you very much indeed for sending us that book, with that precious wobbly signature. You baystard, you stinkeroo. We prize that, because we know what to prize. (July 12, 1962)

On the Text of the Letters

The symbols **[P]** and **[B]** at the head of every letter signify the Pattee and Beinecke collections respectively. Whenever possible, through evidence extrapolated from the content of a letter or discovered on its accompanying envelope, the point of origin and date, when not included within the context of a letter, have been placed within brackets. Where intentional wordplay has contributed to eccentric spellings, we have let them pass; simple misspellings have been silently corrected. In a few instances where the date of a letter has been at odds with the contents of the sequence of a conversation (Oct. 29, 1925; Nov. 10, 1947; Nov. 1, 1952), we have seen fit to honor the coherence of conversation over the date, which was obviously an error.

Notes

1. Matthew Josephson, *Life among the Surrealists: A Memoir* (New York: Holt, Rinehart and Winston, 1962), 72.

2. Ibid., 77. At the time of their first meeting, Josephson was twenty-two; Kenneth Burke, twenty-four; William Carlos Williams, thirty-eight; Robert McAlmon, twenty-five. Dr. William E. Williams, Williams's son, who still lived and practiced medicine at 9 Ridge Road in 1994, remembered that even in his early youth the river ran "a different color every day." Dr. William E. Williams, personal interview, November 18, 1993.

3. Paul Jay, ed., *Selected Correspondence of Kenneth Burke and Malcolm Cowley, 1915–1981* (New York: Viking), 63.

4. Ibid., 75.

5. Ibid., 77.

6. Ibid., 73.

7. Robert McAlmon, *Robert McAlmon and the Lost Generation: A Self-Portrait,* ed. Robert E. Knoll (Lincoln: University of Nebraska Press, 1962), 145.

8. Williams to Burke, January 26, 1921.

9. Josephson, *Life among the Surrealists,* 74.

10. Thirlwall, *Selected Letters,* 48.

11. Patricia Willis, to the editor, March 10, 1994.

12. Charles Mann, to the editor, October 26, 1993.

13. Michael Burke, to the editor, May 5, 1994.

14. The letter from Burke to Florence Williams after Williams's death is in the "Williams mss II" at the Lilly Library, University of Indiana at Bloomington.

15. Burke to Williams, December 20, 1941.

16. Paul Mariani, *William Carlos Williams: A New World Naked* (New York: Norton, 1981), 177, 405.

17. Ibid., 406.

18. Ibid., 403.

19. Ibid., 394. For reference to Milton, see Paul Mariani, *A Usable Past: Essays on Modern and Contemporary Poetry* (Amherst: University of Massachusetts Press), 40.

20. Jay, *Selected Correspondence*, 153.

21. Michael and Kenneth Burke, personal interview, November 17, 1993.

22. David E. Shi, *Matthew Josephson, Bourgeois Bohemian* (New Haven: Yale University Press), 174. In the same work, Shi also relates an account of Burke and Josephson's having been asked if they were prepared to kill for the movement (29).

23. Armin Frank, *Kenneth Burke* (New York: Twayne), 24; Jay, *Selected Correspondence*, 154.

24. Malcolm Cowley, *The Dream of the Golden Mountains* (New York: Viking, 1964), 279.

25. Burke to Williams, June 12, 1952.

26. William Carlos Williams, "At Kenneth Burke's Place," *The Collected Later Poems* (Norfolk, Conn.: New Directions, 1963), 257.

27. Michael and Kenneth Burke, personal interview, November 17, 1993. Michael Burke, Burke's second son by Libbie, pointed up one of the interesting ironies of life at Andover, that while they did not have indoor plumbing installed until the late fifties, they had discovered a sizable clay deposit near the house that allowed them, with little effort, to construct a fairly decent tennis court. Too, in their outhouse they boasted a paper dispenser carved in the shape of a hand—its longest digit serving as the spindle for the roll—carved by Alexander Calder (1898–1976).

28. Williams, *Autobiography*, iii.

29. Josephson, *Life Among the Surrealists*, 305.

30. For a discussion on Williams's "variable foot," his attempt at describing a device to capture the American idiom, see Hugh Kenner, "The Rhythm of Ideas," *Sagetrieb* 3, no. 2 (fall 1984), 37.

31. Anthony "Butchie" Burke (b. 1936): Burke's first son by Libbie.

32. Michael Burke, letter to the editor, December 2, 1993. This passage is excerpted from an unpublished essay by Michael Burke.

33. *The Autobiography of William Carlos Williams* (New York: New Directions, 1967), iii.

34. Dr. William Eric Williams, personal interview, November 16, 1993.

35. Kenneth Burke, *Language as Symbolic Action* (Berkeley: University of California Press, 1966), 283.

36. Burke composed a poem with such a title that does conclude with a wry diagnosis not unlike Williams's own: "The Momentary, Migratory Symptom," *Book of Moments* (Los Altos, Calif.: Hermes, 1955), 6.

37. Kenneth Burke, "Heaven's First Law," review of *Sour Grapes*, by William Carlos Williams, *Dial* 72 (February 1922), 197–200; and "The Method of William Carlos Williams," *Dial* 82 (February 1927), 94–98.

38. Burke here is responding to Williams's frustrating attempt to explain his own ideas about the "variable foot." See Kenner, "The Rhythm of Ideas," for further discussion.

39. Burke may be referring either to his *A Grammar of Motives* (New York: Prentice-Hall, 1945) [Williams had a copy: see Williams to Burke, December 14, 1945] or *A Rhetoric of Motives* (New York: Prentice-Hall, 1950).

40. Robert Lowell. "William Carlos Williams." *Hudson Review* 13 (winter 1961–62), 530–37.

41. Williams, *Autobiography*, iii.

42. Jay, *Selected Correspondence*, 101.

43. Ibid., 109.

44. In order to help Williams's through the structural problems of the current book of *Paterson*, Burke had passed Williams a passage from page 37 of John William Mackail's *Virgil and His Meaning to the World of Today* (Boston: Marshal Jones, 1922).

45. The letters from December 1946 through January 1947 focus on the Reich text. Wilhelm Reich (1897–1957), *Die Funktion des Orgasmus* (New York: Orgone Institute Press, 1942).

46. These are hardly adequate summations for the prominent issues in each of the texts Burke published during the span of their renewed relationship with one another (with the exception of the first): *Counter-Statement* (1931; reprint, Chicago: University of Chicago Press, 1953); *Permanence and Change: An Anatomy of Purpose* (New York: New Republic, 1935); *Attitudes toward History*, 2 vols. (New York: New Republic, 1937); *The Philosophy of Literary Form* (1941; reprint, New York: Vintage, 1957); *A Grammar of Motives* (1945); and *A Rhetoric of Motives* (1950).

47. Michael Weaver, *William Carlos Williams: The American Background* (Cambridge: Cambridge University Press, 1971); Jack Selzer, *Kenneth Burke in Greenwich Village*; David Blakesley, "William Carlos Williams's Influence on Kenneth Burke" (paper presented at the Modern Language Association Conference, Toronto, Ont., December 1997); Mariani, *A New World Naked*; Brian Bremen, *William Carlos Williams and the Diagnostics of Culture* (New York: Oxford University Press, 1993).

48. Milton Hindus, ed., *Leaves of Grass; One Hundred Years After* (Stanford, Calif.: Stanford University Press, 1955). Williams's essay included in that volume was "An Essay on *Leaves of Grass*" (22–31); Burke's contribution was "Policy Made Personal: Whitman's Verse and Prose—Salient Traits" (74–108).

49. Williams and the Hungarian composer Tibor Serly tried to write an opera based upon the life of Washington. Although *The First President* was never completed, Williams's libretto was published in 1936 in *The New Caravan*, edited by Alfred Kreymborg, Lewis Mumford, and Paul Rosenfeld.

50. Kenneth Burke, "The Five Master Terms, Their Place in a 'Dramatistic' Grammar of Motives," *Views* (June 1943): 50–52.

51. William Carlos Williams, "A Fault of Learning," *Partisan Review* 10 (September 1943): 466–68.

52. William Carlos Williams, review of *The Granite Butterfly*, by Parker Tyler, *Accent* 6 (spring 1946): 203.

53. Burke, *Language as Symbolic Action*, 38–39. Compare this passage to the paragraph from Williams's autobiography to which Burke refers—Williams's discourse on the objects of his poems, the people (*Autobiography*, 288).

54. Blakesley, "William Carlos Williams's Influence on Kenneth Burke," 1.

55. Jay, *Selected Correspondence*, 77.

56. William Carlos Williams, "Improvisations," *Little Review* 6, no. 2 (June 1919): 52–59.

57. Williams, *Autobiography*, 265.

58. Ibid., 265.

59. William Carlos Williams, *I Wanted to Write a Poem: The Autobiography of the Works of a Poet*, ed. Edith Heal (Boston: Beacon, 1958), 67.

60. Burke, "Heaven's First Law," 197.

61. Mariani, *A Usable Past*, 53.

62. Ibid., 54.

63. Josephson, *Life Among the Surrealists*, 32–33.

64. Burke, "Heaven's First Law," 200.

65. Paul Jay, "Kenneth Burke," in *Modern American Critics, 1920–1955*, ed. Gregory S. Jay. Vol. 63 of *The Dictionary of Literary Biography* (Detroit: Gale Research, 1978), 71.

66. Burke, *Counter-Statement*, 124.

67. Ibid., 107.

68. Ibid., 111.

69. Mariani, *A Usable Past*, 54.

70. Burke, *The Philosophy of Literary Form*, 31.

71. Ibid., 100.

72. Mariani, *A Usable Past*, 70.

73. William Carlos Williams, "Prologue to *Kora in Hell* (1920)," in *Selected Essays of William Carlos Williams* (New York: Random House, 1954), 11.

74. Mariani, *A Usable Past*, 48.

75. William Carlos Williams, *Paterson* (New York: New Directions, 1963), 11.

76. Burke, *Counter-Statement*, 210.

77. Jay, "Kenneth Burke," 74.

78. Ibid., 74.

The Humane
Particulars

1921–1929

William Carlos Williams (1883–1963)
Poems 1909, *The Tempers* 1913, *Al Que Quiere!* 1917, *Kora in Hell* 1920, *Sour Grapes* 1921, *Spring and All* 1923, *The Great American Novel* 1923, edits *Contact* 1920–23, European trip 1924, *In the American Grain* 1925, *Dial* Award 1926, *A Voyage to Pagany* 1928

Kenneth Burke (1897–1993)
Withdraws from Columbia 1918, writes for *The Dial* 1920–29, buys Andover house 1921, helps edit *Secession* 1923, "Prince Llan" 1924, "Psychology and Form" 1925, research worker for Rockefeller Memorial 1926–27, music critic for *The Dial* 1927–29, *Dial* Award 1929

[P]   [Rutherford][1]
Jan. 12, 1921

Dear Ken Broke,

This time it is my fault, not Bob's.[2] I received your story from him last week and have neglected to remit it to you because the weather has been cloudy and clear by turns of late.[3] I enclose it. Bob has given up the idea of getting out an issue of <u>Contact</u>, at least for the present, but he didn't like the story. Perhaps some day when I have so reduced my residue of sense that I have more money than it, I shall continue <u>Contact</u> here among the skunk cabbage where it belongs. Until that time I'll buy books. I hope you sell your story.

I met that Russian, Gilbert Seldes, ten days ago for the first time.[4] He told me that <u>The Dial</u> was preparing to use your essay on my place in our America.[5] He did not, most positively, say that you would put me in my place. They are also printing two new poems of mine.[6] Damn you, if your article slams me my poems will show you up, so there!

Should you be planning to move to N.J. I hope you will give me the opportunity, as a native of that state of introducing you into its mysteries. They resemble in some measure the Eleusinian, the celebration being by means of a liquid core extracted from the center of a barrel of frozen cider, etc. etc.

I did not see the article in <u>The Times</u>.[7]

I send the books at once. I read De Gourmont's novel with the greatest pleasure; it is <u>tres agreable</u>.[8] The poems I should like to read had I ever the time to do so but time is too swift in passing. The few I did read and absorb, though they fascinated me, did not invite my study as closely as say the present day work of Scribe[9] whom I admire most among the Frenchmen that I know at all. I suppose I am somewhat influenced in my shyness toward Laforgue[10] by a knowledge of what a too close study of his work has done to Eliot—and others, even Pound—the unhappy cripple. But I intrude upon your game park. As a poet I prefer—well, Scribe. Is Scribe a Jew? I can't imagine that he is one but somehow—No I am sure he is not, he is so little ornate.

Well, as I have said so often before—Well, this is the end.

Yours,

Bill

[P] January 24, 1921

Dear Williams,

Enclosed find documents. I am afraid they may make McAlmon froth a bit. The essay, "The Armor of Jules Laforgue," is sent purely as a matter of orientation.[11] It carries the double stigma of having been written to sell and not having sold. However, it is much nearer the issue than McAlmon's claim that the appreciation of Laforgue is based on one's familiarity with Flaubert. . . . As to the long story, it was done last summer, and is a bit too much Huysmans and Little Review to satisfy me completely now.[12] Still, it has turgescence, and I am anxious to know your reactions to it. Let me especially call Chapter V, "Tonnage," to your attention, in case there is too much measles and child-birth this week for you to read the entire shaydevver. I realize that it is too long to serve in CONTACT, and am sending it, also, for purposes of orientation. . . . I do hope, however, that you will agree with my little three page "Tone-Picture," in spite of its somewhat Griegish title.[13] For it is thoroughly representative of the sort of thing I am writing at present. And I do not think that the direction, scherzando, is idle, as it signifies the basis for my excursional dips into a sort of artificial emotion. . . . The other thing I am enclosing is a poem of Cowley's, somewhat Jules Romains[14] but still very much Cowley. It is my personal opinion that 7 and 8 should be reversed; I remember that Cowley once agreed with me in this, but I see that he has not changed them.

The French books are being mailed at the same time.

Burke.

[P]   [Rutherford]
Jan 26, 1921

Dear Burke,

God bless your bloody American heart I want to print all you have sent—and shall sooner or later in some way or other. The Laforgue article pleases me. I object to appreciative articles on foreigners being written for us from Europe. The environment gets into the writing every time and it is inimical to me. I resent the feel I get from the composition and so I am led to antagonism against the appreciated. Criticism must originate in the environment that it is intended for. Laforgue is a new Laforgue in America. Our appreciation of him creates him for us and this I feel in your work. You have taken what you want from the master in order to satisfy your needs and your needs are the product of your environment. (I wish to God I dared print this note somewhere in the next issue where your paper will be used. What do you say?)

You fairly illustrate what Bob and I mean by contact. Why the last paragraph, the quotation, is a perfect exemplar of our attitude. Laforgue takes what he has and makes it THE THING. That is what we must do. It is not even a matter of will. It is fate. We are here under one—Hell, you know all that as well as I.

The stuff apart from the Laforgue thing I have not yet read though the story where I have dipped into it seems to be full of well formed blocks rich with good words.[15] I want to look it over more carefully with a view to bringing it out in installments. We'll see.

Damn it man you encourage me. I want to go on and on with this damned magazine as long as men like you can be doubtingly approached and dragged forward against their wills. It is the way it must be done. Bob and I thought that geniuses would rush forward and fling masterpieces at us.

We will be the greatest gainers by this venture if we learn what CONTACT with the Americans we want to meet means. It's a hell of a job meeting each other. It's a battle. We have not means of transit.

Shit. Cowley's poem is also good. I agree with you however that 7 & 8 should most decidedly be transposed. We'll use it though either this time or next but please try and have the man do what you suggest.

If you see Bob tell him what I have said here. Oh of course you won't. You're an American. Never mind.

I haven't forgotten the promised evening at that place on 3d. Ave. Next week, is it? on Friday.

THERE IS HOPE! It's a damned lie. There is BURKE.

Yours,

Williams

Don't mind this god damned letter. I really mean something or other, as you shall see. <u>W</u>.

⟿

[P]   [134 West Fifteenth Street][16]
January 27, 1921

Dear Williams,

Judging conservatively from the excessively fervid tone of your letter, it ought to take just about two weeks for you to cut me on the street. McAlmon, however, assures me that the case is not so serious. Still, I can't help conjecturing the exact nature of the cross I am to be Jeezuz to.

I am writing you to make a suggestion which I woke up with in bed last night, and which I can't nurse until next Friday. As follows: we assemble a group of men for the purpose of getting out of a periodical. Each of these men buys a certain number of pages in each issue. Thus, the 24–page <u>CON-TACT</u> which McAlmon says the De Pamphilis press would get out for seventy-eight dollars could be portioned among twelve or twenty-four people. Each of these men has his own page, is his own editor, and pays the expenses of printing this page. At the figure of the De Pamphilis press, twelve people could divide up a 24–page magazine at a cost of about seven dollars each, surely a nominal amount. And any outside contributions in the way of money could be used to pay distributing costs and perhaps even a bit of advertising. Such a paper would exist formally as a permanent symposium, and could adapt its size entirely in accord with its list of contributors. In this way, each man could unburden himself without in any way involving the others, and the paper could be issued entirely free of the necessity of ass-licking, a predicament which I suspect stigmatized <u>CONTACT</u> at its very inception. Was sagst du darüber? I am pleased with the idea because it would be a business proposition, and I don't see why the echt-Amerikanisch in art should differ from the echt-Amerikanisch in anything else. And I, personally, should be willing to give up smoking to own my page in such a venture.

The organization of such a paper would be a sort of American Unacademy of Arts. After the original group was formed, each new man would be admitted by the consent of the others, the one requirement being that the candidate's output should represent something more affirmative than a masturbatory adolescence. Also, in the interest of all these seven-dollarses, the only censorship would be to stop the publication of anything which would cause the total suppression of an issue. Each contributor would guarantee to take a certain number of pages regularly, although arrangements would be permissible among the various contributors whereby one man could transfer his pages to another in one issue and have them paid back in another, thus enabling the publication of longer articles without running them serially. (Surely, a most business-like system, which I learned from my study of the Tidewater Coal Exchange, and which I have explained exhaustively in my article on Exporting American Coal, to appear in the March issue of <u>Dun's International Review</u>. I must certainly send you an inscribed copy.) However, what do you think of the idea? And are our avid self-expressionists really avid enough to remain keen in the face of a seven-dollar expenditure?

McAlmon came in last night, and I took him around to Cowley's but things went off quite funereally. In this spiritual copulation both parties failed to come. Cowley, I suppose, was still a bit disgruntled at the rap McAlmon took at him in the last <u>L.R.</u>, and no doubt doubly so since McAlmon's objections had been anything but clearly formulated, so that there was very little grounds for discussions.[17] So we all contented ourselves by a barren litany of the people we should care to shit upon. . . . As to the arrangement of the stanzas, by the way, Cowley is perfectly agreed to having 7 and 8 reversed, and asked me to tell you so.

I am enclosing the <u>Dadaiste Litterature</u> I have here, with the original copy of an analysis of Dadaism which I sold to the <u>Tribune</u>, and which—I pray in the interest of the fifteen dollars involved—will appear some day.[18] It is, as you will note, criticism doped up for Sunday supplement consumption, but nevertheless it says something. It should be read in the following order: front of first sheet; front of blue sheet (insert found in handwriting on back of blue sheet); back of first sheet; and front and back of second sheet.

I shall see McAlmon later on in the week and make definite arrangements for our meeting at McSorley's.[19]

Good luck,

Burke

I had a number of the <u>Dadaiste Litterature</u> here, but I can not find it.

[P]   [Rutherford]
Thursday [1921]

Dear Burke,

Nothing doing for this Friday night. Things have happened too rapidly since we last met for me to be able to arrange them in order. Have you spoken to Bob lately?

Your article goes into this issue of <u>Contact</u>. We intend to print this time. If possible I want you to correct your own proof but if you prefer I will be glad to do it for you.

In any case keep all that should be up, up until better days.

Yours,
Williams

[P]   [Rutherford]
[February 24, 1921]

Dear Burke,

You're a damned irascible Irishman with more sense than you deserve to have. Of course you have Typhus; couldn't anyone tell it by the smell of your letter?

Meanwhile—am awaiting death—I'm damned sorry for your eyes & your headaches. I want to see you and talk with you. I have a few old soiled pairs of underdrawers under the lounge or piano or somewhere which you can mop your tears on.

And quick as you are, you have been as quick to interpret my idea of <u>Contact,</u> etc. I want to see you. Last Friday was an impossibility for me. Bob's sudden demise <u>etc</u>.[20]

You haven't known me long enough to know how I have been knocked out by Bob's going away.

You call me a Whitmanite (Jezus Christus what lightning like penetration) then you want me to admit Josephson[21] to my cellar closet—I am raw and stupid—

I like <u>you</u>.

C'est tout.

Yours,
Williams

[B]   134 West Fifteenth St.,
New York City,
March 21, 1921

Dear Williams:

Thanks for the CONTACT's. The prize, I think, goes to "Apotheosis to Extinction."[22] I have been getting bumped in the nose quite generally of late—hated, where known at all—so that McAlmon's scathings seem harmless enough, especially as they are written in a style which was satirized by de Gourmont before 1890. But McAlmon, being pure of literary influences, can write in such demoded fashions without sullying his bland virginity. While gnarled I, weakened by knowledge, am cursed by the awareness that it has been done much better thirty years ago. Vive l'ignorance! However, I do think a great deal of the lines

> No man exactly expressing himself
> Would be understood by anyone else . . .

no doubt because they do express my attitude so perfectly. The entire fallacy of McAlmon's viewpoint, it seems to me, is expressed in the line

> For sensitivities have a suture that closes to discovery.

As a matter of fact, sensitivities have a suture that closes in <u>invention</u>. The process of discovery is involved in those inexplicable accidents which occur when the artist focuses his feeling for the uncertain and yearning for the certain on one subject. In some, this process may be limited entirely to that last moment when the work of art is being produced. In others, however, this process may be at its height in the synthetic attitude toward the whole, and thus begin operating long before the actual process of writing—or composing, etc.—has been undertaken. Simply because I try to envisage an entire work before turning to any part of it, it is not just to diagnose this method as "yielding no point to temperamental discovery," for the elaboration of a personal form is as much of temperamental discovery as any wild shot in the dark. (Please do not misunderstand me. I do not "resent" this poem. Indeed, McAlmon showed it to me the day after he had written it. I simply pick on it since in its immediately personal application it comes so close to the source of all our discussions.) To quote, or instance, a page from my diary which traces the development of one part of a story:

As to our present story, it might begin this way: He pulled through the draft all right, without having to do his share for the Dupont interests. . . . Still,

I had wanted to start with the general orchestration of his life, making it a little less definite before actually pulling out the thin string of himself. America . . . cities . . . adolescence . . . they hit Humpty Haas'es bat with a lemon . . . in short, all sorts of general orientations of the conditions under which he ripened. Then perhaps, we could suddenly jump into the above sentence. Or better still, since the beginning will be generally ideological, the second movement should get away from ideology altogether; thus, the argumentative note of the proposed sentence would spoil the contrast. No, the style here must be as exclusively narrative as possible. Parts I and III, as they are now seen:

Part I

1 General orchestration of background

2 Specific narrative

Part II

1 Final annihilation of protagonist (by annihilation I mean his ultimate non-register or shrinkage)

2 General pessimistic batting of wings

3 Return to specific character for a few sentences

(Note: Not necessarily the annihilation of the protagonist. One could perhaps better do the annihilation of the protagonist's background—as in the success of a bad play—and then annihilate the protagonist in those few closing sentences in the "return to the specific.")

As to Part II, it should be some sort of pivotal point between I and III. I think that the love-affair with ample footnotes would be the desired thing, since in this way there would be no motion either one way or the other—a sort of way-station. Thus:

Part III

1 Matter-of-fact discussion of love affair

2 Lessons learned therefrom; also, other details of wisdom acquired by protagonist in course of life.

(Note: The expressiveness here will be greatly dependent upon the accessory paraphernalia.)

I am certainly not asking the semi-Whitmanites to write after this manner. Indeed, I am not even asking that any other man in the world write after this manner. But what I do wish to point out is that every turn in the development of this story is a purely <u>temperamental</u> turn; the only difference between my method and yours is that in my case the temperamental begins working as an agent in a <u>conscious choice</u>. That is, the actual set of my medium can be discussed from the standpoint of co-ordination of parts. (What this produces is another matter, as I am not discussing excellence now but method. Even if I wrote the damnedest truck on earth this method would not be affected. Also, the final sentence will always be of necessity a temperamental discovery.)

I am, by the way, leaving New York for the summer, leaving in about three weeks.[23] Since last seeing you I have "discovered" a remarkably expressive method of attack which I should like to talk to you about. Do you want to see me? Do you want correspond with me this summer? Let's get these things cleared up once for all. If there is the possibility of a spontaneous relationship, God bless us . . . if not, I might as well have spared myself this letter.

Burke

[P]   [Rutherford]
March 22, 1921

Dear Burke,

Wont you and your wife and baby[24] come out to spend the afternoon with us a week from this coming Sunday. Arrive here sometime about noon. We'll have dinner then after which we can disport ourselves as may best suit our fancy. And wont you lift yourself to this province of darkness and cellars and four-months-old puppies that are mistaken for senile hounds sometime earlier. Come out Friday late in the afternoon if you like this Friday and stay for supper. Let me hear from you.

We shall hear from each other this summer. It would be a pity not to have some traffic between the poles. I have long wanted to have a correspondence with someone very dissimilar to myself, the thing to be planned as a dialogue criticizing the universe (literature), which might be published later. Procrus vs. Aprocrus. In any case I should like very much to write, though I feel, without meaning to spoof, that I'll be the gainer rather than you.

As a rule I detest argument—no one is ever convinced by it since it is nearly always a mere confusion of terms, like a football game. But your objections to McAlmon on the score of his general ignorance of French literature and Rémy de Gourmont's 1890 satires in particular almost stirs me to reply.[25] But after all it would be no use. We are too far apart yet to indulge in talk profitably. Perhaps someday we'll get some sense out of each other.

I like your ill-natured jabs at myself so come on out and lets fart around for a couple of hours and see if we can't amuse each other—perhaps even complement each other in something serious.

I received word from Bob in London. He's having a noble time of it. My word what a chance!

Have you received notice of Stuart Davis' new periodical—SHIT?[26] Two hundred copies to be privately circulated each month. Come on in the shit is fine.

Don't forget to let me hear from you, Mr. Whitman.

Yours,
Oscar[27]

[P]   [Rutherford]
[March 23, 1921]

Dear Burke,

That thing of yours in the present <u>Dial</u> is breathless in its power to hold. Very good Eddie.[28]

Were not Thayer a helpless false-alarm he would accept your new story at once.[29] It is by far the most modernly gripping thing of yours—or any one else's I have seen in years. Your reference to myself makes me think my <u>Improvisations</u> may have interested you. Well, God is kind and gives us a few men of sense every generation. He is kind too in refusing recognition to them while they live.

But the final bolt that fastens up your tin image in my "chur'," as my Greek boot-black calls the temples they dig up in their gardens at Samos (pardon the digression), is that goddamned cuntlapping shitwaggonhound Floyd Dell's[30] dislike for you. He is to me the last syllable of the universal fart. Now I KNOW you amount to something.

You should hear my Greek speak of the blocks of stone two miles from the sea, the sea having receded during the past two thousand years, where "them fellas" used to fasten their boats. It is thrilling. Ancient Greece does not live in Homer as it does in that man's talk.

I'm sorry you can't come out on Friday but I can wait. I know all about babies so don't let that concern you.

Someday you may even understand what—What?

Yes SHIT is the immortal word. Imagine a temple to SHIT with little booths ranged along the sides. But after a meal, what more important compartment exists in the two great N.Y. railroad stations than that where one may shit. Eat and shit. Someday they will dig up these stations and investigate our sad, disused toilets—into which man has slowly disappeared from year to year, teeth and all. It is too sad.

Yes, do not forget the diapers.

Yours,
Williams

I have read your story all through again—yes it is a very tight jobby.[31]

Congratulations.

[P]   [Rutherford]
March 31, 1921

Dear Burke,

Sunday then, before noon. I'll try to be at the station to meet you but should this not be possible I hope you'll not get lost. It is only a very short walk.

May the day be bright; in this day of popular neurasthenias the weather is one of the few things a man can tolerate at its best. I'll try to have all the crocuses up, the narcissi also and all leaves neatly brushed and polished.

I hope you're not a vegetarian or cannibal or any of that ilk. If so you'll be good enough to tell me what you DO eat at once by return mail that we may have the dish you prefer before you. Speak up young man.

You make me tired with your Whitman guff. But then I suppose you make very important distinctions between _merde_ and shit, so I can't quarrel with you. Art is <u>so</u> complicated. My God I stepped in some the other day. It was on my first spring walk. Some American gentleman had dropped it beside the road at the entrance to a culvert. Bla! It was not nice. I had an immediate and almost irresistible desire to study French literature—Oh well, how can one help waxing enthusiastic over such a subject. Please pardon me.

Should anything arise to prevent you from showing up on the Sabbath please call me up by ten (10) A.M.

Regards to your wife.

Yours,
Williams

The American Ideal![32]

**[P]   [Rutherford]
April 27 [1921]**

Dear Burke,

In Maine yet?[33] Well, I'll know if you answer. I don't blame you for waiting until July Fourth before a comeback in view of my own lack of speed. I haven't written a word to a soul for a month. How flattering that always looks.

Then again I wanted to curse you for implying what you implied about my remark anent the <u>Freeman</u>. I know nothing of an article about my book which Fletcher has written[34] and probably never shall know anything about it. I said the <u>Freeman</u> was not so bad because I enjoy its political bunk. As a literary magazine it is of course nonexistent. I like to read political bunk when it is served frankly as a viand.

May I use your very good spring poem in the next issue of <u>Contact</u>?[35] Do not refuse. The issue I speak of will appear in May sometime.[36] I'll surely mail you a copy.

Your damned theorizing about—about—about—Well, what the hell do I care whether you theorize or not so long as you occasionally write something I like. Anyhow all I want to say is that your theories are very pretty especially the one about screwing your sister in the Pullman car.

I can tell you all about how hair grows on the female pubis and that's about all I can tell you these days unless it be—what? Something else, I suppose.

Just damned rot—

I went in to see a picture show—not the movie kind—a show of pictures by Stuart Davis, etc. very nice but rather disappointing. All French—somehow. God when will an.American be born? Quoth the Raven: Nevermore. It will have to be a Mongolian I suppose. Not a mongol tho'. I bought two books the other day. A corking normal physiology and a great (in bulk) treatise on the brain and all it does to itself. You and your inhibitions make me tired. The world has fucked itself with Freud too long. The two most useful things I can think of right now would be to destroy Freud and the French by some capable Manifesto. Somebody ought to be able to invent a full stop before the whole works dribbles out—

Anyhow, it's a letter—

Yours,

Williams

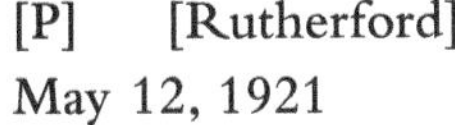

[P]   [Rutherford]
May 12, 1921

Dear Burke,

Bob is about to bring out an international issue of <u>Contact</u> in London.[37] Please send us a story[38] or anything else you want to send. I'll give it my best backing with Bob so that I am sure it will go through. Remember however your international reputation will be at stake. You will be judged in Jerusalem and Bangkok by the quality of what you send—etc. tempo rebato D.C. con fuoco Wurtlebacheimerdoodlesacmachergeselle—etc.[39] i.e.<u>1/2¢/?1/4@5#$% &"*—bla!</u>

Come across.

No, dearest anal—asist (with apologies to farmer in the Dell Floyd) lock-jaw does not come from skin wounds, barking of the knuckles, splinters in the glands or any such light affair. Tetanus is the result of infection with the tetanus (ha,ha!) bacillus, an anaerobic bug which cannot grow or do harm until it is in a location from which the AIR is excluded. No, I did <u>not</u> say vagina. It delights in deep wounds the external opening of which has closed up leaving a focus of infection deep in. This is the reason that one is annoyed when a four inch spike penetrates the shoe and the foot carrying infected horse manure etc. deeply in there to lodge and do harm. If you are thus wounded put your foot in your mouth and yell for help. Meanwhile suck the foot as hard as you can being careful not to bite it off at the ankle as men are not crabs and a new foot would not grow on the stump in the old one's stead. Spit out the blood and bacilli as soon as your mouth fills up continuing in this way till you are unconscious from loss of blood. At that time your foot will automatically unbutton itself from your lips and you are cured.

Rheumatism is hopeless. You probably have it already and will not live more than eighty years from today. Unhappily rheumatism does not kill but causes the poor sufferer to writhe with agony twenty five hours a day so that if he is not a poet at the beginning of his illness he rapidly becomes one, witness Aesop and Paul Scarron,[40] so that death approaches in the end as if it were dawn.

Shift your cud, you have a cold.

Yours,

Bill

I'll be glad to have you read proof on <u>Contact</u>.[41] Thanks.

[P] [Rutherford]
[May, 1921]
<u>Sunday</u>

Dear Burke,
Dear Ken,

Please send story or anything else you have on your mind or elsewhere to Bob:

>   1 South Audley St.
>   London, EG.1.

He is mad, insane, hipped. He has hit Paris and remains unconvinced that America is banal! Jesus—a Daniel come to judgment. Write direct and at once.

Send a car load of MSS.

I am ill with Shit[3] x $\frac{\text{hell}}{y^x}$ = no writing

Wife in hosp. small operation on neck.[42] O.K. now. My eldest son danced at a local function last night: Peter rabbit.

Yours before Cream of Wheat,
Bill

Tell Gould to write Bob.[43]

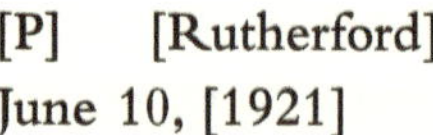

[P] [Rutherford]
June 10, [1921]

Dear Ken,

Read Victor Hugo. You remember in <u>Les Miserables</u> how beautiful the gardens were where the city emptied its sewage? In other words instead of piddling from the porch and killing the grass why not shit among the beans and do some good in the world. The cucumbers of course may need special treatment but a soliloquy on Shitting among the Beans by Moonlight, should make Beethoven green with affection.

Thank God you have the woods and water to rest you. The antiphony from Paris should not bother you in the least. Have you not read my <u>Improvisations</u>.[44] I have said there at least five hundred times that all things have their perfections and that perfection and perfection are equal. It is my sole contribution to the world of my own senses. Drink.

Here the world of art is non existent. I have had a fine rest of late fighting the town in order to get the shitasses to take their hands off the lid long enough for us to get a new high school built. It has gone through at last. We are to have our school. The net result to me is that I have had to address two large and excited audiences, 900 souls, to this effect that I have found myself using words like fine instruments to cause an effect. I felt cool, detached, able to feel each word as it appeared and I uttered it with conscious knowledge of its purpose and effect. It was queer and delightful to be standing there quite collectedly and steering my words into those ears just as I would drive a car through the street. I never had that sensation before. It only shows how unexpectedly such a valuable experience can come to the surface, even in a local school fight. I am wealthier for having faced the music. And I won the fight.

I couldn't help feeling though all the time: Ah, if this energy were only going into art! If only this excitement had some literary matter for its concern!

—★ Bla!

You might know it. The first literary pleasure I have enjoyed in weeks (this letter) has to be interrupted because some bastard of a butcher is bleeding to death, has cut his wrist. Yet I have written these last four lines. Good-bye.

Write more. Tell me more.

Yours,

Bill

[P]   [Rutherford]

July 6, 1921

Dear Ken,

Bob is in Paris having an illuminating time of it—judging from the two letters I have had. He is meeting the best of them constantly and it is having a serious effect on him. He will develop—wait and see.

The MSS of your story is in his hands.[45] He is holding it but cannot bring out another issue of <u>Contact</u> until he has more American material. I'll mention your story in my next letter and tell him to send it back if he can't use it soon—

(Third interruption)

I'll have my issue of <u>Contact</u> out some time or other.

Yours,

Bill

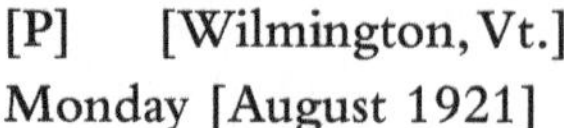

**[P]   [Wilmington, Vt.]
Monday [August 1921]**

Dear Ken,

I suppose I am very dense to the literary impact, everyone, including the Barrenass, says so, so it must be true.[46] I see almost nothing in what I read except short leaps of the machine when it leaves the ground for a word or two. The Dadaists are very proud but they fly very little—even they.

Well, to tell all that is in my head about your things (the two stories) now that you have defended them—would take a week of academic talk.[47] I can't do it.

Send along more stuff please. I may find the key later on. So far, I feel these stories as cerebral brickabrack—to hell with them.

I leave here in 8 days.[48] Why I go back is hard for me to say.

Bill

**[P]   [Rutherford]
Friday Noon [August 1921]**

Dear Ken,

By the speed of your reply to this letter I'll know whether or not to mail you proofs of the new <u>Contact</u>.[49]

c/o E. Haslund
Wilmington, Vt.
Fine weather

Yours,
Willie

**[P]   [Wilmington, Vt.]
August 10, 1921**

Dear Ken,

I won't send the proofs which I am returning to the printer at once. It will be the best printed affair I have yet been identified with.

I want your stories with interest—let us see.

Thanks for your "honey" speech. I say "thanks" because surely beggars are a nuisance.

Yours,
Bill

[P]   [Wilmington, Vt]
August 23, 1921

Dear Ken,

Your horrible allegory so disturbs me that I can't tell whether it is good or bad.[50] I don't like it a bit though bits of it seem like hell itself let through. It is too unreal, too granite-like, bloodless for my taste. It is perhaps bad because it is based fundamentally on a moral issue. That is all I can say.

The other piece also I dislike. It is too uneven. I feel the places between the bricks. In places I feel your genius but you seem to thwart yourself sense-lessly for some meaningless external purpose.

I feel angry at you for not shitting more gaily. You take it too much to heart.

Yours,
Bill

[P]   [Rutherford]
Oct 21 1921

Dear Ken,

Congratulations on the sale to <u>The Dial</u>.[51] May the god of all good men shine in the minds of that editorial staff until you get tired of writing essays—which I hope will be never. I enjoy your essays.

As soon as <u>SOUR GRAPES</u> appears you shall have a copy.[52] It should be out at any moment—but it may not be out for a month. It would be fine to have you do it. I have been least interested. For this reason, perhaps, it will turn out to be one of the best, though I think not. It has been more "composed" than any so far, which, if it is discoverable, should please you. The fact of its appearance is due more to the pressure of ordinary circumstances, such as hav-ing a lot of stuff lying around than to anything else. Yet, one hopes—proof that

I am not yet an artist. An artist is always beyond hope—please do not remind me of it.

You "hay stackers" are the naive children of genius. Yes, medicine pays. Bless your heart, it is easy for me to admire you, surrounded as I am with paying dirt in the form of grippe, tonsillitis. Each to his own filth.

I'll see you someday—I expect soon.

Do you want to come out for a rest and a meal some day?

Yours,

Bill

∿

[P]   [Rutherford]
Nov. 10, 1921

Dear Ken,

Bravo! Best yet.[53] S.O.B. not to show it to me. Quite right, though. Read it almost all without knowing it was you who had waked me when I was so damned heavy eyed I could scarcely see the page. Capsicut.

Most interesting to compare it, in texture, with French stuff in same copy. Your quotations from De Gourmont stand out awkwardly against Morand et al. It is America stroking its cock—But that is not what I want to say.

What I want to say is that I take great pride in saluting you as—well, the foremost writer of your place (Is it an anticlimax?) Yes, it is. T&h$e G#r% r&r★e%"t(e)s#t WRITER—★#68%# of your time—Shit. When all I want to say is—All I want to say would be so much more hydrocephalic than basilar lues is likely to become by looking at a "the" through a prism. In other words, intelligent and all knowing as I am I find your David Wasserman brilliant, thrilling, interesting and the best you have yet accomplished.

I wrote Bill Saphier that your story laid upon the French stuff in the <u>L.R.</u>, as a group, resembled woolen fabric upon linen.[54] I warn you that I wrote this to him in a letter today, in case you should meet him.

Now let me suggest that—ha, ha!

Yours,

Bill

∿

[P]   [Rutherford]
Nov. 19, 1921

Dear Ken,

I accept your apology.

English being, as you imagined, the lousiest language on earth, you thought to write well by writing lousily. You wrote better than you imagined. If I could tell you why, I would, flower from the crannied wall, tell you all you don't know.

Besides, didn't you once tell somebody that the only reason my own work was readable was that it was so damned mediocre—in tone, that is, with itself and its natural circumstances of being?

I suppose I am at heart a mystic. But who isn't until he clarifies his meaning or dies trying to. Even the Arabs or the Phoenicians, or whoever it was that invented the rule of three, were mystics until they found out pretty damned clearly that they were fooling themselves and so had to invent the science of mathematics to save their faces. Contemplate that last sentence awhile and you'll know a hell of a lot more than I knew—once.

I like your theories—they're so puerile that they don't count, so you have plenty of opportunity to write and save your face. Kiss me again Merdito. Because you CAN write.

I'll do all you ask concerning Bob.[55] In fact, I have sent your stuff on already.

No, I have not contributed to Alfred's <u>Broom</u>.[56] I may someday soon. I haven't much to send.

Crazy about your Matthew Arnold tidbit.[57] You really delight my heart. Do you think me a fool if I say that at present I find you to be the only interesting character writing in America today. Paul Rosenfeld seems good in his way but he has no flare or flaire or insanity to temper his bricklaying.[58] Yes, writing is bricklaying.

L'architecture c'est poser un cailloux sur un autre.
You like that? My brother handed it to me.[59] I wish he really knew what it means.

Up Irland! You knife.

Yours,

Bill

[P]   **[Rutherford]**
Dec. 5, 1921

Dear Ken,

I'm really ashamed.

Yours,
Bill

[P]   **[Rutherford]**
Christmas
is here [Christmas Eve 1921]

Dear Ken,

Quite so, quite so. Room enough for both. Thanks for copying out my lovely sentence, I wanted to see it again. Your comments, continued, might make fine reading if done at length in the manner of Mozart or Bach or whoever it was that would write variations on a theme. Really quite wonderful even as it is. I enjoy your achromatic lens.

Whenever you write the thing you want me to see, send it on.

The book is, as usual, delayed.[60] With me it seems always the same: obstetrics one way or the other and always difficult deliveries.

So I say, let us die talking, do I? Go ahead and die then if you think it's so damned smart. People talk about death as if they know somebody who had died. Ah, I am at one with you there, my deah boy. Talk might even convince a virgin that she is ready to cast her light into the dark heart of ye poet. And when this happens, America will be cut open and found to be full of mushrooms. Yes, I am one of these, i.e. Mushrooms. Talk is not the drip it is for, it is a drip that may not be a drip but the trip of ye jazz, quite right. Nebuchadnezzar—blaaaa. But TOMORROW—GLOOOOOOOOOORY—OOOOOOOOOOOOO

Meanwhile see if you do not like my interpretation of the Apollo.

What shit I really do spit.

Spit

Spit

Oh. Ah
at last
a poem

Yours truly,
William Carlos Williams

Order is heaven's first law
Order is heaven's first law
Order is heaven's first law
Order is heaven's first law
Order is heaven's first law
Order is heaven's first law
Order is heaven's first law
Order is heaven's first law
(Order is heaven's first law)
Tweet tweet

After this, I really cannot bring myself to send you the poem questions.

[P]   [Rutherford]
Feb. 3, 1922

Dear Ken Burke,

It is perfectly proper that you should have answered, as you have, the letter that I have been sending you for a week past. This is the proof positive of the existence of the soul for which all men have sought since Jesus' ass was wiped—or before the first anthropoid's was licked. The trouble has been to find the words. I have carried your sentences in my head—also my spleen (some of them) ever since I had my advance copy of <u>The Dial</u>.[61] You have ·pleased the little tin—No, that's not it (I'm in a hell of a rush, writing in the kitchen because I happened to leave the machine there last night)—in a damned wordless rush to get—That's why I waste so much time I guess.

I enjoyed reading your article because it went at the work as if it were an interesting problem and not a sign board to be painted—therefore you thought enough about what you were doing to keep the facts scientifically before you.

Come out at once and show me your throat. I mean at once. I would come and getch you—or go and fetch you but I really think I'll be able to take you home again even if I can't do the first.

Wallace Gould is here.[62]

Come out for supper or something. Call up first. Come out in the morning if you like or any time at all—lunch is a good time. So is breakfast.

Please phone first—not that I have to make any adjustments but Flossie must go out and buy the pickles.

I fell at once for the propositions in the tail (under the tail) of your letter. To write of the aesthetic of writing has always fascinated me. You could do it and be interesting. Do it.

Yours,

Bill

[B]   [Spring 1922]

Dear Bill,

Sitting in a station, with nothing to do but wait. I discover an envelop in my pocket. Use it! (Waiting in a station, to go to Andover, to put the sturdy little seeds all in a row and see what happens.)[63]

Well, I'll say this: it looks like a new magazine, edited by Matty Josephson, me, myself, and I.[64] We already have 5000 you-knows underwritten for the first year. That alone would get us get us something, so we can with reasonable safety say that we shall get out something.

So be holding back some of our stuff from the Saturday Evening Post, to let us have it instead. Contributors are to be paid! Dial rates.

Greetings. Hope all your poor-paying clients are healthy. You must try to come out this summer. (We're going to there this Saturday and Sunday— so look in if you happen to be about.)

K.B.

[B]   R.D. #1
Andover, N.J.,
June 3, 1922

And a hell of a June 3 it is, dear Doc. Boredom sits upon me like a cloak. And it sat upon me yesterday idem. Concerning our certain Guterrez, I have a sonnet which touches on the matter. I quote herewith, to pass away the very heavy hours:[65]

> Imagine this: a new Balboa . . . heat . . .
> Trampling of horses . . . sweating in the sun
> He stormed eight thousand miles . . . unstopped . . . <u>ensuite</u> . . .
> Just one more mountain . . . and the ocean!

Imagine him as last word supermannish,
And over-weighted with the Small Specific . . .
"Turn back," he muttered in a weary Spanish,
And died, with vague regret for his Pacific.

Thank God, at least, our hero undertook
By far the major portion of his journey . . .
Is there some oh, but no there is no book . . .
Sonatas die, while we go on with Czerny.

Why not include in our nosologies
Such neo-Post-Parnassian ennuis?

Alas! It <u>is</u> the philosopher who will turn back, but that simply proves that Columbus was the first traveling salesman, and discovered a continent which was to be made in his image. I vote for a certain Guterrez. And I'll venture further that it was not Guterrez who took syphilis back to Europe.

Gorham B. Munson, Esq. has been here to see me by the way, and he informs me that you met his request for contributions—aesthetic and not economic—to his nascent magazine with a deaf ear. Why, pray, so highty-tighty? There is just the least possibility that the magazine may actually amount to something. At least, the ambition is to carry on an experimental fiction and poetry department with a solid critical department to bully with. Munson intends to finance the thing for two years. His editorial policy is still very vague. The first issue was rather weak, except for Cowley's poem.[66] The second, I think, will be much better. It contains four poems by Cummings (two of which I liked considerably; the other two looked fishy), two by Cowley, my Book of Yul, a story by Josephson; he has said very little of his intentions.[67] As he has gone mad on Dadaism since being in Paris I challenged him to a duel on this subject, a symposium of contrasted views to be published side by side, but have not yet heard from his seconds. But the next two or three issues after this are to be gotten out under the tripartite editorship of Munson, Josephson and Burke. Our aim, as I see it, is to get stuff which is good, as good as possible, stuff in which the virtues have transcended editorial taste or have been over-ruled through fear of censorship, advertisers, etc. By Munson's printing in Vienna he can get out about five or six issues for the price it costs to print one issue of Contact in America. The thing which I am trying to instill into my somewhat overly advance-guard co-editors is the need of a certain critical solidity, authority, sitzfleisch. I am so sick of these customary vomitoriums for the professionally young that I feel like cutting off my cock and telling the world I am eighty-five. We hope in the fall to inaugurate some sort of sittings for our little group of serious thinkers. And in the meantime why not send us some pet which has been rejected by the Dial, Broom and the Saturday Evening Post?

I hope you really will be able to get out here. And I am very sorry to hear about our boy's illness. Are mastoid operations imperative? I understand that Josephson has been dodging one for years quite successfully.

Sincerely,

K.B.

⸛

[P]   [Rutherford]
[June 10, 1922]

Dear Ken,

Glad you opened your shell again. There is a nice story about my friend Columbus in the book of Leopardi's[68] dialogues, which I read, alas, in translation only. On the <u>Santa Maria</u> with the admiral, it seems, there was a certain Guterrez, an officer of the Spanish crown, a gentleman and a philosopher— a philosopher. After they had been sailing westward for a month he one night arrested the admiral in conversation; he asked Columbus how much longer he intended to sail westward in view of the increasing dangers and the likelihood of a not far distant death for the entire outfit. Columbus replied that he intended to sail westward until he found India. But, answered Guterrez, we shall all die. Hard luck, answered Columbus. I believe he was referring to himself. You see he had so much to lose.

I know the road to Cranberry lake very well.[69] I shall be with you some day before July first.

We have had serious illness in the family during the past two weeks. The smaller boy has been on the verge of a mastoid operation but happily seems so far to have escaped.[70]

Sorry about the apple blossoms and azaleas. Best luck.

Yours,

Bill

I'm writing poetry.

> How do I write?
> By the weather.
> Fine days fine verse
> Dark days, better.

[P]   [Rutherford]
[June 20, 1922]

Dear Burke,

Which Frenchman is it from whom you imitated your contempt for Columbus? Blaa! Let's start a new radical magazine. Blaa! Let's make it pay. Blaa! Let's imitate Dada! Blaa! Let's purify our philosophy until we discover the way home! Blaa! Let's ask Josephson to contribute to it! Blaa! Why not turn your penis inside out, furside outside inside, inside juiceside outside, treat the act seriously, sincerely—Imagine having the entire surface of the body secreting semen, or laved with it. Then imagine one big juicy cunt to crawl into where one can shake himself as a dog who has been drenched. Why do you upbraid me when I do not answer every letter that comes? Who the hell is Munson?[71] And what the hell difference is it to him whether I contribute to his sheet or not? Who the hell am I? I am busy thinking. The ship is sinking, Columbus has diarrhea and has built himself a small shack near the wheel. Guterrez must have time in which to wax his moustaches.

But if Munson really wants something from me I think I have it.[72] It is in French. I went to school in Switzerland when I was fourteen so that I assure you what I have to contribute is in French.

One thing only I would insist on: my contribution must be kept from all eyes save the editors until it actually appears in print—THAT MEANS YOU. And it must not be translated, not even <u>in camera</u>. Its meaning must not even be surmised. If the editor sees the word <u>quand</u> he must close his mind to it, it must mean <u>bread</u> to him until it is in print. Under those circumstances I have an epoch making contribution to the new magazine—perhaps it will pith the thing.

Family is well. I'll surely see you before July first—if you are there when I arrive. Best wishes. Yours.

[B]   R.D. #1
Andover, N.J.
June 21, 1922

Dear Doc,

All right, two-gun Williams, culture's bad man, the cowpuncher of Eighth Street, but I'll swear to God I don't know whether you're just letting off steam, or kidding me tail off, or whether Munson's great-grandfather once robbed your great-aunt. It is all very vague and distressing. The French poem doesn't sound inviting. We are, you know, strictly anti-poodpullers, a rare group these days, you must admit. Better advance a few more years and send us something after the first night.

I, thank God, am a wretchedly busy man. My job starts with the Dial on Monday, the twenty-sixth, and lasts until December.[73] In the meantime this prolonged wet weather makes it almost impossible to kill the weeds out of the garden. I must get some wood carved up before starting to work. I have about twenty thousand words of German to get off my hands . . . and here come six cherry trees all ripening at once.[74] Thought is only possible while dumping. . . . I feel like a Rutherford doctor.

Incidentally, I write this letter lest you some day actually should get it into your head to come out here, and find nothing at home but my quietly fattening vegetables. But if you came this Friday you would be treated with great deference and respect, given fresh peas, and perhaps could take back fifty cents worth of free cherries to make up for your four-dollar expenditure in gasoline.

But it is long after twelve. I fail.

KB.

⤳

[P]   [Rutherford]
[June 1922]

Dear Ken,

You're a fool but then, so am I: you make me tired but apparently so do I you. And your accuracies are the remainder. Such is my enjoyment. This morning, in any case, I am in your hands. What I have to dispose of shall be sent to you for Munson's use. I really have very little work ready to be shown.

My trip to your farm is one of the incidents in the imagined farce of my existence. It is a trip that has more possibilities unmade than made I suppose—since I do not make it. But the composition of bank books is the drip from uneaten apples. It is stupid to remain here waiting for butcher's wives to calve while my plans wait and nothing happens in the end anyway—the woman misses her time—but such is my life.

Returning to Munson's project: I haven't a grain of interest in it aside from your letter this morning—how could I, of course, not having seen it? I suppose you stung me a little with your favorite taunt of 'poodpulling.' It seems so, damned if it don't. In any case, I'm interested and amused. Two or three poems, more or less finished are in my case together with a quantity of prose notes on the subject of "contact" with which idea I have not quite finished. But this is very uninteresting. I'll look over the things.

The fourth stanza is sympathetic. What do you know of a Frenchman called Blaise Cendrars?[75] He seems to have heard of me in some way, not from my friends. I presume he must be a leader in French fashion!—literary fashion. I hear that he has collected an anthology of African Negro poetry. Having exhausted that he turns to New York. It is soul destroying to imagine what might be done, in French, with my masterpieces. It seems he wants to translate me. Am I not interesting?

Best luck,
Bill

I am sending a single poem—all that I have—one that Demuth wants dedicated to himself: Demuth is one of my longest standing (tours Eiffel) friends.[76] Please rave about it.

It is about a year old.

[P]   [Rutherford]
Monday [July 1922]

Dear Ken,

When in city call me up Lenox 10195. Please do not hand that phone number on indiscriminately; I am in a sort of retirement here. My address is 54 E. 87 if you want to write, which would be better.[77] Might still arrange to go out with you to Andover, would like to very much in fact if we can arrange it.

Have you seen the slam I got in <u>Poetry</u>?[78] Pound has also just finished shitting on me in a personal letter. Also McAlmon's book and his story in <u>L.R.</u> haven't made me feel exceptionally fine.[79] I enjoy Bob however.

Have you seen the complete <u>Contact</u> publishing list? Hemingway is a star I think.[80] His poems especially are noteworthy but the prose is thrilling. Who is he anyway?

My best wishes to your good wife—that climbs cherry trees and picks cherries.

Yours,
Bill

[P]   [Rutherford]
July 15, 1922

Dear Ken,

Thank you a thousand times: my work is diseased and theatric, as if taken out of a hat.[81] It's what I've been trying to say for five years. I am really grateful to you.

I want to see you soon and get the rest of it.

Congratulations on the birth of your daughter.[82]

You may not believe it but you've done me the most considerable favor by your acute criticism of my verse that I have known in recent years. I feel free as a condor or a pee-wee or something.

Bless you. I'll call you up some day soon, you may depend on it.

Yours,

Bill

[P]

[undated]

Dear Ken,

What about this Sunday? If the weather is fair I shall try to get away from this sunspot fairly early in the morning, to be with you for broiled chicken. As usual my word is so much tissue paper but I think I can make it this time— probably it will rain, not having rained for a month.

Try to worm something out of Seldes about the stuff I sent him recently. Lola[83] has been hauling me over the coals a little since I promised the poem to her and then sold it, so to speak, to a higher bidder.

Then, damn it, it maybe isn't sold at all. I wish I had it back. Shit.

By—No, not that—Just that I have been reading Cummings' <u>Enormous Room</u> and enjoying it—for the most part, greatly. It is atrociously written in places: impossible sentence constructions—but there are other places of great intensity; while through it all there is a lovely New England Sunday effect <u>a travers le Montmartyr</u>, which I greatly appreciate.

Drop me a line—the contemplation of my navel is growing a little thick this week. Is it a perversion to be happy with a pencil and paper? Ah, it is an old question.

Yours,

Bill

[B]   R.D.#1
Andover, N.J.
September 4, 1922

Well, well, old Doc Bill Billiams, and how many bedpans have you looked into since we last communicated? With the rain falling upon the saturated sponge of my seventy-three and fifty-three hundredth acres, and with a third holy day on my hands—the first I slept, the second chopped wood, and the third, becoming cultured with this excess of leisure, I write letters—all this being so, I rite to Rutherford's Romulus. Professionally speaking—being undermined with business—I first lay awake for a week with ivy poisoning, and then lay awake for a week with acid poisoning, and this week I move under the Damoclean sword of a growling tooth.

Concerning Secession, your two poems are appearing in issues three and four.[84] The third issue should be along in a few days now. Other pearls therein will be a story by me, and a story—the dirtiest story—out of Frank's City Block.[85] Also, as the stinking poem of your two will be included, and as there are rapes, exhibitionism, seductions, nigger-fucks, and other gems included, we might gain our coveted suppression; in which case the fourth number would appear punctually, but under a different name. The first two numbers, to my mind, have been by no means negligible affairs, and we have received a really surprising number of correspondence, and even subscriptions. Number 4 will probably contain a review of Cummings's book, by Munson, your poem dedicated to Demuth, a poem by Wallace Stevens, poem by Hart Crane, something by Cowley, and my In Quest of Olympus.[86] Eventually we shall probably eliminate the Frogs, and perhaps after we are all back in New York we shall attempt to organize into some sort of drive, very likely a drive against the stupidity of the progressive critics. For as a matter of fact, people like Irving Babbitt and Paul Elmer More are worth a damned sight more than the Van Dorens and the Burton Rascoes and the Johnny Weavers.[87] Munson really seems in earnest in his guarantee to continue the paper for two years. And we are determined above all to let no thoroughly weak number get through us, a determination which I can assure you will have been lived up to for the first four numbers at least. We shall exist, I hope, as the Dial's most formidable overflow organ, and we should pick up a great deal of value as the Dial has comparatively few pages to allot to our non-continental reputations. I say this, not in ire, not in wrath, but as an observation, a point to be considered in our calculations for a vivid sheet.

Best wishes. And here's hoping you will get around to the Dial offices some day.

K.B.

[P] [54 E. 87th]
Tuesday [Oct. 3, 1922]

Dear Ken,

I'll be out to see you Wednesday eve or Thursday morn. I'd say surely Wednesday eve if it weren't for the walk from the station. I suppose there is a train sometime. I'll get hold of a timetable today.

Must be back here Friday in time to take Floss to see Mary, Mary. We'll fart and talk and walk in the usual literary way I guess. But I'm glad you said Pound should not have shat on me. He won't get a second chance this season, in any case.

Don't have supper kept for me on Wednesday. If I get there at all I will have had supper. If it rains the game is off.

Best wishes,
Bill

[P] [54 E. 87th]
Wednesday

Dear Kennebunk,

Happy to hear from you. I know I am forgiven when I say that all my omissions in keeping promises to write and visit are due to causes from beyond the dragon sky.

Will you take tea with me in the Abstract City this Friday: I will call for you at the Dial office. Wouldn't it be possible to have Munson with us? Any time before seven P.M. I am to meet Mrs. Williams at the Grand Central at 7.36 or whenever Poo Bah admits the train to his garden.

Secession is well worthwhile.[88] I want to give myself to you all. I do so in fact most heartily. I can't help my antipathy to Josephson whom I heartily dislike and in whom I do not believe for one moment.[89] It was my irritation at his image appearing above Munson's first letter which caused my first failure to erect. You will of course look into my Jewish ancestry and invoke Freudian aid in order to explain my emotion but the reaction is far simpler than that as you will find out later, I am sure. In any case that is all past and I hold back nothing now. God bless you all, may the frogs die quickly. Be sure they won't.

Also, I have not by any means given up my wish to see you in the Jersey wilds. Some Sunday soon.

Cummings in the present issue of <u>Secession</u> is most delightful.[90] I haven't read the whole issue as yet since I have only been able to sit down by moments since my appearance in these parts day before yesterday.

I had a rest such as one might liken to a long draught of spring water on a hot day. I feel ready to drive the cow across the barnyard with my final shove—reaching to the region of her neck, inside. It is done every day—in the mountains. Ya ya.

Best luck

Yours,

Bill

[P]   [54 E. 87th]
Sunday 1:30 P.M.
Just home from halfway to your blood dung hill.
W

Dear Ken,

God dam. I left here Sunday morning promising Florence to call her up after I had been an hour on the road. I got as far as Rockaway and had to return.

My regrets are two: the first that I did not see you, the second that you may have prepared a dinner which may have partly gone to waste. The next time, perhaps on the twelfth—oh, blessed thought—I shall arrive sans announcement of my arrival. At least I now know how much time to allow for the trip.

The hour of Columbus' discovery was two A.M. but if I arrive at your crisp farm it will be at another hour—When? Je ne sais pas: so don't prepare for me.

WILL YOU BE AT HOME ON THAT DAY?

I'd like to tell your bunch of thirteenth street pimps what I think of them and to yank my poem and prose back across the river—but I'll wait till I see you first—Why in Christ's name should I wait for anything?[91] Like all excuses it is hollow.

Wont you loosen up on a newsy letter? What about <u>Secession</u>—What about everything? What about this winter? Where? When? Why? Who?—but I know that.

Yours at the breech—in a few minutes.

Horatius

WCW

[P]   [Rutherford]
[1923]

Dear Ken.

What about Wednesday or Thursday—for visit to Andover, I mean? The roads are too congested on the Sabbath. Are you there all day or in N.Y.—or what? Answer pronto, yes?

? ??

?

Am sending copies of <u>CONTACT V</u>—perhaps you have already rec'd.[92]

Pound says my novelette will be out soon.[93]

If THAT don't please you then there is no use our recognizing each other any longer between the sun and the moon.

Ain't the juice a various pricker though? Now we write a ream and now we—Or is it I only. No I cannot flatter myself with eccentricity any longer. Now a poem and now five years gone by without a ripple to show a wind to interest a fish.

Oh but Evelyn Scott sells a novel fairly regularly and her husband goes on writing and I even saw a cheap circular of some jobbing house making a public bid for sales of Kreymborg's PLAYS for marionettes—[94]

Somehow you survive my hatreds—I knew you'd be pleased. It WAS a nice thing to have Christ feed the crickets that way—then flit off, fairy like, over my house into the sunset.

<u>W</u>

[P]   [Rutherford]
Friday night [June 18, 1923]

Dear Ken,

Once more ye laurels and once more ye myrtles ever sear—I come to say that THIS Sunday I cannot visit you. I am the slave of circumstances: half the M.D.'s in town are vacationing which leaves me possessor of the seat of crap.

Have you seen <u>THE GREAT American Novel</u>? It is out. It is in America. It is beautifully gotten up. The best of the series I think. Does <u>The Dial</u> get a free copy or not? Speak, O Andoverian!

I'll call perhaps in two weeks, perhaps in the fall. Flossie appreciates your frau's kind wishes and says she will come with me when I next go—and with pleasure.

Best luck,
Bill

[P]   [Farmville, Virginia]
Sunday [September 30, 1923]

Dear Ken,

I wonder if I shall ever see you again: I am in old Virginia and never expect to rise from among these happily damned ghosts.[95] It is a world too mysterious for poetry.

In New York I'll signal again.

William

[P]   March 26, 1924
Rome[96]

Dear Ken,

Leaving this ripe center of everything in a couple of days, to my sorrow, but I think I'm carrying away half of antiquity with me. The other half is what we have left today. I never so fully realized as in the smell of these relics of the old battle, how maimed we are, and how needlessly we are crippling ourselves. Frascati in full "wildflower" yesterday won me again just as I have been won over and over here by the bits of wisdom that I've seen even in museums, the statues, the whole colossal record of their old time fullness and our unnecessary subservience to our crippledom.[97] We love it. That is the "Shit" of it. We eat it, lie in it. Sing about it and build our monuments on it. "Gentle Jesus Bacchus' whore open up your cellar door."

Well, so here we are again back where I started.

One night, you are right, I let loose and said what I have said before: "to hell with Ken Burke, I can't see what it's all about (his short story theory). If he'd write and to hell with his mechanics, <u>etc</u>, <u>etc</u>." I said what was uppermost in my mind at the time. But Caracalla built great baths to wash himself in.[98]

Good Christ you are curiously a whole man to not mind the crap you hear. What to hell?

Your letter was really in a fine climbing mood. I'm thrilled when I think of you planning your house in the mountains. <u>That</u> is you for me. Someday you'll write twenty words with <u>that</u> in it and I'll say you are Prince of Cranberry Lake and ask you to meet me in Paris for a good bottle of Pommard (Vieux) 1883.

You have the right idea about a magazine.[99] The print shop in the cellar is the only way and what will come off that press will be good for delight.

In fact, Ken, your letter was the perfect answer to my present need. Everything I am doing now is unprintable. To hell with printing and selling work. McAlmon is with us on that, or we with him. There is a perfect unanimity there on all sides; no use to quarrel there, nor can there be offense to fastidious preferences of humor. Print and distribute here and there until we all land in a (patriot's?) jail, it will come to that in the end, you wait and see. That or Paris for us all. But <u>never</u> silence.

That sounds heavily serious but it isn't, don't give it a thought.

The print shop must be forwarded. And it amounts to this: how much?

I think you must have received my last letter by this time so I shall not attempt to remember it. The point was only that your story ("January Broom") seemed to rise up out of the dead wood of your theories, so I wrote the letter.[100]

Yes, my <u>Gr. Am. Novel</u> never found a beginning. It was that I must have wanted to say. And that's how you get me, one of the ones with <u>that</u> that I am after. It's got to be said to be read. I <u>am</u> trying to <u>speak</u>. To tell <u>it</u> in the only way possible, but I do want to <u>say</u> what there is. It is not for me merely to arrange things prettily. Oh purple anemones! (you get what I mean? I mean "Shit." But I'm through with that now. No more "shits." It is dead, that kind of slang.)

Rome that <u>did</u> shit, in its later emperors should make us humble forever. We may pick, there I go again. But I'm another man today.

It's all too new yet but no more "shits." Get out your printing press, that's all.

Fucks and booze, and whatever else we can gather of ourselves and a <u>printing press</u>, Christen it with Champagne and semen if you must but <u>not shit</u>.

Write again, I'm delighted that you are south and that <u>Dial</u> will give you money.[101] It's its only use now as far as I see.

We go to Vienna in 2 days.

Yours,

Bill

[P]   April 14, 1924
Vienna, Austria

Dear Ken,

<u>Secession</u> No. 7 was handed to me here the other day by one Gaspar co-editor (apparently) with Kassak of MA—or AM or whatever it is.[102] My excuse for this ignorance is that they had never heard of James Joyce.

Anyhow I was astounded to find your story, "A Progression," so thoroughly enjoyable and so—able.[103] Please pardon my astonishment. In this piece you have done a fine thing in retaining a classic (or Gothic or Persian) hold on the material of composition, on each word, I mean, and on ideas—but at the same time you use the latest way of composition—I begin to see a little light.

I don't know whether it is that I have gained better insight into writing and things by my present experiences or whether you have improved. Perhaps it is something of both. The <u>MA</u> people speak very highly of your works. I had only a glimpse of them and their wives in a café, I'll see them again in a few days.[104]

To my further astonishment I was completely captivated by Munson's work also.[105] I think he has a blind spot toward Waldo Frank, but it may be that he knows it (judging by the Scientific trochee he hands us on the back cover).

These people are totally ignorant of things American, barring the names of you newer writers: yourself, Munson, Cowley, Josephson and E. E. Cummings. Yes, they had heard of me. Of everything else American they live in an ideally black ignorance. They want reproductions of our paintings, they asked me if any of our men admired the newer Frenchmen, if there had been any artists in America! I didn't believe such questions possible.

They are trying to get hold of "Our America."[106]

It is very nice over here, as I said before. Oh well, why not? I'll be glad to get back—in spite of it. The only sensible thing to do over here would be to go mad and kill yourself. At least that is the way I feel about it. I have heavy bones I am afraid—there's little here for me—gravity must drag me down—over the horizon—I'm too slippery—and it doesn't matter—but so it seems.

Paris would be wonderful if I could be French, and Vienna would be still more wonderful if I could only want to forget everything on earth. Since I can't do that only America remains where at least I was born.

Yours
Bill

[P]   [Rutherford]
Monday 15th [September 1924]

Dear Ken,

Once again I must put off my visit, this time for a week only. This week must be counted out because of an appointment I have, this Friday, for the removal of my tonsils. By Sunday I may or may not be on my feet but I shall certainly not be able to talk. The only hope is that my throat may not be sufficiently healed from a recent tonsillitis to permit the digging and pulling and tying, but I fear it will be in perfect condition for the assault.

Your note concerning meat has been read and proper need has been given. I'll write again, from the hospital!

Yours,
Bill

[P]   [Rutherford]
Tuesday [September 23, 1924]

Dear Ken,

Thanks for the book <u>The White Oxen</u>, it has just arrived.[107] By Sunday, when I expect to see you, I shall have read it, the result of which reading will be at once apparent to you in my face. It was good of you to think of me.

Dinner with you will be out of the question. I am in fact going in another man's car to a Sunday afternoon party at Cranberry Lake so by noon at the latest it will be necessary for me to pull out of Burkes Center. Perhaps I shall not arrive before eleven. In an hour, however, I am paralyzed from the knees up at most meetings—especially today, so for the moment say, I'll see you for an hour this Sunday morning should the weather be clear.

If however I feel strong enough after my recent loss of tonsils, sleep, and food, I MAY drive my own new car up to your door by nine A.M. on the appointed day. I'll do it if I can because I really want very much to see you and to talk with you, the frequent postponements mean nothing save that the distance is awkward and the stars crooked. I presume that you do, also, want to see me.

The snipping out of the tonsils was amusing to me in a small way since there was no pain to speak of and the sensation of having a pleasant fellow cutting little chunks of flesh out of your own throat was novel—with a pretty sidelight on other people's states of mind, in retrospect, under similar conditions. The recovery since Friday on the contrary has been anything but amusing. My throat has hurt like hell. Only today have I been without fever. My knees are still very feeble and my heart beats madly even as I lean to pick up a pin—so that I shall have good luck.

If you have anything important to say to me please squeeze it into small compass so that in our hour there may be chance for at least one full series of questions and answers.

Best luck and best wishes to you all.

Sincerely,
Bill

[P]   [Rutherford]
Wednesday [September 24, 1924]

Dear Ken,

I <u>am trusting you</u> to return the enclosed to its living father after you have read it. I have just this minute typed it out of my fertile bean—and can't be bothered to read it over. Look at it, say the neat word and let me have it back. It will show you at least that I am still militant, in spirit. God damn it to hell, twice as much, god damn it to hell!

And so summer is passing.

Yours,
Williams

[P]   [Rutherford]
[Sept. 1924]

[To Ken]

I wrote you a letter but my wife confiscated it. She said you'd only tear it up but she wanted to keep it: ain't that a wife? Have you read the pages I

<u>lent</u> you? Return them then Sir Kenneth—the Scotch Heine. I received word from Woodstock about a new magazine with copies of said mgzn.[108]

My return is too fresh upon me to do anything yet.

Bill

[P]   [Rutherford]
[Sept. 1924]

[To Ken]

Your letter and the returned MSS have just caught up with me. Thanks. We give each other no credit for sense or virtue. It is embarrassing but not necessarily fatal, just <u>gauche</u> and asinine. I liked your letter hope to see you soon.

Bill

[P]   [Rutherford]
Oct. 21 [1924]
cold as the state of letters!

Dear Ken,

I should say I did notice those lines of Winters', they were a breath of fresh air to me, the strongest impression of reality I have had since the journey.[109] I wanted to write to him at once but not having his exact address handy and needing to put time upon the reorganization of my practice I let the opportunity slip by. If you write to him, provided you have not done so already, put my name beside yours in homage.

Your letter was a good one. No time now for a lengthy reply. I agree with everything you say this time. More heft to your spade when you would "dig deeper."

But it is an event in American letters when simultaneously two men in the desert have come with such a violent and ready rush upon such a tiny spring as Winters' lines afforded us. We are at least beginning to communicate on some kind of an intelligent basis. It gave me nearly as much pleasure to have you speak so whole heartedly of Winters' achievement as it did to read the lines in the first place. They DID stand out like a pyramid, didn't they!

How long will you be in the hills? I'm hoping to see you there once more and for the day this time.

Yours,

Bill

[P]
Aug. 28, 1925

Dear Ken,

I thought you were in Europe.[110]

What's the use of meeting or seeing anyone in a degenerate country such as ours? It makes me weary to go expecting to hear or to say something and then to piss against some other poor bastard's shin and leave him.

I have just had a letter, after seven years or so, from Alfred Kreymborg and I wish he hadn't written.

Still, I want to see you if only to look at your lawn and to say that Carnevali's book, <u>A Hurried Man</u> is the best thing I have seen this year.[111]

Not that I feel alone: I should feel so perhaps but I do not—it is merely that we are neither primitive nor cultured, just inarticulate.

Yours,

Bill

Go see my friends, the Spences, on Cranberry Lake some Sunday.[112] They will be glad to see you.

[B]   [152 W. 13th St, N.Y.][113]
September 27, 1925

Dear Bill,

Poppycock.

When you talk with a literary man, go a scouting for literature, the way you would in talking with a nigger mammy or a one-legged trainman. You might find that Burton Rascoe[114] has his finger on the pulse nearly as often as the usual dementia praecox hebephenic.

Signed,

Senex.

No, no Nanette!
   Unsigned
     Parallax

P.S. What the hell are you talking about?

"No one's home."[115] I referred to your cynicism of a former letter, concerning literary commerce, artistic intercourse.[116]

Ever onward,

Exlax

⤳

[P]   **[Rutherford]**
Oct. 8, 1925

Dear K.B.,

Yesterday at <u>The Dial</u> they said you were in the wilds for three days or more.

May we visit you on Sunday, boys too, also Florence? If you will wire or phone us, or send special delivery letter <u>at once</u> it will ease our spirits. <u>Rain Checks</u> attached to all tickets; we'll come, in that case, another time.

Ask Mrs. B. to arrange her dinner to go with a sirloin steak.

And will you let me have some new work for the second <u>Contact</u> collection to be published in New York.

Yours,

Bill

⤳

[P]   **[Rutherford]**
Oct. 14, 1925

Dear Ken,

Suppose Friday should be a fine day and suppose that I should drop in at about one o'clock, at the farm, would you be there? Or, are you at the farm when you are not Dialing?

There is no great hurry about new work for another <u>Contact</u>. In a month.

Yes, I'll see you in N.Y.

Yours,

W.C.W.

God Knows(?) When my debut.

⤳

[B]   [152 W. 13th St., N.Y.][117]
October 20, 1925

Dear Bill,

Sure, make it Friday, although once again you happen to hit upon a quasi-relative day. One of my sisters-in-law is coming over for the day. If you are coming alone, this would not matter, however, as you and I would saunter off after lunch.

How about Sunday, with all the family? That is, if others are coming with you. If you are coming alone, then come alone still, and come on a Sunday with family. But I hesitate to invite family on Friday without first consulting the Mrs., as I do not know what she plans to do with her sister.[118]

Sometimes they drive to the Gap, and so on.

Write me at Andover, so that I hear from you Thursday morning, or at the latest Friday morning. Come with an empty belly and bring no meal. I am sorry that all this business makes us look inhospitable, but we really do hope that you and entire outfit will come out sometime. But I would not say Friday without first consulting the Mrs. So come Friday and then all come again, and write me your note.

It's damned fine out, on way over, and we could walk over by the lake, and I have three cherry trees to cut and haul to the house, and I'll have one of them for you. And being in the publisher's trade I learn from the inside that young Mencken is to honor me next month with a scathing attack on <u>The White Oxen</u>, and I wish that he had a head like Ernest Boyd's so that I would pull it, and I wish I could pull Ernest Boyd's.[119]

Yours, as ever, for DeTay. It's when I think of Mencken that I yearn for pure—material power—like, say, the Hearst papers.

KB

[P]   [Rutherford]
[October 23, 1925]

Dear Ken,
     Sunday midday
Sirloin
     if clear*
family

W.C. Bill

[P]   [Rutherford]
December 13 [1925]

Dear Ken,

What ho! what ho! Where in hell is your contribution to the new <u>Contact</u> collection that you can't sell to anyone else (nor to us) and has <u>Dial</u> fired you yet and if not why not?[120] Answer in one word—and don't say maybe.

D'ja read my book any?[121] Is that why I haven't heard from ya? Others have survived and written to me.

Best wishes to Madame Burke and to the small ladies. Is it cold up there? There has been no snow to speak of, at any rate. A man I know who is more than half an Indian and whose job it is to rescue agricultural lore from Indian memories then to rediscover the lost species of plants the Indians used to cultivate—this man wants to send out seeds of forgotten American food plants for cultivation. I have put your name on his list. Next spring you may hear from him.

New work is stirring, in my insides, soon 'twill out I hope, leaving me again at peace.

I may send you a couple of stories to read soon, work of a youngster John Riordan whom you may meet some day in N.Y.[122] He is strong for you as I believe I have already told you.

Loosen up on something for the <u>Contact</u> collection!

Yours,

Bill

[P]   [Rutherford]
Dec. 16 [1925]

Dear Ken,[123]

Your enemies know where you are while your friends look for you. Tomorrow, Friday, evening I may be in New York; if I succeed in getting away from my work, I'll look you up at your new place about six or six-thirty by the clock; there may be a friend along with me; do not eat till you've given me a chance to arrive as I'd like you to come out to supper with us. I'm writing to Cowley to come too, but that is only a chance shot.

Yours,

Bill

⟨⟩

[P]   [Rutherford]
December 31 [1925]

Dear Ken,

If Malcolm Cowley leaves some MSS. at your house for me put them in a corner so that I may find them when I call.

This midwinter period of celebration and general distraction being over we shall have to go on with our conversations.[124] Do not forget that I want something of yours for my <u>Contact C</u>. Josephson sent me a chapter from his book.[125] It is worth printing I am sure. I'm sending it to Baer.

The French publication containing Joyce's bit I'll bring in when I call again for a <u>punchino</u> and a talk. The last evening was well spent, must try another.

Hope your bratlettes are cold free and that Mrs. B. keeps able.

Yours,
Bill

⟨⟩

[P]   [Rutherford]
Oct. 29, 1925

Dear Ken,

It rained.
See you in the city soon.
Enclosed submitted to <u>The Dial</u>.[126]

Yours,
Bill

<u>Fight</u>
Get into a fight
with a man
and you feel light
in the tail

Blaze up
about a woman
and your back
is broken.

William Carlos Williams
    Oct. 28, 1925

[P]   [Rutherford]

April 13, 1926

Dear Ken,

These tickets are for you—use them or—as you are able.[127]

I'm to speak at St. Mark's on the Bowery this coming Sunday at 4 P.M. Party.

Yours,

Bill

[P]   [Rutherford]

March 15 [1928]

Dear Ken,

We have designs on your wife, we want her out here to speak to a small social club on gunplay in and about a Carolina schoolhouse, or something of that sort. Come along with her a week from this coming Saturday night, come to supper with us. If necessary bring the children, modern life must regain the old flexibility of social intercourse even at the cost of final disaster—we'll find a place for the kids somewhere. Lemme know how you decide, each and both.

The review was worth reading, that is it was worth my while to read it— which is doing well for a review.[128] Whether or not anybody else read it is another question. I disliked the title as too flat a statement of the facts. I thought I had altered the original matter with enough historic material to have escaped the bald statement "Subjective History," perhaps I miscalculated. The distinction between hero and genius is worth remembering. I didn't like the implied association between poetry and bravura. I liked well your careful desire to say something intelligent and truthful. I wish however that you had sensed a sweep to the book as a whole. Maybe it isn't there but one or two friends have gotten it. The ideology seems to me not so low in the evolutionary scale as you believe; it is simple and more over the writing than in it —which induces an imagistic style that can never be satisfactory to you I know—but it is there. It is not complicated however, not worked out, you're right. I have never been sufficiently devoted to that life.

Sold a story to the <u>New Masses</u>.[129] That is they have kept one of my new stories, they say nothing of paying.

Boni Brs. have finally quit on the American edition of <u>Contact Collection</u>.[130] I am about to return the MSS. to the various contributors. You escaped an annoyance by refusing to contribute.

Hope to see you soon.

Yours,
Bill

[P]   [Rutherford]
Nov. 14, 1929

Sure Mike,[131]

We'll be up for stew on Sunday if the weather doesn't look too unpleasant. Do we swim? Yeow!

Didn't see your betrayal in the <u>Trib.</u>

A Pollock from Passaic brought us a case of beer made by his Ma-in-Law in her kitchen (usually Temp. 110 by the stove all summer and through the winter—the kitchen, not the beer) maybe we'll bring up a flask or two or three or so.

No particular news. Cowley is quite interesting at times in his these here Sunday talks.[132] I like his account of the savage tribes of young men who cock suckingly inhabit all the large cities of the Up Stuck States of the Umpty Stump, or what have you not?

Say, <u>Pagany</u> is going to be interesting.[133] Yea, take it frum you Uncle Dudleigh.

Yop, I got the check from the <u>Horny Hound</u>.[134] Many thanks.

Sure, Wall-nut Street has been plucked and the sound of the cracking remains with it still.[135] I hev a few stucks but es I owen um outrite I jus sez to meself <u>Dial</u> or no <u>Dial</u> m sez I, I aint a gonna sell em, not ef I has to use em instid uv corn cobs in the old cannery next year.

See you Sunday about noon.

Yours,
Bill

[B]   Room 3004
61 Broadway
June 6, 1929

Dear Bill the Bold,

I seem to be sending you a lot of non-paying customers. For long I have been intending to write you and thank you for your kindness in helping Mrs. Farnham-and recently I made so bold as to suggest to Ruth Laughlin that you might be able to suggest some place for her mother. I believe she is coming, or has come, out to see you. If my fluttering heart flutters one more flutter a day, I shall be next. Meanwhile it remains strong enough to crawl around with.

Why not, you and the family, come out some time? We are there every Saturday and Sunday now. And probably after the sixth of July, I shall be on the rounds steadily every day until September. You should bring bathing suits, or else big stockings, as the lake now works. I shall not press you to make your tummy ache with amateur cider.

Incidentally, the demise of The Dial has caused some of us to look about—and the only thing on the horizon seems to be The Hound and Horn, in Cambridge, Mass.[136] They print beautifully, and pay modestly. Cowley has given them poems—I have given them the Seventh Declamation, and shall give them others when as and if written.[137] They publish, unfortunately, but four times a year. The magazine is effete, but intelligent—intelligent enough to become less effete if mightier contributions come in. Why not send? Particularly they want fiction. Blackmur, with whom I have corresponded, asked me to stir up anybody I know. And you are obviously anybody. He is R. P. Blackmur, Box A, Cambridge, Mass. Why not ship him that poem about a chancre which you tossed off only this morning?

Greetings, Friend Bilious—and have you read Gide's Les Faux Monnayers?[138] The old buck is a stinking fairy, ripe as a cheese, but I come fresh and glowing from his book, he too is intelligent. He moves about in his subject easily. He and Thomas Mann are the two examples of meisterlichkeit in contemporary letters, and I have thought of comparing and contrasting them in one article.[139] Each concerned with the morality of art, the German tight, conscientious, intense—the Frenchman suave, competent, light. The one knotted, the other relaxed. The adjectives are hasty approximates, but you get the idea.

K.B.

[P]   [Rutherford]
June 29 [1929]

Dear Ken,

All you say in your letter has been duly (what does that mean?) noted and mentally registered (I know what that should signify).

While you were writing to me I was writing to you. What does that mean? I wrote to you at Andover after paying your house a visit. I wrote you a very nice letter too and left a French magazine inside the screen door at the rear of your domicile. If you do not find it there this weekend, I'll send you another for I want you to see it and to have it.

The poem for <u>The Hound and Horn</u> was written last winter.[140] It is not about a chancre but about life, thus you see it amounts to the same thing. Or do you find heart disease more convenient?

At the present moment I am suffering from the after effects, so to speak, of a double circumcision, performed not upon me but upon twin Yids of my recent acquaintance. They had good whisky and excellent cigars.

I have a book of Gide's, <u>Si le Grain ne Meurt</u>. I will read it this summer. I'd like to read, <u>Les Faux-Monnayeurs</u> but I read too slowly to read more than one French book of any size each year.[141]

We'll be out to see you some time in July no doubt. And you are quite wrong, the cider was excellent.

Write again. I have not seen Ruth Laughlin. Please greet your wife for me, I really expected to have a nice talk with her last Tuesday.

Yours,

Bill

1930–1943

<table>
<tr><td style="text-align:center">William Carlos Williams</td><td style="text-align:center">Kenneth Burke</td></tr>
<tr><td>

Guarantor's Prize 1931, *A Novelette and Other Prose* 1932, *Collected Poems 1921–1931* 1934, *An Early Martyr* 1935, *White Mule* 1937, *Life Along the Passaic* 1938, *Complete Collected Poems* 1938, *In the Money* 1940, $5,000 lawsuit 1940, *The Broken Span* 1941.

</td><td>

Counter-Statement 1931, *Towards a Better Life* 1932, Divorces Lily and marries Libbie 1933, Music critic for *Nation* 1934–36, Guggenheim Fellowship 1935, *Permanence and Change* 1935, American Writers Congress 1935, *Attitudes toward History* 1937, Lecturer at New School 1937, Lecturer at Chicago 1938. *The Philosophy of Literary Form* 1941.

</td></tr>
</table>

[B]   Room 3004
61 Broadway
February 11, 1930

Dear Bill:

Among those things which have occurred to me recently is the following: that you had talked of a handy, inexpensive, tootsy little place for weekends. And that the bootleggers' place is now vacant. You remember where, beyond Colby's, when coming down hill towards our place, you turn from the Cranberry Lake road into the road from Andover? You remember that, Bill? And you remember the none too palatial house which stands about a hundred yards or so from this turn? It is vacant. It rents for about ten dollars a month (you could probably get it for a little more). It has a place for a telephone. It is rented by Colby, F. G. Colby, who owns the slightly transplanted Spanish villa that you may have noticed falling down now and then.

The fact is that some friends of ours have just arranged to rent another house of Colby's near there—the log place on the road to Andover. And it occurred to me (among other things, naturally) that you might like to help us fill the entire valley with sad cries, and of course peeing in our pond whenever you chose.

This is a mere random idea, Bill, a damn fool notion, one of those crack-brained imaginings which are always happening to you and me, Bill—so I know if it seems unusual to you, that you will pardon the unconventionality of my letter, being as we are both writers.

It would be so sweet to have you near me.

K.B.

[P]   [Rutherford]
Sunday [February 16, 1930]

Dear Ken,[1]

Many thanks for thinking of me re. the house to let at Andover—or there-ABOUTS (mere slip of the shit key). We have recently lost our zest for tying ourselves up with a place in the country.

(Erratum: "shit" in third line above should read "shift"—awfully sorry.)

But do not for that reason lose your spontaneity in suggestion, we do and I do appreciate your thinking of us. I should like nothing better than a crib for my bones in your valley where one year is divisible into two summers. I am restless divided against myself. I shall never be able to sit down. Yet that seems my desire.

They tell me, ask me, confide to me things about you (1) You despise a certain Calverton.[2] Why? He seems a decent enough chap. (2) Why do you not send some work to Johns, 109 Charles St. Boston.[3] He is well worth your attention? (3) You were at the Peggy Joyce tea, drunk as a Senator (should be l.c.).

Cum on, send something to Johns. And if your antipathy to Calverton is not too well founded, forget it—tell you why later, unless you already know. Oh hell, would you make one of a group to write chapters of a modern symposium re. American letters?[4] Say yes. (prisoner) Yes.

My best to your wife and her sister.[5]

Lots of new magazines. Met <u>Horn and Hound</u> a couple of weeks ago. <u>The Miscellany</u> is well printed.[6] Second number of <u>Pagany</u> will be better than No.1, so 'tis said.

The <u>Last Imagist Anthology</u> is to be published March: original contributors only. Rebecca West answers my attack (see Bookman: Jesus some answer.)[7] Nice gal too. There should be a better answer and I like her dog. England can't be so bad after all.

Buttercups and daisies. Is that the way to spell daisies? Don't literature play hell with splqelling anyway? Doesn't it?

Yours,

Bill

[P]   [Rutherford]
June 20 [1930]

Dear Ken,

I wasn't trying to snoot your party last Sunday.

I'd like to have come over but I was too damned lazy, too blarsted tired to move off my backandbuttocks to get over there. We'd been up too many nights immediately prior to that particular flight from Egypt—or whatever the hell you want to call the flight from the present dominion of the machine and brain environment.

But the chief reason I am writing is that I don't want you not to wish to invite me again. Yes, we have our bananas.

So let me say that the visit has been postponed and that within a week or two or more you'll have the blistering delight of seeing me and I thou.

For after all Proust's letters do show him to have been not only a little but very much of a climber.[8] Not that I have read them. And what has that to do with it? So many, so many, so many.

This spring has been a sweaty one for me. I don't seem to be doing much but it uses up all the time and me along with that. Perhaps it's my advancing years or the fruit of the borem-borum tree. Anyhow I'm weary as hell, haven't much to say, couldn't rape a jar of orange marmalade—not even if I tried.

(A kid was clipped by a car in front of the house just now so I had to beat it—excuse the interruption. He was not badly hurt—just knocked blotto for a moment)

To resume: what about the new magazine? and why? Why not? But anyhow, what about it? <u>Transition</u> is about to resume, so I hear, and then there is <u>The New Review</u>.[9] What are you writing? What are you thinking? How's the swimming? I'll bet it's good this year. I'll be there.

Best to the family,

Yours,
Bill Williams

[P]   [Rutherford]
April [1931]

Dear Ken,

Glad to hear from you. Glad you are on your way toward summer. I suppose "glad" is a Saxon word, sounds like it. I have been reading bits of translation centering around Beowulf recently. I like the place where Ethelwyn (is it?) comes down to the shore to tell the Danes to go to hell and they have to wait till the tide goes down before they can begin fighting.

Glad the new magazine is on or about to be on.[10] What's its policy? Pro anything or just anti? Anyhow I have work for you whenever you want it. I write and there it lies, I don't even try to get published anymore. But I haven't much poetry, just one short thing that's any good. But I have a ten page story that I like muchly—yes, I like it plenty and it aint even censurable.

Did you see Zukofsky's criticism of Ezra's <u>Cantos</u> in the recent <u>Criterion</u>?[11] I think that it is fine stuff after he gets going. I'm sick of this God damned hair splitting that so many of the critics, the erudite critics, go in for. All that means nothing to me. But when Zuke speaks of Pound's excellences and lays the thing open for the eye and the ear it is clear and it has power and I can feel the weight of it and enjoy. If you haven't read the thing, do so. Skip the first page or two.

Then, as a diversion, read what I myself said on the same subject in the last <u>Symposium</u>.[12]

I've been looking for your name recently but found it not. What t'ell? Whatchadoin these days? And yes, we'll be up to see you soon. It may be age but I've been physically fat, but this spring. Not that it has made much difference in what I have done—only spring aint what it has been other years. Probably a good sign. Let 'em bloom, is the way I feel this year.

My best to your lady and the brats.

Yours,

Bill

[B]   Andover
New Jersey
July 20, 1931

Dear Bill the Bold,

Barring the unforeseen (I ever bar the unforeseen), John and Mavis are going to be out here the week-end that is a fortnight from the one just past. I mean that there is a week-end coming, and another week-end thereafter, and on this second one we are expecting John and Mavis. So why not try to appear then if our patients can all be persuaded to remain undoctored for a few hours?

How goes litrachoor? I just, the other day, saw the first proofs of my book of criticism, Counter-Statement, which is (barring the unforeseen) to appear in the fall.[13] And this week I am scheduled to conquer the fourteenth Declamation (it looks as though there are to be eighteen in all, and as though I shall get out from in under them this summer).[14]

As for the magazine, all is yet uncertain. Josephson and I seem to disagree on every matter of policy from the name to the placing of the office spittoon —we are, I think, just about on the edge of writing Open Letters of mutual revilement to the press of the metropolis.[15] And besides, this is the great year of wrangles anyhow. Let's see, have I wrangled with you yet? I believe there are about seventeen friends of mine who, if the old theories of witchcraft are true, are slowly wasting away as I blast them with mute wishes.

Ho hum Harry—here I am, sleepy at ten in the morning, from having lain damnably awake with home brew and the poet's own birthright, predawn suicide. Here I am all shot to hell on Monday morning, when Chapitre XIV is to begin to be disposed of. I shall go up and kalsomine the walls, fit in this shattered state only for physical toil (when weary, one can build houses, crush rocks, climb mountains, haul lumber, but one can write only when his vitality is at its top-notch).

Greetings,

K.B.

Am reading Ouspensky's New Model of the Universe.[16] It is, I gather, the primer of mysticism, the introduction to wisdom-of-the-East wisdom. Now I am all for wisdom-of-the-East wisdom (on the grounds that anything must be better than Occidental thinking as now conducted). So who knows—perhaps I shall become an Arrow Collar Mystic after all? The chapter on the five Yogas made me want, just a little bit, to learn Sanskrit.

Am conducting my hero into the mysteries of Iscariotism, the piety of sin and crime.[17] A writer can, out of the depths of himself, invent but one new aspect of vice. No wonder he prizes it so greatly and dignifies it by having it cause the destruction of his favorite character.

[P]   [Rutherford]
July 29 [1931]

Dear Ken,

Did you ever say anything about Ezra Pound or his work that you'd like to see reprinted? If so where did it appear? I'm collecting that sort of thing—with an ulterior motive in mind—or—in view,[18] perhaps.

I'd like to see you Sunday, you and the others, but as usual the stars are relatively against it. Howsomever, if—and if—and again, if—the weather—the this, the that—I may drop in anywhere between 9 A.M. and 5 P.M. But don't count on me for dinner—I won't be there for dinner.

The thing is I'm passing through that country on the 5th—so feel disinclined to jog the eighty odd miles there and back on a Sunday—but by starting early and returning early—pussossibly I'll do it. I'd like to.

It's been interesting to hear about your writing projects. More power to you. I'll even buy a copy of the <u>Declamations</u>—maybe two—when the thing appears.[19] I'm curious to know what happened there.

If I don't get there, please remember me kindly to Mavis and Jawn.

You know, I just came across a medical article, which I know will interest you. It seems that men are not of course all male, as women are not all women. Well, the proof that men are not all male goes something like this: remove the ovaries of a female mouse. Let the gal recover. Then take a pint of male piss. Extract it with alcohol or acetone or ether or what not—I've forgotten. Do this again. Then again. Finally evaporate the stuff down until it is a thin jelly. Of this jelly take a tenth of a cubic centimeter and inject it into the muscle of said mouse. The mouse starts to menstruate!

Now this is due to the fact that men excrete female hormones in their urine. Ain't that something. So always take a piss before or after you jerk off or you might end some day by finding yourself pregnant—with a castrated mouse perhaps.

Anyhow this is all true.

Regards,

Bill

[B]   **[381 Bleecker St., N.Y.]**[20]
October 15, 1931

Dear Bill,

Katherine Anne Porter, whom I earlier in the season asked for contributions when it seemed that we were to get out a gazette, has sent the enclosed, which I think has considerable quality.[21] I send it to you because she asked me, in case we could not use it, to pass it on to <u>Pagany</u>, and I assume that you are still now and then assembling material for that organ—though I hope Katherine Anne fares better on eagle-day than I did.

Harcourt, Brace have accepted my <u>Declamations</u>, which are to appear around January or February. I am not at all modest about them—and the editors have promised to give me a nice fancy book, with type, paper, binding and format of my own selection. So I shall at last have a book of mine done in such a way as I should like to sleep with—and I don't give a damn if I have to sleep with the whole edition.

My book of essays, <u>Counter-Statement</u>, is out.[22] The first reviews appear, I believe, this week. So far, the volume sleepeth on.

What next? Am eager to spend a couple of months on a long political tirade, but who would want it? All poets should now attempt to write Areopagiticas,[23] proclaiming anew the dignity of their craft, outlining the good life, and vilifying every authority and public institution that fails to place the aesthetic far above the practical. The reign of business is over—and we return to the erratic, the unpractical, the picturesque, the Bohemian and mad. We now have the documents. We saw the thing at its best. We know that, even if Black Friday had never come, it would have been a hell of a way to live. But now that Black Friday has come besides, the Taylor system is without rejoinder.[24] All poets should sally forth, to taunt, to reaffirm, to make the debacle unforgettable through the use of skilled metaphors. This is the year for obtrectations from the sewers. Above all, this is the year for attacking the growing myths of Fascism. The damned country went to the devil because of centralization, and now they want to cure things by making it more centralized still.

But I am sleepy. I was out of town too many months. I have forgotten how to sleep in city noises. So I toss all night, and then nod like Homer over my typewriter.

Greetings,
K.B.

⌒

[P]   [Rutherford]
Oct. 19, 1931

Dear Ken,

And when I die (and when I die!) don't bury me all (don't bury me at all) just pickle my bones (just pickle my bones) in al co hol:[25] 'tis a consummation devoutly to be wished.

I'll be glad to be the purchaser and owner of a copy of your <u>Declamations,</u> which I have always admired. Good luck to you.[26]

My poems—the droppings of a decade are going the rounds in N.Y.[27] I suppose somebody will take them some time or other. Or at least the supposition being pleasant appears to me to be reasonable.

In answer to your high advocacy of the poet's present duty may I say that perhaps I may have published this fall a "Political Poem"—

Or something.—(in al co hol)

Yours,

Bill

I'll take care of the Porter thing.[28]

[B]   [381 Bleecker St., N.Y.]
January 11, 1932

Dear Bill,

As things look now, on the twenty-eighth of January, Thursday afternoon, about five o'clock, Harcourt Brace plans to have a little alcoholic tea for gents only, and I hope you will be willing to be among them. This is the day when the <u>Declamations</u> are coming out, and 'twould be nice if you could let a few people die that afternoon and yourself be present at the vernissage.

When the book comes out, I want to present a copy to you, as one who was kind to it in its earlier stages.

Greetings, dear Bill, greetings, Bill the Bold, greetings, Bilious Billiam, greetings, two-gun Will, good-night, ladies, good-night, sweet ladies, good-night, good-night.[29]

K.B.

[B]   [381 Bleecker St., N.Y.]
January 18, 1932

Dear Bill,

Oot do hell? Aren't you coming to the five o'clock?[30]
Busy? Mad? If not, why so? If so, why not? You have no reason to be mad at me just because you got out a magazine and didn't invite me to contribute to it.[31] You should be charitable, and forgive me for that.

Be a nobody, and say yes.

Thine,

K.B.

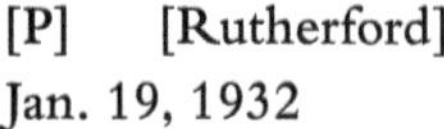

[P]   [Rutherford]
Jan. 19, 1932

Taint fair! Who the hell ever pays any attention to me and my doings. Here an obscure little bookshop wants to start a small literary organ and I very hesitatingly takes the job on.

Well, of course I'm coming to your party. Do you expect me to send an engraved acceptance?

And let's see if you'll send me script—

Yours,

Bill

I kept the mag. dark expecting to ask my friends for contributions later— <u>if</u> they approve—on
   W.

[P]   [Rutherford]
March 3, 1932

Dear Ken,

It's been a pleasure to read your "Better Life" which I finished last evening.[32] It's been a mixed pleasure, for often I didn't know what to think. There was an uneven effect of stark reality breaking through masses of words. That is, there were two effects, the words as word calling for a reaction to pure thought and a very human story—which left me floating at the end.

But no doubt this was your desire. Certainly the demonstrations of a method makes a solid effect. Nothing is trivial. You have found a method for using complex and accurate words for subtleties of thought without making the reading either "English" or precious. It is good straight writing of a satisfying kind. It is what it is by purpose.

In places the emotional force is wonderfully effective, precisely so because it has been bred (the effect that is) in the rhetoric. Perhaps this is special writing. It is very human tho. It has been a pleasure.

Yours,

Bill

[P]   [Rutherford]
7/20/32

Dear Ken,

Thanks for letting me see the speech.[33] It is a speech, and as I read it I realize that that's its chief virtue. We can't use it much as I'd like to. It should be "given" rapidly, in a hall, an armory <u>etc.</u> in a loud voice. That is its place.

But this job of rejecting scripts is disgusting me with my job. Often a rejection comes from no more than a vague feeling (in me) made up of things like—"no space," "we have one like that," etc., etc. (and acceptances the same: reversed) it's hell.

I tried to find time to drop over for a visit this Sunday but-but
Shit.

W.C.W.

[B]   [381 Bleecker St., N.Y.]
January 5, 1933

Dear Bill,

I wonder how the enclosed might strike you, and whether you have any MSS you would care to see issued in this way.

And I also wonder whether you might have any addresses of the various young-bloods (such as wrote for the <u>Caravans</u>, for <u>Pagany</u>, and your past and present <u>Contacts</u>) to which you would let me send this circular?

This might turn out all right. In any case, as you will note by reading our song, an author regains the rights to his MSS after four months, and so does not tie himself up, to his regret, in case of subsequent glory.

And perhaps also, if something comes to you which is too long, and which you nonetheless greatly prize, you would refer the author, with his wares, to us?

Franklin Spier, who is trying to make this go, is an old hand at book promotion (does the advertising for Farrar and Rinehart, for instance). He thinks that the facsimile feature gives him the chance to make the books "collectors' items." Dunno. Only know that he must know more about it than I do, which obviously is grand—and I should like to get together twelve books that I liked.

Ever thine,

K.B.

[MANUSCRIPT EDITIONS]

This is to announce the tentative formation of a new publishing venture, and to make a request for the submission of manuscripts, preferably of average book length.

If such work as we are seeking comes into our hands, we plan to publish a succession of twelve volumes, at intervals of a month—and as far as possible we want these volumes to vary greatly in both subject and treatment. While we have in mind primarily prose fiction, we would not limit ourselves to any one category—criticism, verse, biography, history, etcetera also falling within our range. And while we wish to have work apropos to contemporary situations, we are aware that there are very many ways in which a work can be apropos without necessarily being a circumstantial account of such happenings as one reads about in the daily press. Accordingly, we should be interested in sound work of any sort—so long as it is sound, and can be felt to involve the apprehensions, wishes, speculations, bewilderments, ennuis, or any other aspects of thinking or feeling that are stimulated or irritated or soothed by the processes of living.

The only difference between our purposes, in this respect, and the purposes of other publishers, is that we are deliberately concerning ourselves with such ways of involving the stimulations, irritations, and soothings as are likely to confine a book's appeal, when it is first issued, to a public of 1000 to 1500 readers.

The depression has caused this kind of book almost to vanish from the current publishers' lists (except insofar as the publishers may grievously miscalculate, and end by selling a thousand copies of the work with which they had planned to flood the country). As a matter of fact, conditions in the publishing business as a whole have got to the point where the representative publishing plant is as thoroughly geared to mass sales as the manufacturer of any nationally advertised commodity. Thus, it is not editorial bad taste that is causing the elimination of many valuable books from the publishers' lists—it is the economic factors involved in the conditions of production and distribution.

To combat such disadvantages, some of which have accumulated out of the past while others thrive by their own right, publishers have been gradually forced to eliminate more and more of the books whose virtues are not deemed to be of a sort making for a wide and ready acceptance. In this policy they are thoroughly justified. To issue the sort of books which we have in mind, and which they are being forced to neglect, one either must be subsidized against loss or must alter the conditions and methods of publication. It is the second course which we propose to follow in MANUSCRIPT EDITIONS.

In the light of the past publishing experience of those connected with this venture, we have reason to believe that we can organize, by mail, the minimum body of readers necessary to guarantee the minimum public necessary to the workings of the plan. They will be asked to subscribe in advance for the entire twelve books.

The books themselves are to be issued by methods which will cut the expenses of manufacture considerably, eliminating type-setting charges entirely and reducing almost to zero the costs of binding. They are to be fac-simile reproductions, page by page, of the author's manuscript—thus not made by type composition and letter press, but by photography and the litho-offset process. The pages will be clamped together, and laid in a cardboard folder.

The author will receive an advance of from $100 to $200 (depending upon the nature of the manuscript). He will receive in royalty a flat 20% of the receipts, his earnings being paid regularly and promptly, bimonthly after publication. Should we, finding ourselves happily in error in our calculation of sales possibilities, discover that the reception of a book justified a regular printed edition, we should ask only the conventional agent's fee for placing the book with a publisher. (In this respect, MANUSCRIPT EDITIONS might be said to give an opportunity for a "trial run.") Otherwise, four months after our date of publication, full rights revert to the author.

In substance, we plan to organize a group of discriminating readers that should provide an audience for authors whose books might not otherwise get a hearing under present conditions, or even under improved conditions, unless some such devices as we propose are adopted.

The Editions will be printed on good paper, will be neat and easily read, and will have the added appeal of the facsimile. They will not be merely sub-stitutes for printed volumes, but will have distinct and unique qualities to rec-ommend them to the collector, as well as to the general reader interested in substantial literature. Thus we hope to profit by a double advantage: increasing the allure of the volume itself and cutting the cost of its manufacture, both at once.

Manuscripts, accompanied by adequate return postage (or inquiries of any sort) should be addressed to:

Manuscript Editions
2 E. 45th Street, New York
Kenneth Burke,
Franklin Spier, Editors.

(This circular is printed by the process we intend to use for MANU-SCRIPT EDITIONS.)

[P]   [Rutherford]
Jan. 6, 1933

Dear Ken,

Nothing could have come more pat, I have the book you want lying here in my strong box just screaming to get out—has been waiting to piss itself forth on the world for twenty moons or more—

THE EMBODIMENT OF KNOWLEDGE:[34]
(First Writing)
THESE ARE THE WORDS.

—that's the title. It is a series of writings—very random in general arrangement but with one burning theme running through the whole with many historical and other examples—such as French painting as a whole—the character of Shakespeare and the precise value of his work—the education of the American male—and all the agglomerate and conglomerate bellyaches I have suffered for the past ten years—to one end that there is no knowledge (everyone else to the contrary) but my own, and may God pardon me!

The only drawback is that it is typed on foolscap. And if I have to have that book length script retyped—well, I'll have it done if you want it.

I could hug you for the opportunity to have the thing presented to the to-be-stunned-to-extinction reader in EXACTLY the format in which it now lies generating purple mold. And if the need for what you plan can be a criticism of its timeliness and other virtues in the case of any one writer, your scheme has about it the earmarks of genius.

Besides which I'll keep a sharp lookout for the work of others in a dilemma similar to my own. Can it be that dawn is at hand? I should say not. So, many thanks for switching on the light.

To which you may add that I'm always and in a clean way glad to hear from you—which can't be said in all cases—that of recent communications to

me from Yvor Winters for example with whom I hope to have broken forever—he <u>is</u> buried and stinks, nice as he is personally.[35]

I'm thrilled to be quit of <u>Contact</u> which is "<u>out</u>" as far as I'm concerned.[36]

Yours,

Bill

[P]   [Rutherford]
Jan. 26, 1933

Dear Ken,

Yes, of course. The examples are missing tho' present in my head as circus performers, net makers—anything but machines—possessors of knowledge in the flesh as opposed to a body of knowledge called science or philosophy. From knowledge possessed by a man springs poetry. From science springs the machine. But from a man partially informed, that is, not yet an artist, springs now science, a detached mass of pseudo-knowledge, now philosophy, frightened acts of half realization. Poetry however is the flower of action and presents a different kind of knowledge from that of S. and P. If I am wrong then it is just too bad— but I should never want to write reading matter that would be dull: hence my reluctance to show anyone my notes save as "my mode of procedure."

I thought what you were after was something to print which would amuse, puzzle, entice people suffering from the depression of their equivalents in some other category.[37] I didn't expect you to be convinced. I sought only to present to you an object.

Your letter would make an excellent prefatory note with my own abject apology following it. My object in much that I do has also an ulterior motive. I have to go on and want to go on living for a few years more perhaps. As I grow older I hope to get rid of medicine—the sooner the better if only I can fulfill certain obligations and still have enough money for bread, wine, honey, beefsteak—travel, adultery (tho' that's cheap enough) and a nice garden, maybe a swimming pool—and guest rooms. So, I have gradually made enough notes, here and there to keep me busy clearing them up and developing them for a long time after I retire—if ever. I should dread an old age divorced from the thoughts and actions of my more vigorous years. Age should be a commenta- tor and what better than to comment upon one's own existence. Thus I have many projects in mind. And if I never catch up with them—wouldn't that also be a misfortune. But I intend to try to do so. These notes on what the hell would then be straightened out, illustrated. I do want to make the thing clear and I fully intend to drive myself into all the corners possible. What the hell, I'm no bigot. If I could convince myself or have anyone else convince me that I were merely following in the steps of Dewey, I'd vomit and quit—at any time.[38] But for the moment I don't believe it—the poetry is offered not too confidently as proof.

If you want the object to print it's yours, if not I have absolutely no feeling about it. Send it back I'll love you just the same.

Regards to the family, I doubt that I shall be able to come in on Sunday, these are working days.

Yours,

Bill

[P]   [Rutherford]
Feb. 11, 1933

Dear Ken,

Since the script I sent you will not do (and, by the way, you are the only one besides myself that's seen it) perhaps you'ld care to use the first seventeen chapters of <u>White Mule</u>, the original (corrected) scripts in most cases—complete.[39] Together these comprise the first year of the infant's life.

Or you might care for a full size book of poems—all my unpublished (in book form) poems that have been collecting for the last ten years—and more.[40] Plenty!

But if either of these attracts you I'ld want to go over the copyright phase of the thing very carefully as I already have conditional offers on both of the above. Which shouldn't affect your plans.

In any case, I agree with you relative to the subject spoken of in your letter: the good President, etc. etc. The only drawback to living in the country is the lack of city life with all its heats and humors—odors, perhaps would be the better word. You may rub it hard, you may scrub it well, etc. etc. Yet we all desire it—in season (an'out!)

And—I am still waiting to receive my <u>Embodiment of Knowledge</u> back home. Everything I have said above is contingent on that coming back first.

Yours,

Bill

[P]   [Rutherford]
3/6/33

Just to let you know I'm not idling my time away but, on the contrary, that I have been working steadily—if not always hard—to clear the way for sending you the two scripts. It turned out to be more of a task than I had anticipated involving much typing, copying, checking and rechecking. I may be able to send one of the items off by Saturday, I hope so at any rate.

Bill

[P]   [Rutherford]
3/21/33

It's been a task to dress the carcasses for you. They are about prime now however so I'll be shipping them by express in another two or three days. If you don't get them Saturday it'll be Monday surely. I think you'll like them but if the work isn't satisfactory it won't be because I haven't given the time to it. Hope your friend is satisfied.[41] <u>The White Mule</u> may be a little tough in spots due to a lot of checking I tried out and the other may be against your taste but it's the best I can offer. Pretty good too <u>I</u> think.

Yrs.,
Bill

[P]   [Rutherford]
April 3, 1933

Dear Ken,

No doubt the messy scripts have reached you by this time. The poems I have sent to Maxim Lieber along with the clean scripts of <u>White Mule</u>.[42] I thought it best, after all, to let him handle the whole matter of disposing of these things for me if possible. It would be best for me not to prejudice his chances of placing the work by a separate distribution of them, in any form. He says he knows you. You may wish to speak to him of the matter. Or maybe you'd better not just yet. I don't care only I don't want to create confusion.

The thing is this: I have considered your venture quite a separate one from the usual publishing game. Am I wrong in this? I have felt, or understood, that you wanted facsimile scripts as such for their direct interest value as much as for their content. That is why I have sent you the things I did. I gave Lieber the poems and the first fifteen chapters of <u>W.M.</u> I did not tell him that you had the scripts of <u>W.M.</u> so, if you please, if the matter comes up don't get me in wrong at the start. I'll tell him too.

Sincerely,
Bill

***

[P]   [Rutherford]
April 15, 1933

Dear Ken,

Maxim Lieber says he is showing you my scripts as a first step in his selling campaign. Can you not do them both? I wish you would and so an end to it. If I could be assured of this, that you'd give both scripts the light, I'd be extremely happy.

Sincerely Yours,
Bill

Please show this note to Lieber when he comes in.

***

[P]   [Rutherford]
[June 6, 1933]

At least return the corrected "original" scripts of <u>White Mule</u>—since Lieber has (or says he has) shown you the final scripts of it. Please do this by Express. Best regards.

Bill

***

[P]   [Rutherford]
Oct. 9 [1933]

Dear Ken,

Would you do an introduction to Reznikoff's[43] <u>Testimony</u>, the stuff copied from the law records, bits of which you have seen, and of which I spoke to you recently? If so kindly write, yourself, to the man, saying you are interested and that you'd like to see his script. He is difficult through diffidence—of a sort. Wouldn't bother anybody, etc. etc. Mention my name as the intermediary. It would be of great help to our budding Press if you'd take on the job.[44]

Yours,

Bill

Charles Reznikoff
3900 Greystone Ave.
Bronx, N.Y.C.

[P]   [Rutherford]
Dec. 6, 1933

Dear Ken,

The Pap of our Country's coming along fine—in a general way.[45] There has to be so much strategy employed though that the actual weaving together of the words and music seems to be almost incidental. The first act is scheduled to begin intercourse on or about January first, in other words I have promised to have the revised revised revised revised revised and revised libretto of the first act ready by then. May I say that your hint relative to soliloquy may prove helpful.

And what about the Reznikoff introduction. Have you done it? I hear very little of what's going on in the city but the fact that R's book is in the page proof stage and that no one has said anything about what you've written makes me wonder. I hope your plans haven't fallen through.

My own book of poems has just been corrected in the galleys. By moments it flares up before me as a real entity—then it falls apart again as so many printed pages. There will be no answer until the thing is finally printed. Stevens' preface is surprising.[46] It is not what I expected but I think I detect general appeal in it. It may sell the book yet—especially if the right Sunday Supplement guy sees it and falls for it. Paradise by the back door! Or who assed you in.

Reminds me of the stories I enjoyed at 12. The height of impudence: Shit on a woman's doorstep, then ring the bell to ask her for a piece of paper to wipe your ass. There was one about the height of improbability but I can't remember it. But why I'm remembering these things is more than I can say.

Perhaps it is that I wrote a short story for the little mag. <u>Blast</u>.[47] I sent it to my pal Miller last week.[48] It was quite a story with plenty of Communism (unorthodox) in it. I think it probably wounded the guy. Hope not; I'm sleepy from childbirth, pneumonia, and all the other posies.

Yours,

Bill

[P]   [Rutherford]
Dec. 22, 1933
Friday

Dear Ken,

Reznikoff wanted to give you some sort of gift. I suggested cash. He said, How much? I said, twenty five. He looked at me. Well, I said, there's no reason for giving him anything; make it ten if you want to, but I think he could use the money better than anything else—provided you like what he has written.

I've been going mad this afternoon searching for the clean script of <u>White Mule</u> when it flashed across my mind: The guy who was going to bring out Manuscript Editions has it. Verify this for me and get me the clean script back again if you have a soul. I have the carbons but, if I remember rightly, there are various corrections on the script your side-kick has which are unique. The mass of script which you gave me when I saw you at Andover is the original, very much corrected copy—that is not what I mean. What I mean is the stuff which my agent at the time, I've forgotten his name, sent to you direct. Max Lieber. Please don't delay in at least reassuring me that the thing is safe.

My book will be out Jan. 15th—unless it doesn't come out till later.

The season's greetings, color of brick-bats, color of verdigris. And little red balls on twigs of holly.

Yours,

Bill

[P]   [Rutherford]
Jan. 3, 1934

Dear Ken,

Lieber, I think, is mistaken, so are you, unless I, in turn, am mistaken, mistaken.

The script which Lieber gave to Martin Jay was a script of the poems, not the script of <u>White Mule</u>. That of the latter was turned over to the man who was working with you on Manuscript Editions. He it is who should have it now. Please verify this, I haven't the name.

Meanwhile, I have asked my friend Bud Miller to get in touch with you re. the same. If the script is located you may safely let Miller have it.

My book of poems will be out in a few weeks.

Yours,

Bill

[P]   [Rutherford]
[January 6, 1934]

All's well. Lieber had the script right in his office all the time. Not that there is a chance to publish but I want Miller to see the new chapters. Best wishes. I have made a note of the phone address.

Bill

[P]   [Rutherford]
May 7, 1935

Dear Ken,

Yezir, I'll be good for five bucks toward the book and I'll come to the party if I can, where'll I send the check?[49] What in bloody hell are we all going to do? The shits get the prizes (Yeah, you got a prize.[50] I know that.) and all we get is the shits. And it's too far into the distance to pray for a pre-literary Communism—which would probably vote for just another set of shits. There ought to be some more simple, some shrewder, inventive method of getting printed. Hell, we act like a lot of lost sheep. Yet I have no answer. Are we so impotent that we can't do anything but yell for a Lenin or else go pantsless? There must be some way, some regular (in the sense of historically practiced) way of getting on.

I've begun to think it's inside myself. I can't be thinking straight. I'm not interested in being a martyr and I'm not resigned to my fate, not by a damned site. But where's my invention, my imagination. Even a cheap advertiser knows the ropes better than we do? I think we're crazy—or really impotent. We should really work, really sweat for each other. If we did that we'd damn soon get attention. But we haven't the least sense of solidarity or loyalty. Every man for himself seems to be the stupid rule. I wish I knew how to get us together on even the most purely selfish front—barring theory or god damned economics which has Pound ball-tied and cock-trapped.

I'll be seeing you this summer. If I hear of anyone who wants to live in your barn I'll tell them.

Regards to the family and good gardening to you.

Sincerely yours,

Bill

[P]　　[Rutherford]
Aug. 5, 1935

[To Ken]

Somebody says you'd know the address of the <u>Southern Review</u>[51] or Wm. Penn Warren or something. If you do may I? If not never mind or mind or spirit but & hole. So tell me: 9 Ridge Rd, Rutherford, N.J.

W.C. Williams

[P]　　[Rutherford]
Nov. 25, 1935

Dear Ken,

Fer God's sakes! What in 'ell 'ave you been drinkin'? Any time to want to do that review, critique—and my! how I'd like to see what the lucubrations of the philosophic Meester Burke would do with me—say the word and I'll send you the books you haven't got, if any.[52]

Many thanks for the good word. I saw Dr. Latimer a few weeks ago who told me of your physical misfortunes this summer. It sounded as though you really had something this time but I suppose the bugs got mixed up trying to get through the intricate maze of your psychologic entity and just lay down and died of starvation without reaching the spot where they could piss on your essential fires. Anyhow the lady doc said you were in a bad way for twenty-four hours or so.

There's no overpoweringly great news to pass on—no great victory won —just guerrilla warfare as usual—and common in an uncivilized and overgrown terrain. But the boys are in college and I have my garden all in order for spring.[53]

My best to—whoever remembers me.

Yours,

Bill

⬳

[P]   [Rutherford]
Sep. 4, 1936

I may be up your way for a call or so Sunday.

W. Williams

⬳

[P]   [Rutherford]
Nov. 16, 1936

Dear Ken,

Thanks for laying yourself open to a visit by yours truly of the <u>New York Times Book Review</u>, etc. etc. and points west. The only times that look to be possible for such a visit would be the Tuesday before Thanksgiving and the Friday following—Maybe the Saturday following. If I find it possible to get away I'll arrive around five o'clock and stay for a couple of hours. I'll come alone, most likely—and try to let you know before hand. Most uncertain.

It's good news about the book[54] and you have my best wishes for its success. Hell, you don't want to do me. Why in hell should you? In about ten years it might be worthwhile but right now there's such a whale of a lot of work for me to do to get my head clear—or clearer—just beginning—that I don't know that anything would do me much good. Hope you do me anyhow.

Yours,

Bill

⬳

[P]   [Rutherford]
Nov. 22, 1937

Dear Ken,

My thanks for your worthwhile redefinition of newspaper terms in the <u>New Republic</u>, there's a lead that cries for a follow up, you hit something that time—and what a book it would make![55] It is just such primary work that is needed in the laborious campaign toward a really better life, for the well intentioned but preoccupied reader of today hasn't the skill to clarify his own terminology but with assistance could be counted on to act with commendable precision in the good cause. How many people are there who realize the full significance of words? And since they do not differentiate between the meaning which they seek and the false term which misleads them they remain tools in the hands of the thieves and liars. A breath of truth here comes close to being a veritable blast of genius. Go to it, it isn't everyone who has the power. Floss joins me in sending you this greeting.

Sincerely yours,

Bill

[B]   53 West Eleventh Street
New York City
December 21, 1937

Dear Bill:

And it's thanks a lot for taking the trouble to say a kind word about our elucubrations on the "spontaneous combustion" kind of propaganda. I was all steamed up to do a lot of that sort of thing, a year and a half ago when I sold the article to the N.R., but the long interim during which my paragraphs were allowed to mellow in the editorial basket made me think I was _still_ on the wrong track (as one who would talk to his fellow-countrymen).[56] So I perforce went on "developing"—and now it would be a bit hard for me to regain that particular kind of stride. (At the same time, for instance, I analyzed a speech by our beloved old potato-eater, Al Smith, to display the clockwork whereby he is able so repeatedly to strike late; but that one didn't even get as far as a chance to be put on editorial ice—and thus did we die once more.)[57] But a good word from such as you enkindles, so maybe I'll try again some time, possibly when some other address by a great leader is hot in the news.

Incidentally, I wonder if I could burden you with one of my problems as a papa. Young Butch is now about ten months old; and as he is growing interested in things on the floor, I keep wondering how many little bugs we are willy-nilly bringing in, because our shoes walk on spittle-laden streets. In particular, wonder about the matter of diphtheria and the walking sticks (if I remember my Greek aright) of same. Should I get little Butch systematically polluted as to blood stream? And if so, could you suggest what agency or individual hereabouts you think could be relied upon to do the task with the minimum expense consistent with maximum virtue? Any suggestions you might offer would be gratefully, very gratefully, received.

I am in the midst of much disgruntlement over reviews of "Attitudes Toward History." (A) They are slow in coming out, and (B) when they do come out, they cause me much sleep-destroying fury. So I am wasting hours and hours, annoyed particularly by the fact that each reviewer seems to select some one paragraph or footnote and write about it as though it were the whole book. Irony: one tries to put a lot together—and the reviewers, thinking primarily of their own comfort and convenience, take it all apart, isolate one part, and play it up as a totality. Heck.

Seasonal greetings,

K.B.

[P]   [Rutherford]
December 29, 1937

Dear Ken,

Yeah, I heard about Butch from a patient here in town only last week.[58] It was the wife of a Russian-American sea-captain; why 'n Heck don't you send out announcements? The brat has a natural immunity against diphtheria until about the age of ten months or so. After that let someone (maybe next summer since most dip comes in October) give him two doses of the alum-precipitated toxoid—a month apart. I prefer to shoot at the buttock, more meat there. If you don't want to wait too long start shooting in April. I'll do it for you if you want me to, but any clinic or other private doc will do.

Nothing else to think of for the moment unless you care to improve the time by giving whooping cough vaccine: six doses, two each time for three times. Right in the ass—as most things come in this world. If you want to start that now he'll be all set for the dip shots in the spring. Take it or leave it, it isn't essential.

Scarlet fever immunization isn't advised. If the kid by extraordinary chance gets a vicious case of that there is a serum that will cure him—usually in twenty-four hours <u>if given at once</u>. This is not given in mild cases. They're mild.

Vaccination against smallpox can be delayed until the kid is ready for Mexico City or school.

What else? Tuberculin test. Fer Chrisake! We all got T.B. more or less, tha's what makes us so able to keep going. It's the truth I'm tellin' yuh. I actually feel a bit uneasy because my son Bill has a negative test for T.B.[59] I don't like it. He'll have to be unusually careful, I think, because it means he has no acquired protection against it. Paul is, on the other hand, positive for it. I'm just tell' yuh how it is.

Then there's syphilis, gonorrhea, chancroid, the itch, impetigo contagiosa, athletes' foot, poison ivy and liver spots—no cure for them except a healthy life in the fog and mist, lots of salt fish, snails fried in onions (no kiddin') and— Vodka!

So the world degenerates and I'm doing an essay on the development and significance of Spanish poetry.[60] What a subject! And how much more important to us than the blight of English literature under which our cocks have all but rotted away into each others ass holes.

Yours,

Bill

[P]   [Rutherford]
May 5, 1940

Dear Ken,

I <u>will</u> read your essay.[61] I'm already ⅓ the way through it—among the usual distracting interruptions. It fascinates me and looks to be something valuable in my case. I want to see more of you this summer. I'll run up soon.

Bill

[B]   [Andover]
May 24, 1940

Dear Bill,

I admit it, it's a very nice poem. Since people got everything backwards, poetry is the art of getting backwards what they got backwards, so that it will be frontwards. Hence, maneuvers for turning the inside out, so that us tough bums can be peered at by virgins (we-looking-at-the posies becomes posies-looking at us). Yet, it's a good poem, and I could use my calipers on it until you cried out that I was as delicate as a coroner's jury.

I am still resolved, by the way, that I shall some day do that essay on you I once wrote you about.[62] Using the "cluster" business (or did I mention "clusters"—anent Coleridge—in the Freud piece, and with mention enough to make it apparent what I had in mind?).[63] I.e., I should look for "blue," "yellow," "room," flower faces, etc. elsewhere, to make sure by citable scissor-work what is telescoped here. I wouldn't dare to interpret "cherry" frivolously, for instance, unless I could offer substance from other passages.

Also, I had an especial desire to get the essay done right away, that time I saw the Horton crack and your crack back.[64] I ran across the guy who has Horton as his understudy at Harvard (or had then), and gave him hell for letting Horton be so stupid. And I felt it wrong that you had to do the chastising yourself.

Sure, let's arrange to have you declaim some of your poems here. You can pass the hat and probably pay off that lawsuit.[65] We'll set a definite date later— and I'll arrange to get some extra people here over the weekend, to augment the ones that usually accumulate in the summer.

Sorry you couldn't stop at Syracuse. My friend Leonard Brown is there (English dept.) and you would have enjoyed talking with him.[66] Also, Eaton is very nice. (I've been up there for a week three different summers, and am scheduled to be there this summer, but may have to crab, in that I seem to have got to a point where several days of consecutive verbalizing get me too bestirred.)

Meanwhile, turn up—and greetings,

K.B.

[P]   [Rutherford]
Oct. 14, 1940

Dear Ken,

I'm glad somebody is interested enough to think and to write in the manner and with the authority in which you wrote in <u>Poetry</u> on the matter of verse making.[67] That sort of thing, taken as an act, is indispensable to any civilized society. It indicates the way growth takes place. No poet would be likely to stop to think as the philosopher would think of the materials he, the poet, uses. But he can accept the support he gets from that kind of thinking and, in turn, reward that thinking by example. There's a word for it perhaps it's symbiosis, I'm not sure. Very good exposition, very useful. I don't know why I don't see you other than my inability to exist in two places at once.

Bill

[P]   [Rutherford]
April 21, 1941

Dear Ken,

The enclosed more or less explains itself. May I add that Floss and I have been to Puerto Rico where I attended an Inter-America Writers Conference.[68] We returned not two hours ago, the motion of the plane is still in my semi-circular canals.

The notice which I received just before we set sail last week concerning your new book touching the general problem of modern poetic form suggested to me that you would be an excellent one to take my place at the N.J. Writers Conference to be held at Princeton next Saturday and which I cannot assist at. I disagree with Mrs. Hutchinson that any slight is implied in asking you to take my place, we approach the subject from different categories of thought. I wish you would accept the office and carry on the good work, it is a legitimate opportunity for the forwarding also of your book on the subject. Please do not turn me down.

It might be expeditious for you to reply direct to the letter from Mrs. Hutchinson.

By the way, I have ordered your book from the U. of Louisiana Press. I always want to have a talk with you over those things which concern us jointly —I have already told you how much I liked the essay in <u>Poetry</u> which appeared a few months ago—so that now that you have assembled the essays on poetry I shall make a special effort to get up to Andover this year.

Yours as ever,

Bill

I'd be curious to know what you think of Hem's new seven decker.[69]
    W.

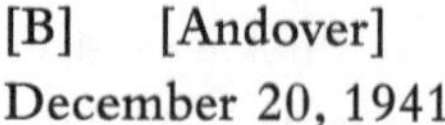

[B]   [Andover]
December 20, 1941

Dear Bill,
    Merry Christmas.

Going through my sack, I came upon the enclosed, which you asked me to return. Here it is.

I guess we mean well, you and me. And maybe we even really intend now and then to have a session together. But we just do go along his or her individual way.

It's too bad, probably.

Anyhow, best seasonal greetings—and know we'd always be glad if you dropped around some day.

Sincerely,
K.B.

[P]	[Rutherford]
July 12, 1943

Dear Ken,

Criticize this and make it more effective.[70]

How ah yuh? I enclose postage for return mail. Or if, being a professional, you don't want to touch it, leave its cherry intact.

The war goes on and more and more of our youth become involved. Paper is scarcer and a book of poems next to impossible to get printed—yet the very youth are the ones who demand the poems. I feel gratified but thwarted.

The writing goes on—mostly in the small magazines as usual. I can sell isolated poems. The difficulty is, as usual, to find time for the writing. This job of being a doctor is worse than the Japanese beetles, it eats up all the foliage.

Haven't you anything to say about Pound and Eliot—or skip Eliot. It seems to me that Pound today as a logical development of Pound yesterday holds an interesting position for the philosopher bent upon investigating the means of expression. My little dribble wanted to mention Pound and his end products as of today but—it didn't fit.

I enjoyed the coolness of your developments in the <u>VIEW</u> piece.[71] My piece was written before, during and after my reading of what you said there.

As ever,
Bill

[B]   [Andover]
July 30, 1943

Dear Bill,

How.

Gladda hear fromya. Why don't you breeze in this way some time? Or we'd be glad to make it a definite time if you'd prefer it that way. Say, for dinner, some time during the week? Or weekend? No matter.

The article—I don't know? It isn't among your mightier compositions. No? Maybe my trouble is this: when Eastman and Dewey write on international politics, I can never feel that they write as philosophers, simply as small-time politicians out of office.[72] Thought it got better towards the end, though I challenge you to parse the final sentence.

I guess what threw me off is that you don't suggest what a despicable figure the man is. (I admit I never had anything to do with him personally. But I felt that his <u>Digest</u> line merited simple contempt. As for Dewey: he's done a lot in the past that I respect, but when he talks about Russia he is simply a prisoner of Hook and his ilk.)[73]

You speak of Pound.[74] Didn't he simply get into it step by step? Not as a "philosopher," but simply as a literary prima donna. (I.e., did some good writing, but wanted it to do more for him, in lay channels, than he should have.) Then, as the result of dialectic, he found himself saying this because somebody else said that, and that because somebody else said this. Which was a harmless enough thing for one to do in the realm of pure art, but has all sorts of surprises in store for anybody who lets it be amplified against the sounding board of contemporary politics. First thing one knows, a few innovations in the writing of a sentence have become transformed into treason against one's country (I don't mean that the innovations are treason—I mean that the banding-together, which came as the outcome of them, happened by the accidents of political exploitation to put Pound in a band on the other end of the seesaw. And what was in the twenties literary expatriation becomes in the forties the placing of oneself at the disposition of conspirators. But "essentially," this man functioning as a political traitor is still motivated by the motives of the literary twenties.)

Maybe your article puzzles me because I don't know what you want. "What should we do next?" I do indeed agree that we should go beyond the kind of thinking done by man in the <u>Digest</u> whoredom; but I don't think you give any concrete ways of doing so. (Lerner mopped up Eastman in <u>P.M.</u>)[75]

I guess the main thing to be said against the article is that it has no twist. As per your use of the anecdote about Grant and the whisky.[76] A good anecdote— but isn't some twist needed, if one would use it again? (Or am I talking like the twenties myself?) (I guess I'll always talk like the twenties.) (Datsa mah home.)

Speaking of such: went up to Newton last night, and saw Joan Fontaine in her latest.[77] After she died, I came home and lay awake two hours feeling very melancholy. That wasn't very professional, was it? Her mobile face—made Boyer look like a billboard.

Hello. Best greetings,
Sincerely,
K.B.

[B]   [Andover]
August 12, 1943

Dear Bill,

Have arranged to take a teaching job.[78] Hence, after Aug. 26th my times here will be quite irregular. So if you're minded to be in these precincts, hope you'll be so minded before that.

If you're grouchy about what I said, drop around and tell me why you think I'm an s. of a b. Topics like that are always good for a couple of bright hours, aint they?

Meanwhile, goodes gluck.

Sincerely,
K.B.

[P]   [Rutherford]
Aug. 14, 1943

Dear Ken,

Damned nice of you to write again. I didn't in the least object to your comments on my little article,[79] in fact I thought you were very mild, perhaps too considerate. I expected you to tear it to shreds.

Delmore Schwartz, now taking Dwight Macdonald's place on the editorial board of <u>Partisan Review</u> wrote saying they would use the article or communication with a reply to it by someone and would I object?[80] I told him I would be delighted and hadn't the least compunction in saying whoever attacked me should be given free rein. My only object was to bring the subject into the light. I told him also that you did not at least froth at the mouth at my amateurishness or at my opinions.

I'm rather glad you're taking on a teaching job. It may be a poor way to earn a living but, properly guarded, it might prove stimulating to your thought.

I wish I could see you sometime at leisure but more than ever this has become close to impossible. I went to Cranberry once this summer for a short visit but you know how it is, the time is eaten up by swimming, fishing and canoeing, talking to one's host and friend—then there's a rush to get off in order to be able to get home on time. I thought of you but didn't want merely to say hello good bye, which was all I should have had time for.

During the past six months or more I've been collecting, sorting and arranging various poems of mine that have not heretofore appeared in a book.[81] It makes a rather formidable collection but no one will print it (did I tell you this in my last?) I am not greatly concerned—just passing on the news.

The work at my profession is hard, very hard and trying but so far I have managed to survive and still keep an edge for writing. I suppose I'll never give up that, come what may. But the work is very hard and will get much harder the coming winter with more of the men in the profession going into the armed forces.

The impossibility of meeting all situations emotionally has been a great lesson to me. I have to a great extent succeeded in keeping my body at a sort of ease even when I am harassed to the point of complete exhaustion. I have even had the experience of going into the office after twelve hours of continuous hard work, for evening office hours, and coming out three hours later refreshed. Now that's an odd thing. It is pure emotional restraint that makes it possible. I suppose with a little more practice I shall be able to chirp like a cricket even at the very moment when my bones and muscles finally collapse.

I was telling the girl on the obstetric floor this afternoon that when I get old I'm going to look for a job as houseman in a whorehouse. I'm still crazy about the women, I just like 'em around and having enjoyed them and given them some enjoyment I feel now that I have earned the right to be right in among them no sexes barred—just for the relaxing hell of it. Rabelais[82] is my patron.

Best luck, Ken, and if they tear me apart in <u>Partisan Review</u> don't forget to send them a polite letter in rebuttal—if it should amuse you.

Your old friend,

Bill

1945–1963

William Carlos Williams	**Kenneth Burke**

The Wedge 1944, *Paterson I* 1946, Lectures at Washington 1947, *Paterson II* 1948, *The Clouds* 1948, *A Dream of Love* 1948, *Paterson III* 1949, *Selected Poems* 1949, *Collected Later Poems* 1950, National Book Award 1950, *Collected Earlier Poems* 1951, *Paterson IV* 1951, *Autobiography* 1951, first stroke 1951, Consultant to Library of Congress 1952, Bollingen Prize 1953, *Desert Music* 1954, *Selected Essays* 1954, Lecture tour 1955, *Paterson V* 1958, *Pictures from Brueghel* 1962.

Teaches at Bennington 1943–61, *A Grammar of Motives* 1945, Elected to Institute of Arts and Letters 1946, Lectures at Princeton 1949, *A Rhetoric of Motives* 1950, Chicago 1950, Kenyon College 1950, Indiana 1952 & 1958, *Book of Moments* 1955, Stanford 1957, Drew 1962, *A Rhetoric of Religion* 1961.

[P]   [Rutherford]
10/5/45

Dear Ken,

A swell bit in <u>Sewanee Review</u>—that Swiss Cheese (you remember the holes) to me the best thing in the issue.[1]

If only I could read, read, read as I'd like to but my special destiny, at that, saves me from that I suppose.

But I think of you at these times with the warmest regards.

Yours,
Bill

Regards to the ladies. What a work they are doing!

[B]   [Andover]
October 12, 1945

Dear Bill,

Thanks a whole lot for your note. That means something to a guy.

Many times I have wondered why you don't mosey over this way. And I wish you would.

Incidentally, I wonder if you could suggest whither I might wend anent this one: Always asking what is to be the death of me, I think I should not neglect much longer getting someone in the know to diagnose a bony protuberance in the roof of my mouth. I first noticed it, I believe, about 30 years ago. Gradually it has got bigger, until now, bejeez, it seems damned near as big as a jellybean. So I guess I should consult some saw bones, begging to be assured that it aint really so bad as all that—whereupon I could go back to worrying about my heart trouble. Do you have any place to suggest? Some place where, if there is chiseling to be done, most of it could be done on the roof of my mouth?

Whether accidents could have started the thing, I don't know. I am the proud possessor of a broken neck, as disclosed by X-ray photographs taken at a hospital some years ago. I had a bad fall when about three years old, and spent many years of my childhood in terror, a sense of being elsewhere, or dropping through the bottom. I guess the fall did its part in that. And I wonder whether it may also have got things to growing a bit wrong too, as my head sits awry. And then at another time I had my front teeth batted out, an accident that might have dislocated the maxillary bones a bit. Anyhow, there is the egg, and I'm finding it more and more difficult to give priority rating to my other worries. So, if you had someone to suggest? Particularly some thoughtful soul like me who might be more prone to diagnosis than action. I'd be very grateful for the tip.

Am just about at the end of the business of seeing my <u>Grammar</u> through the press.[2] I hope very soon now to be at work on the next volume, the <u>Rhetoric</u>—for which I have all the notes already, and which I hope to write within a year.[3] (We hope to bundle the kids, the notes, and the typewriter into the car sometime in December, and roll down U.S. 1 to somewhere in Florida.) Finishing a book always gives me an end-of-the-world feeling; then there is this dismal fall; then there is the fact that I gave up my teaching job, for a year at least, to write full time again (and when that great amt. of externalizing, in personal relations, has become a bit of a habit, the many more hours with the self make one all the more mindful of the self's burdens—how nice it would be to be worrying about other people, and then all of a sudden be gone, except insofar as the sudden going itself might inconvenience those about whom one had been worrying, say we legalistically).

Meanwhile, weather permitting, I sally forth with my scythe each afternoon, to clear the weeds from the fields about the house. I have driven the wilderness back quite a bit, since the last time you were here (at least in some places, though it is patient, and ever ready to catch me napping, and moves in here as soon as I go there). So, while scything, in a suffering mood, I worry about our corrupt newspapers, about nucleonics (for where there is power there is intrigue, so this new fantastic power may be expected to call forth intrigue equally fantastic), about things still to be done for the family, about a sentence that should never have been allowed to get by in such a shape.

But duty calls. I must stop this letter now, and turn to less joyous matters.

Best greetings,

Sincerely,
K.B.

[P]   [Rutherford]
Sunday [Oct. 14, 1945]

Dear Ken,

If you want to get here next Sunday somewhere around 11 A.M. we'll go up and see DeBell.[4] Stay to lunch if you will when we'll give you a drink and plan between us when we might best run up there for a visit—I realize there's not much time left before the cold weather but every season has its compulsions and attractions for the imagination, we'll go when we can. Which, by the way, means just what it says.

Someday! Someday! we'll be free: no babies will be being born, no one will have a cold, no one will have miscarriages—there will be no committee meetings or clinical conferences—or cocktails or Anais Nin or Shapiro writing about Rime or rime on the windows or sumac or talks to be given at Briarcliff or printers or even Shakespeare to tempt us and torment us.[5]

There will be only philosophers and bombs.

Quote, Mrs. Androla (after I had told her we would all in all probability be blown to high grade manure before her baby shall be born and only a few Esquimaux be left to carry on): Maybe those barbarians will do better than Christianity did.

I <u>love</u> the past tense of it. It has already happened in many minds.
RSVP

Bill

[P]   [Rutherford]
10/15/45

Dear Ken,

A hell of a good younger man is a Dr. DeBell a friend of mine in Passaic. Maybe some Sunday morning.

Or, if you want to go to a clinic, the Memorial Hospital in N.Y.C. at E 68th is headquarters for all lumps, knobs, buttons, protuberances. You'd need a note from me.

Damn it, I <u>must</u> run up to see you now the war is over and gas is free-er.

<u>You</u> depressed, you a philosopher? And when you have taught yourself to write so lucidly and well? Your other piece in <u>Kenyon</u> is fully as interesting and well done as the other.[6]

Tell me what you want to do and I'll make the arrangements and I will definitely try to make the trip to Andover during the next few weeks.

Both my boys still in the Pacific area.

Wish they were here.

Yours,

Bill

[B]   [Andover]
October 17, 1945

Dear Bill,

How! All this time I had been thinking that philosophy was the road to freedom; yet you would have it deny me my constitutional right to bellyache. And does not no less an one than Goethe praise above all else fear and trembling? (I used to like to cite the gag I found in Aulus Gellius. Of the philosopher and the merchant, in a dreadful storm at sea. The merchant took it quite calmly; the philosopher was very agitated. Then, after the storm had been successfully weathered, the merchant began twitting the philosopher. "You, who are supposed to be an exemplar of philosophic calm—look how much more frightened you were than I was." And the philosopher answered: "True, but look how much more I had to lose.")[7]

Fact is: all is tolerable when I'm moving ahead in my work. But at the moment I'm lying sluggish sans breeze, not yet having got the new direction going for the next book. And at that stage I'm just a plain simple taker of my own pulse.

Thanks very much for your suggestions.[8] I'd like to take you up on that jaunt to Passaic some Sunday morning. Any one you suggest. (Not counting this coming Sunday, as I might not hear from you in time to come then.) I'd drive down.

And some time when you can come out here, let us know beforehand—and arrange to come with the wife and stay for dinner. What say?

I did not know your boys were away off there.[9] Glad to hear that they're safe. I have one son-in-law and one prospective son-in-law who have seen quite a bit of action on the continent of Asia, and are now in China. Another, a strapping guy that would make about three of me, turned up with a minor leg ailment, and has been placidly playing his drums in a jazz band at army training camps in U.S.

Best luck—and many thanks indeed for your prompt reply to my piercing outcry.

Sincerely,

K.B.

[P]   [Rutherford]
Oct. 23, 1945

Dear Ken,

Talking to DeBell, the surgeon, today he said—after I had described your palatal lump to him—that it was in all probability what is called <u>taurus palatinus</u>, a fairly common appearance (though I have not seen it), non-malignant and of no particular importance unless it proves annoying.[10] He said it can be knocked off any time you like with a mallet and chisel like any other osteoma.

I'd be inclined to think from this that you needn't bother to come down on Sunday unless you feel like it—we're always here. Drop me a note.

Yours,

Bill

[B]   [Andover]
October 24, 1945

Dear Bill,

Many thanks indeed for your note. Old Falling Apart will plan to be there, then, as you suggest, circa eleven next Sunday morning.[11] One possible hitch is that he plans to come in his car, which has been acting up a bit of late. So there might be delays due to the agues and shiverings of Falling-Apart the Second. I hope not. I shall leave early enough to give me plenty of time. (The ailment in the case of my pal is a leaking water-pump, which I am trying to get replaced, but which probably will not be replaced by that time. Ah! would that old Falling-Apart Sr. could likewise get his pump replaced.)

But don't bother about lunch for me. I'll just bumble along back hither. But I'll gladly take you up on that drink.

Yestiddy, went to the Great Market and there gave final O.K. on proofs for my book.[12] Due to appear in early December. I was recd. with smiles by men in the sales dept., which is about the most Olympian thing that can happen to an author. It seems that the advance orders from booksellers have been quite good.

Yes, by all means, we'll arrange Sunday about your visit here.

Sincerely,

K.B.

[B]   [Andover]
October 24, 1945

Dear Bill,

Holla! Just got your latest, with the bit telling my fortune.[13]

Palatine bull! That's fine! Sounds just like me. So now I can joyously return to my heart trouble.

I'll not trek thither on Sunday. Particularly inasmuch as the car is so unwell. But how about your trip in this direction? Do say the word, and pick your time.

Many thanks.

Sincerely,

K.B.

[B]   [Andover]
October 31, 1945

Dear Bill,

Many thanks indeed for sending me the W.C.W. number of the <u>Quarterl. Rev. of Lit.</u>[14] I read your poems with my usual delight, and your critical bleats with my usual bepuzzlement.

I remember how, some years ago, in the fall, when I was in one of my just-about-through moods, and was trying to bring myself to say good-bye to this world, I got a note from you, telling how you had the garden all cleared for next spring. That was a good jolt, though at first it made me feel even more about-to-depart. (It stinks, and I am ready to de-pot, was my then motto.) Well, I thought of that note again, when reading the last lines of "The Bitter World of Spring." About the shad, "midway between the surface and the mud," and "headed unrelenting, upstream." A good fable, is that poem. Isn't that what "objectivism" finally gets around to? Or isn't it? Anyhow, I think the poem is a byoot. The first is good too, but lacks the final twist. Or perhaps the second is the first's twist. And "The Goat" and "The Hurricane" are also two sturdy evidences that your diagnostic savoring hath not lost its salt. Just what you are making of your clouds, I am not yet quite sure. The heavenward glance is decidedly qualified. Shrewd rather than pious?

Would it be correct to say that you have learned how to make a poem out of notes for a poem? I have in mind particularly such a one as "The Rare Gist."

As for me: I hope that, some time before I'm through, I'll be able to carry out my plans to do one of my studies of "equations," in your work. I'd like to do you and Stevens, somewhat along the lines of an essay I did on Marianne Moore.[15]

Hope you'll be turning up before long. And we can hear more on you on Eliot on place.[16] Didn't you start off too soon? There are also some remarks in "Little Gidding," on England, mind, nowhere and everywhere—and these also might figure in?

Have been, for better or worse, batting away on the <u>Rhetoric</u>.[17] Finally got started.

Sincerely,

K.B.

[P]   [Rutherford]
11/1/[1945]

O.K. Ken,

It is the opposite of piety that I am concluding in "The Clouds"; the unknowability of knowledge and the professional asses who trade on that basic fact—pontifically proclaiming this or that.[18] Did I say "asses," I beg the donkey's pardon.

Disease has no connection with medicine, nor philosophy incapacitated from knowing anything of disease. To him it is "cute" or "important" or something else. It is never disease, as it is to the person who has it. The proof is that when the physician is diseased the disease comes to him as her lover to a virgin. He can't understand it.

In something after this argument I look upon the metaphysician or religionist who uses—the mystic might be the better term—who uses poetry, as that prime mental shit Eliot uses it, for his own purposes.[19] My resentment toward him is as deep as I am. I stake everything I've got on it. He is a subtle defamer of poetry, the more contemptible in that he is smart enough to wrap it in his stopgap religion.

The man as a man is plaintive, unable. I do not hold that against him. But when the weak hold their resentment against the strong as a virtue, I resent it —profoundly. It is all right that he must live as he can and write as he is able to write and of the things that concern him, that is his own business—but Jesus Christ, that doesn't make the world outside his restrictions an evil thing.

It is evil to him, of course—etc., etc.

And when this permeates down through a plastic technique to torture its modes—and the distortions of thought and plastic, shielded by subtlety and "knowledge" presented to the exclusion of other work as the norm. At this point I attack.

Eliot as a mystic is to poetry a disgusting disease. But if it is the idea of disease only that we are considering then perhaps we may, logically, speak of placelessness. He hides his disease well, but it is hidden, not cured. Take off his mental clothes and I think "place" will get a new meaning—in his case. I have not heard that even at Lourdes do they cure chancres by prayer.[20]

Tomorrow, Friday November 2, Floss and I will make an attempt to reach you in your isolated valley around 3 in the afternoon—the weather permitting. Don't bother to "feed" us. Sure, we'd like a cup of tea and damned if I won't bring a bottle of spirits for general cheer. See you then. Bad weather would be a bar.

Bill

[P]   [Rutherford]
11/2/[1945]

Dear Ken.

I suppose this is going to be another one of those things. It's now 1.25, the sky somewhat threatening and I've decided not to make the trip. If I don't do it today I know I won't do it this year. That's that.

I'd like to see you and talk with you—maybe I'd be happier if I did, I know I should be—

Nothing much else I can say—except that I dread the expense of energy, of time of—unknown involved. My knees ache, my tongue is coated, my brain (I should say my skull) is over crowded.

I'll end by putting on old clothes and going into the back yard, drink my own Bourbon—take a hot bath.

Cough my guts out.

And wish I had gone to see you in Andover. The worst is you'll be expecting me.

I may even deliver a baby (3 overdue) and use the excuse of being out of town to avoid going to a committee meeting on revision of the by-laws of the Senior Staff at the Passaic General Hosp. at 5 P.M.

I may even work on my play.[21]

Bill

[B]   [Andover]
November 6, 1945

Dear Bill,

Why not try it this Friday, weather permitting? And plan to stay for dinner.

Incidentally, just for safety's sake, might add that we'll probably be away Monday and Tuesday of next week.

Sorry you couldn't get around last week, though I must admit it wasn't a very undiscouraging day.

In haste, as 'tis time for me to get back to the Grind. Lost yesterday; had to go to Babylon, and weep by the waters.

Sincerely,
K.B.

No use sending special deliveries here, unless you just like the ritual of the thing. However, the postman assures me that at least they don't arrive any <u>later</u> than other mail.

Do think on this Friday.

[P]   [Rutherford]
Nov. 10, [1945]

Dear Ken,

We both enjoyed seeing you all. Three things: to get the information as to whether or not the "bull" can be carved off the roof of your mouth under local, how much follow-up there will have to be, the time element, etc.; second, to copy out the poem containing the lines you want and send it to you; three, to say that if we come again it'll be on a Sunday, earlier in the day so that we may get home before dark—it takes too much out of my aging carcass to do it this way.[22] The next three weeks or not till next year. We shall see, though the chances are, after all, slim.

I saw the beginnings of many valuable conversations between us sticking their heads up as we passed them by yesterday—I particularly liked your manner of explanation when you lowered your voice and spoke quietly of the elementals that interest us both, the humane particulars of realization and communication. I woke in the night with a half-sentence on my metaphorical lips "the limitations of form." It seemed to mean something of importance and to have been connected with what we had been saying.

You'll hear from me again in the next two days.

Yours,
Bill

[P]   [Rutherford]
Nov. 18, 1945

Dear Ken,

Dr. DeBell says he can carve that lump off the roof of your mouth under local anesthesia any time you want him to do it—provided I help him.[23] No hurry about it. He'd do it some Sunday morning between now and Christmas or next spring or at your convenience.

Any news on your proposed flight south?[24] Let me know what's up. I dashed off a sketch for a poem following our visit to you week before last, if and when (if ever) I finish the thing I'll send you a copy. Did you like "The Visit"?[25] Any further visit by me to Andover before next spring seems more and more unlikely the more the season advances.

Our best to your wife and kids.

Bill

[B]   [Andover]
November 19, 1945

Dear Bill,

Many thanks for your note, with expert enclosures. We were sorry indeed to learn that the trip turned out to be burdensome to you. Here's hoping 'twas not so much so as to discourage you from taking another. Incidentally, it may be that the Cochrans (Tom Age of Enterprise Cochran) and the Josephsons (Matthew Robber Barons Josephson) will be here on Sunday Dec. 2nd.[26] So, if you wanted to be here then, for Sunday dinner, that would be excellong. (I could let you know definitively, later, lest you be induced thither by added attractions that are fraudulent.)

I await your info. anent the excavating of oral cavities.[27] Await same with much gratitude for your efforts in my behalf, and also with some trepidation. Wd. like (a) to get the damned obstacle knocked out immediately, within the next ten minutes, and (b) to put it off forever. It is really getting to be a mouthful. And as one who works constantly with ideas, I am vastly more worried by the idea of the thing than by the thing itself. I can't keep myself from expecting it of a sudden to disclose urgently malign properties. Suppose, I ask myself quaintly, if it were growing in some other direction too. (Maybe that is simply a ghastly way of taking the childhood pun of "bonehead" seriously.)

Have been batting away at the <u>Rhetoric</u>.[28] (It will become, I guess, a study devoted to showing how deep and ubiquitous are the roots of war in the universal scene and the human psyche—a study extending from our meditations on the war of words.) <u>The Grammar</u> is due any day now.[29] And I dare tell myself that I actually might, when the reviews start appearing, be sufficiently involved in the <u>Rhetoric</u> to be no more than mildly irritated by the misrepresentations of the criticasters and the horesesasters. (I have learned to expect criticastering as a matter of course, somewhat as one expects cold weather in winter.) And though one might grumble at the cold, one does so with quite a different feeling than he would if he had expected that winter would be like summer. The fact is that the trilogy can build up a fairly comprehensive abstract of human relations I am convinced.[30] And if I but get a fair enough treatment from the critics to permit me to go on getting the volumes published, I'll be content. I worry mainly about the reception of the middle section, on the philosophic schools. The pages on Kant and Spinoza may raise much trouble for the reader. For though I am trying to show how the use of our five pet terms assists radically in disclosing the basic structure of a philosopher's system, my ways of simplification are not those of Will Mansions of Philosophy Durant by a damned sight.[31] And insofar as they are not, I may expect resentment on the part of the reviewers. For other reasons (vestiges of the old Stalin-Trotsky battles) I shall expect to see the book beturded by the stinks who get out the Phartisan Repuke.[32] Rhetoric. The War of Words. Logomachy.

Your vatic awakening, with the words of the anonymous spokesman, "the limitations of form," suddenly reminded me that I forgot to mark down a reference I had come upon in Aquinas a few days ago.[33] His three (quoting Aristotle, I believe) were: symmetry, order, and limitation. Anyhow, the scholastics equate "form" and "act"—and, to apply your localization business in another way, one can act only by not acting all over the place.[34] As a matter of fact, the dream words doubtless went back to the old battles of you and McAlmon vs. Matty and me, which were always about "form," though God only knows what we meant by it.[35] I, the same night, was dreaming of being chased by some nameless thing that finally turned out to be a big and very friendly dog. The amusing thing is that you, the imagist, dreamed a concept, and I, the ideologue, dreamed an image.

Glad to have the line anent the concealed weapon.[36] However, strangely enough, I believe I got the quality of the interview better from your telling of it than from the poesy. Why was that?

But to the other notes, which I must get out before the postman arrives.

Sincerely,

K.B.

[B]   [Andover]
November 23, 1945

Dear Bill,

Jeez, thanks very much indeed for yours anent the deboning.[37] What would you think of Dec. 9th? Or, if you thought there was any likelihood of your coming out here on the ninth, then the 16th? (We still hope you all may think fondly of the second, though I do not yet know about the others.)

Figuring out what I missed in "The Visit," I'd say tentatively it was this: It was really an incident that required <u>filling out</u> in terms of <u>dramatic action,</u> to make it fully live for a reader who <u>had not</u> himself been through it; but you treated it rather in terms of <u>imagistic impression</u> which is perhaps the best way of <u>summing up</u> the quality of the experience for one who <u>had</u> been through it.[38] Does that mean anything? And if so, would you grant any justice in it?

Your <u>Improvisations</u> always struck me as the most revealing spot, methodologically, in your poetry.[39] And looking back at them again now, in the light of the formula I just offered, I'd say that in those who were (sometimes almost schematically) dividing your poem into a dramatic half and an imagistic half, one half telling the <u>situation</u> explicitly and the other half giving the <u>impression</u> that was distilled from it (if one can distill an impression!). After the <u>Improvisations</u>, you reverted to the allusive method of letting the situation be glimpsed through the impression. But where the give and take of the dialogue itself (the <u>form</u> of such sparring) is itself the main interest (as, it seems to me, should be the case with "The Visit"), then the summarizing imagistic impression cannot make up for the omission of the dramatic minutiae.

If that all seems too tangled, let's try it again.

Incidentally, I thought afterwards, the dream I told you about may have been left far too ambiguous in my telling of it.[40] Recall that, one of the few other times when you were here, an old woodsman, Gene, stood holding up his hand, with my mean little dog hanging to it as though it were an old rag. And you had to patch him up. The dog was shot the same day. And the whole episode left an extremely troubled memory with me, particularly as I was much worried by the thought that a mean dog reflects on the state of mind of its owner—so I felt mean (a) for having such a dog, (b) for having him killed, and (c) because I was actually in quite a bothersome situation. So, that all had to be patched up somehow—and it took the form of (was summed up in) an imagistic impression involving the happy character-change of a dog. (Among the enacted puns that have beset me, incidentally, is the one which, when I am loudmouthed, could be joyced as Kennel Bark.)

Well, we gave thanks yesterday—and I'm not as much of a wreck as I thought I'd be, as I lay tossing in the night. So I'm back at work on the <u>Rhetoric</u> today.[41] Hence, shall say no more for this time.

Incidentally, am I right in assuming that I could plan to drive in Sunday morning, and then drive out again after the bopping (i.e., bring Shorty [42] along to drive the car on the way back, in case I was too full of myself)? Meanwhile, could I say that I'm very grateful to you, too, for offering to join in the fray?

With best greetings to you and your wife. And remember, if you can trek hither again, we'd be delighted should any of the others you spoke of be able to come too.

Sincerely,

K.B.

Incidentally, I think that "The Cod Head" is a very good poem.[43] I don't believe I ever got around to telling you so before. But would you, for the sake of some of my own linguistic speculations, tell me whether it was literally a cod head? Or was it simply a fish head, which you thought might sound best if particularized as a cod? If it was a cod, I'm not better or worse off than I was before. But if it wasn't cod, or if you didn't know just what kind of fish it was but wanted to call it a cod, then I'm a tiny step farther along. I'm embarrassed to be so pedestrian and pedantic about the matter. But if physicists are willing to blow up the world for the advancement of science, I might at least be willing to ask a blunt question in the same noble cause.

[P]   [Rutherford]
Sunday [November 25, 1945]

Dear Ken,

Did you ever notice that the most brilliant screen representation you ever saw were those in the "advance notices" they show between the regular pictures? With me at least it's always been so. The reason is that the distracting context of any reel has been blasted away and we see the photography as it is, without a "story."

The explanation for your disappointment with my line as seen in the finished poem is that when I first spoke of it you fitted it instanter into a context of your own—to which it applied perfectly.[44] In the finished work you resented a context which was foreign to your first brilliant conception. At least so I believe.

I am sorry but I knew the cod head was a cod head and not just a fish head—for I knew that cod was the only thing being caught at that place and had seen many of the assistant fishermen cutting up the fish preparatory to laying the flesh out on prepared boards to be sun-dried. I saw hundreds of the heads thrown back into the sea. You might, in the same poem have wondered about the "red cross." But there is actually a plainly marked red cross, just like the ordinary "plus" mark in arithmetic figured on the back of the large jelly-fish or stingray, seen so commonly in the waters of Labrador.

Dr. DeBell says any time Sunday morning on Dec. 8 or any Sunday thereafter, he'd be glad to do the job for you.[45] It won't be a particularly difficult or shocking piece of work. He says you will be all right to drive back home immediately after. Bring "Shorty" though to give you assurance. Get here not later than 10 A.M.—here at my house in Rutherford. You know the place.

The "Improvisations,"[46] I can see, have a conceptual quality, which might be satisfying to a man dealing more with concepts than images—but as compared with my "Novelette"[47] they appear rather static to me today. Have you ever seen the "Novelette"? Send you one if you want it.

Not much chance of our getting up there again this season—but we'll keep it in mind.

Yrs

[B]   [Andover]
November 30, 1945

Dear Bill,

You got me wrong. I wasn't disappointed with the line.[48] It serves my context as well as I thought it did. But I felt that the poem as a whole did not reveal the incident in toto as well as your impromptu account of it did. And what I was trying to say, in my laborious distinctions between narration and summation, was that I thought the account of the incident would have profited by a particularized sequence of give-and-take (what she said, then what I said, then what she said, etc.).

I don't know whether you wholly got the sort of speculating I had in mind anent cod. I was concerned with speculations that have to do with the joycing of cod-head as God-head, plus phallic implications of cod (as per cod piece, properly placed btw. the two stones).

No, I have not seen the Novelette.[49] But I'd be delighted to read it.

Many thanks for info anent "my operation."[50] We'll plan to be there next Sunday (Dec.9). Unless one of these damned north easterners turns up at the last minute, and seals us in. Had I been due yesterday morning, for instance, I just simply could not have made it. But I have hopes that the weather has been adequately psychoanalyzed for a while now, and will take more than a week to develop new tantrums. And I'll take every human precaution to be there on time.

Sorry we can't expect you to appear here any more this season. Both the Cochrans and the Josephsons are due tomorrow, and possibly Dave Mandel, a Perth Amboy lawyer who you probably know—though I am half expecting word sometime today that the newest meteorological developments have scared them off.[51]

Sincerely,

K.B.

[P]   [Rutherford]

Dec. 14, 1945

Dear Ken,

Whatever the hell happened to you? I thought I might get a card from Whippany or Succasunna during the week giving me hope that you were on your way and expected soon to get there. But nothing! Nothing at all! Can I have a spare part taken in to you on mule back. Only send me word and I'll do the impossible to rescue you. My mechanic here in Rutherford said we should have broken the opposing blade off by hand, any way we could. THAT IT WAS NOT HARD TO DO. Had we only known!

Drop me a line so that I may know all is well. As for the small black-silk suture, it has probably fallen out long since, but on the chance that it is still in place, untie the knot with the tip of your tongue—or have your wife snip it loose with a pair of nail scissors, the kind used by beauticians, cuticle shears![52] Tin shears would be too heavy.

It was a pleasure to have you here even though the occasion wasn't a particularly pleasant one. At that it must be a pleasure to get rid of that annoying lump in the roof of your mouth. DeBell did a good job on it. He'll be sending you a bill one of these days—not too much either.

I enjoyed opening your <u>Grammar</u> at random and reading here and there for the pleasure of the study as I often do.[53] I happened to hit the Socrates, really a beautiful exposition of the resources at work in that tragic dilemma.[54] Or would you call it tragic, I wonder. I think not, not any more than Socrates found it so at the end. This book is extraordinarily congenial to me as it is a book I used to dream when I was a child at the supper table hearing the wild arguments that used to cross our board. I wanted to invite a stranger, a referee to live with us, at a salary, to lay down some simple rules for us. The stupidity of discussions when no one acknowledges the rules that should govern any controversy used to drive me mad. Any youth, any intelligent child who should be started in life with such a book as this of yours at hand should land in the middle of life ten years ahead of the best I did and ten times as well armed for the fray. The intelligence, a naked flame if you will at its best, needs such shucking as this before it can even reach the metal for its play. Good luck to you. This is a book I shall never entirely put down.

Wrote a poem (first draft) after I returned from my visit to you up there.[55] Some day I hope to be able to sit down to it for the final putting in shape. I'll send it to you then. It looks pretty good.

Best luck all around,
Bill

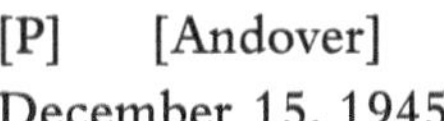

[P]   [Andover]
December 15, 1945

Dear Bill,

Your Dr. DeBell was more than right: though the chunk out of the roof of my mouth never even lost me one meal, the car is still ailing gravely.[56] After leaving you, I found a garage man who removed the opposite blade for me. But by that time the whole mechanism was so dislocated that, some miles further along, <u>another</u> blade flew off, making for such eccentricity as was never before found outside of surrealism. And we have not yet been able to get the parts necessary for the repairing.

But I am writing this to say, I much regret I am such a horse's ass at stating my thanks to you. But I am indeed very grateful to you for your trouble—and more, for your kindness. It is a noble business you are in, Bill, even down to the nagging of the telephone. I am words or nothing; you are words and medicine. Then, eliminating words, as the constant here—oof!

But I was disgusted when you started talking down your next book, while I had such a face full of blood and gauze that I could not defend you against yourself.[57] What bad advertising!

Incidentally, the operation proved to me that my fear of injections in the throat was not mere fantasy. For something <u>must have</u> gone wrong with the shots injected by the dentist, since they did gag me, whereas there was no gagging this time, even though the injections were much deeper in the throat. (There is, however, some neurosis involved too. I had a very bad case of whooping cough when young, did the blue-in-the-face stuff—and that might have left a treasure of memories for the semi-unconscious. And then again, the broken neck sometimes seems to raise some obstacles to swallowing. I remember how, about the age of fourteen or so, it was not unusual to try swallowing sweet potatoes, and have them come back through my nose.) All this by way of apology for the idiotic position of my left arm, which, in the grammar of posture, in some vague way indicated that I was waiting to find that the injections had completely choked me.

As to my business; the word-slinging only: news from the publisher continues to be encouraging about the booksellers' attitude towards the <u>Grammar</u>, though so far as I know no reviews have appeared yet.[58]

Maybe, I'm wrong, but I think you are a bit irritated at some of my tentative speculations concerning possible ingredients of symbolism in your imagery of objects. In part, this is justified, for in my tentative speculations I usually allow myself much more leeway than when I finally get around to the stage of demonstration. Primarily, however, my assumption when approaching an imagist poet is that the imagery is vital insofar as it contains <u>personality</u>. And in its role as personality, it will, in some way or other, embody the ways of <u>appetition</u> typical of persons. That principle, I take as gospel. But in the applying of the principle, there are opportunities for all sorts of stupidities. Despite that, in my desire to figure out the workings of language, I believe that one should risk some of these stupidities, rather than playing safe by purely "appreciative" criticism.

So far, I have not received my billet doux from your D. DeBell.[59] But I'll be promptitititude itself when same arrives.

Meanwhile, do be thinking of a possible voyage here some time. And— our best seasonal greetings to you and to Florence, and to the new generations.

Sincerely,

K.B.

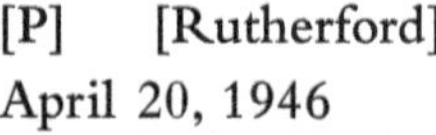

[P]   [Rutherford]
April 20, 1946

Dear Ken,

After struggling with the facets of the Ezra Pound presentation even your illnesses seem comparatively simple to me.[60] I've just finished a letter to a Pound fan (female) living in Elmhurst, New York. He still pulls 'em in, poor guy. She has him down for the modern Jesus. No use trying to explain to her that it's a matter of prose style.

What you complain of seems to originate in your Eustachian tube or the naso-pharynx near its opening. If it is serious enough to warrant a trip to New

York and a ten dollar fee, I'd call on a Dr. Miles Atkinson somewhere in the 70s near Park Ave. He's an expert. Look him up. He's good.

That aside, you could do worse than see Dr. Edward Ehrenfeld in Passaic, not far from DeBell's address. Eddie knows his stuff. His number is Passaic 2-2597, you could see him either during the day or some evening.

Yes, I've read one or two reviews of your <u>GRAMMAR</u>, to me they stink.[61] I don't know what the hell you philosophers want. One thing surely you don't want and that is each other. The sole intent seems to be to destroy; not to work hand in hand for the general enlightenment but to tear everything down to a sort of Caesar's Triumph for the one and only brilliant mind in the world, "my own." In that the philosopher and the poet (not to mention the Jesuit) are one. Oh well.

But what little of your book I have read I thoroughly enjoyed—I have not as yet finished reading it. When? Christ knows. It is looking at me now across my desk.

You know Aiken, why don't you write him a note telling him you miss my name among his lights.[62] Forget it.

I have a poem coming out in the Spring Book number of <u>New Republic</u> —a longish poem.[63] Look it up.

And there'll be an appreciation of a long poem by Parker Tyler in <u>ACCENT</u> sometime in the future.[64] I mention it because I used your statements on the 4 tropes very freely there.[65] Look that up too.

We'll be out to see you this year. Now the old car is having clutch tightened, equivalent, I suppose to a good massage of the prostate in man.

Best luck. "Make your own rules and win!" That's the new Williams motto.

Yours,

Bill

[B] [Andover]
June 1, 1946

Dear Bill,

I'm a bum. The primary victim of my own bad management. I shoulda written you before this, long before this, to acknowledge your letter sent in answer to my pleas. (Incidentally, I have not yet been to see the gent you mentioned, because things have eased up with the easing of the weather.[66] So, in accordance with my one principle, to which I scrupulously adhere, Never do today what can be put off until tomorrow, I have done naught, as yet. I can have that to look forward to, next fall.)

Also, I wanted to say that I read your bearing-witness on Russia, and found it quite moving.[67] There are some strange twists in it, though, that I'd like to ask you about some time. Almost as though your surrender were like that of a girl, asking a Don Cossack to come and lay her. How did that creep in? And another twist, it seems to be, in a roundabout way, saying "Come hither" to death, but the death is made palatable by being given the guise of a political (i.e., temporal) future. Or am I reading too much into it? In any event, I can't take it just as an "occasional poem" such as it would seem to be on its face.

Incidentally, I don't know Aiken.[68] (I met him once, and we dragged out a few words dutifully—otherwise rien.) But what I have been thinking about is a few lines to the NR correspondence columns, saying what the hell all this nobility stuff about Pound, etc. when old inside W.C. was thus o'erlooked, to say nothing of the mood of one-night standers Aiken slapped together, doubtless a bunch of reviewers who said a kind word for him. Am looking for a moment. Wish I had seen the anthology when the issue was in blazing headlines.

Car fixed? Ours is gasping again. There are various settlers scattered about the countryside now. Think of voyaging hither.

Sincerely,
K.B.

[P]   [Rutherford]
Monday [July 26, 1946]

Dear Ken,

Glad to get your letter. You'll meet Auden perhaps at Bennington this year.[69] What you say about Paterson so interests me that I've got to put the finishing of Part II at the top of my work list—but Laughlin says production problems make any near publication unlikely.[70] I don't know how you could have said anything about the poem I'd rather have heard than what you did say—that the blood is still circulating in those veins, nostalgia, constipation, achievement, the flower pressed perhaps between the pages of a book but still retaining a suggestion of the color and even (if you put your nose to the pages) a faint odor through the dryness.

Floss and I are going away for a two weeks rest up a little further north.[71] We'll be home toward the middle of August. During the two weeks that follow we're going to visit some of those friends whom we have wanted to see for a year or more but have been prevented from seeing by the luck of our lives. You're right there—if it'll suit you. Sometime during the last two weeks in August. I'm really looking forward to it.

Yours,

Bill

⬱

[P]   [Buffalo][72]
Aug. 9, 1946

See you sometime later in the month. Enjoying Schlesinger's <u>The Age of Jackson</u>.[73]

A good book. Fine spot here.

W.C.W.

⬱

[P]   [Rutherford]
Wednesday—8.30 A.M. [October 9, 1946]

Damn it Ken,

This just HAD to happen. At 4:30 this morning Alma Cole of 95 Lawrence Avenue, Lodi, N.J., age 26, Para I whose last period occurred January 26, 1946 and whose Wassermann was negative 5–16–46, who weighs 137 lbs, whose urine is normal, whose blood pressure is 110 over 80 and the heart tones of whose belly borne fetus are at 128 in the ROA position—called me on the phone to say she was having pains every ten minutes.

I sent her in leisurely fashion to the hospital whose delivery floor I called just now. They warned me away saying it was a "madhouse" at the moment but that my patient was doing nothing in particular (except, I'll bet, getting an earful of shrieks, groans, lamentations (and jazz from the doctors' rest room)).

That means in all probability that I'll be sitting on my ass all day long waiting for this gal to come down where I can handle her. And the worst of it is that she was due on the 2nd of this month and should have left me in the clear long ago.

But there is a good side to it also, as there is always a good side (they say) even to death, that is that I haven't another maternity case on my schedule before the 20th of this month. THEREFORE I plan, rain or shine, snow or tornado, to drive out to Andover this coming Friday IN THE MORNING to stay and eat with you at mid-day and talk with you and yours for the daylight hours. Floss will be with me.

Which is all very American and infraideational and RIGHT. Our greatest leader was not an intelligence, all our greatest intelligences have always been marginal. Our two party system which saves us from boredom yearly is a sub intelligent maneuvering. THUS we are left to be based solidly on the unvarying emotional substratum of the midbrain area, therefore we are REPUBLICANS today and slaughtered in the field tomorrow. Bitter as it may be it is in many ways what the world is in its seasonal fluctuations, each season bringing emotional relief from the last by thus stimulating the intelligence to every athletic exercise known to apes in a cage—thus insuring the future of the race, I suppose. At least it induces to books—which I like. We are now approaching winter. Thank God I don't live in the tropics.

Cheerio and chuck chuck (but the groundhogs have gone to sleep long since I imagine.)

Best to you all,
Bill

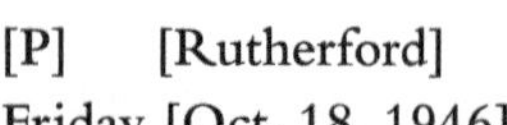

[P]   [Rutherford]
Friday [Oct. 18, 1946]

Dear Ken,

Communication (?) from Ezra Pound enclosed, I presume he is referring to one or the other of his two recently published Cantos. You're a philosopher, what about it?

It should be possible (something it hasn't yet been this fall) for me to get away for a jaunt to the country next week.

I've been tied hand and foot. I still have serious obligations to consider but these should be at least predictable by next Monday, surely, so that I may be able to tell <u>when</u> I'll be free and consequently in a position to tell you what I can do about it.

Two weeks ago yesterday I rushed away to Buffalo to be cited by the University there and presented with an honorary LLD.[74] I put up a rather feeble fight against it, holding out for an LHD but they said they were giving only the one medal and that I could take it or leave it so I took it. I tore out there by sleeper and back by sleeper the following night—costing me, with the two maternity cases I missed in consequence, $160. (I took Floss and my son Bill along as witnesses.)

Thus literature pays for itself—a year's earnings.

Briarcliff Quarterly is bringing out a special issue over me, they have everything except a picture of me with my pants down taking a crap, even my eyes, which Rexroth thinks are like those of St. Francis—animaloid.[75] I wonder if they got a note on my work by T. S. Eliot, the cheap shit.

Yours,

Bill

[P]   [Rutherford]
10/21/46

Dear Ken,

Not a glimmer of a chance! My only time free would be a Friday or a Sunday and both this Friday and Sunday seem already bound worse than Gulliver by the Lilliputians.

I might just seize some other day than the two mentioned but not while maternity cases are pending. I hope to finish up a residue of those within the next six to eight days. Will you be around during the week of November 2 to 9? Let me know for both Floss and I would really enjoy driving out to you for a visit.

There's a lot of crap we could rehash—Horace Gregory's new book, Josephson's new book—oh hell, anything.[76] Even Auden's course on Shakespeare's plays at the New School.[77]

The trouble is I tire if I drive myself too hard physically (as by driving) and I find absolutely no time for work on my play[78] which I've got to get retyped finally (after revision) if I'm ever to get it to a professional copier to put it into shape for an agent. I just can't find the time any longer for my writing.

Yours,

Bill

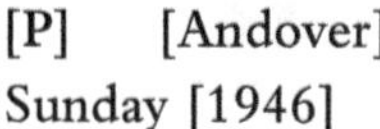

[P]   [Andover]
Sunday [1946]

Dear Ken,

Wednesday, unless it storms—at about mid afternoon. Or if something prevents that, then Friday—but I haven't read your <u>Grammar</u>—not all of it.[79]

Yrs,

Bill

[P]
Saturday [Dec. 22 1946]
New York Hospital

Dear Ken,

This is my last day here and this is my last sheet of writing paper. I came here 9 days ago to have my hernia done over again after last spring's operation which was unsuccessful. I wanted to write you before I left.

First I want to say I'm sending you a book. Throw it out after you've read it. Not a book I have written but one by Yvor Winters on the verses of E. A. Robinson.[80] It is something unique which I think only such a man as you could appreciate, the blankest, most stupid piece of "informed" writing I have ever encountered. It amazes and bewilders me by its complete arrest of the intelligence it represents, and not only that, it besides that gives a perfect summary of its own ineffectiveness in stated words within its own context p.21. It is as I say, not only a book but a psychological phenomenon on the pathological side, Winters' critical rages showing <u>his</u> impotence.

Of course the effect is heightened by Laughlin's[81] miserliness in refusing to pay royalties to Macmillan in order to have permitted the use of the poems themselves (which Winters quotes) instead of merely references to the poems —which is completely stupid. If the poems had been used, the quotations Winters's wanted, they would have distracted the attention from his own atrophies—but there it is amazing!

The rest concerns the work of W. S. Reich, his <u>The Function of the Orgasm</u> which if you have not read it, do so.[82] The paper's at an end.

Yours,

Bill

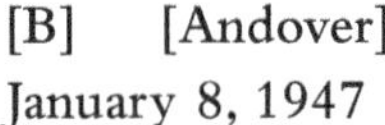

[B]   [Andover]
January 8, 1947

Dear Bill,

Glad to hear from you, and to learn that you are on the mend. (Though I had not known that you were off to be worked over.)

If the old household superstition has any validity, that a good-sized grouch is the sure sign of recovery, I take your letter to signify that you were getting along splendidly. I guess I'm too ailing myself. For I swear I can't get a quiver out of the Winters's confession.[83] Not even the horror you marked on p.39, where the Buddha said:

The vice is the vice of pride in one's own identity, a pride which will not allow one to accept a greater wisdom from without even when one recognizes that the wisdom is there and is greater than one's own; the result is spiritual sickness.

I think the gent here is concerned with a real enough situation. And sometimes the response to it takes the form that we, on superficial inspection, call "pride," though I'd rather call it "fear" (fear of the loss of one's identity, a quite reasonable fear to have, though the possession of it often makes us think and act unreasonably); and I'd take "pride" to be an over-hasty attempt to protect ourselves against such a risk, so that we get into the habit of deflecting alien things even without asking ourselves whether we could assimilate them.

Or perhaps you were objecting to the formula as applying to that particular poem by Robinson. Not having it here, I can't utter on that; but I will say it would seem to be quite typical of a New Englander's temptations in confronting the whole muddle of our cultural importations.

Say more.

And also do please say more on Reich.[84] I haven't read his books, have only heard of them, through a bright, too-bright youngster who seems to see in them a sanction for picking up tail, though he doesn't phrase it thus. A devastating attack on him by Wertham, in the <u>NR</u>, of about five weeks back, gave me great satisfaction.[85] For I did believe that Wertham had been fair in noting how the whole structure of our political necessities was being obscured. But you, as a medico, might have some other angle to suggest. Say more. This "greater wisdom" would, I admit I fear, threaten my identity as I now take it to be. But maybe not. I think nookie is excellong, but I can't see that it is so important as Reich apparently makes it out to be. Human beings seem to have other gratifying ways of short-circuiting, leaping gaps, and just plain broadcast-ing of rays out into whom-it-may-concern space. The important thing is, of course, to eat when one is hungry—but the Reich sort of thing seems to make one <u>think</u> he is hungry for a lot of things that he isn't really very hungry for at all. Maybe not. I speak only from hearsay. But do tell me what is good in the gent, why I should plague myself with him, etc.

If you're too busy to write it (for me, or for the world in general—that's it, why not write an article for the world in general?)—but if you're too busy to write, maybe you'll tell me about it sometime, viva voce. We intend to be in NY from the seventeenth to the twenty-sixth. We'll be staying at Tom Cochran's place, 111 Tenth Street.[86] It is in the phone book, not under Cochran, but under Saint Mark's in the Bowery. If you're going to be in town some time then, with some free time, announce.

Meanwhile, best greetings,

Sincerely,

K.B.

[P]   [Rutherford]
January 9, 1947

Dear Ken,

I'm no expert on Reich's theory of the function of the orgasm for I have not even finished reading his book on the subject.[87] All I can say as a physician moderately well informed on the analysis of clinical material is that as far as I have read his reasoning upon his findings seems sound. Perhaps I am justified in going a little further, in saying that I find his discoveries (clinical data) extremely enlightening on several points, knots of old confusions that have baffled me all my life but which, I think, he has very satisfactorily unraveled.

I haven't read the criticism of Reich's work in the <u>New Republic</u>.[88] If you have the issue containing the article of which you speak in your possession I wish you'd send it to me. I'll return it promptly. But if the criticism is of a political nature I'm afraid it won't interest me much. I'm afraid I'd be inclined to classify it with the objections of the Episcopal Church to <u>The Descent of Man</u>.

In reading this book of Reich's I have been deeply impressed by his criti-cism of Freud's later work. He is in no sense an offshoot from Freud like Jung or Adler but remained Freud's staunch defender to the end. But he strongly dif-fered from Freud when, as an old man, the Master came out with his theory of the death instinct as well as the theory of sublimation, that art, for instance, is a so called sublimation of sex, the artist unable to satisfy his sexual impetus <u>diverts</u> it into music, let us say. This, personally, I have always found to be the bunk. Reich confirms me in that opinion. Art is NOT a neurosis. Certainly sexual denial with an outcropping in some other area is not the history of the artist, the epoch-making artist, in general—or do you believe Beethoven and Dante (because they didn't get their women) produced neurosis in the forms of their arts? I don't.

All Reich has done is reason from his clinical data after which he has used his findings in treating his cases—with outstanding success (or so we are led to believe). You can't go wrong, or very far wrong, in following a man's discoveries from his objective findings, step by step, to his conclusions in the field. Why anybody should fear to take revolutionary steps in scientific discovery, the reports of the sense, I could never see. Reich himself says, for Christ's sake, don't believe a thing I say for authoritarian reasons.

As far as screwing is concerned it's a minor part of his work. Of course that's precisely the part any superficial observer flies to as butterflies fly to a horse turd. All he says about screwing is that we generate energy, biological energy, at our genitals and that it "informs" the whole character of man or woman; that neurosis is a stasis from lack of orgasmic release and that it leads to disaster of various sorts to the individual and to society in general. Of course, it is sidetracked into science, religion and art—BUT you got to have something to sidetrack first, the orgasm is the source.

AND he doesn't claim to have come to the end of the track. All he says is that his clinical observations have led him inevitably to the conclusions at which he has arrived as they have disproved some of Freud's later findings. He admonishes his followers NOT to quit at his findings but to carry them through relentlessly until they can be disproved as false or developed into whatever final form they will take.

As far as the man has gone, I find him amazingly enlightening and en-heartening, he demonstrates health as against pathology—in my own mind I don't know a book more likely to give you, personally, a lift than Reich's <u>The Function of the Orgasm</u> which I will be very happy to lend you at your convenience.

Mind you, I'm not urging you to read it. It is a medical treatise more than anything else (with political and sociological overtones to be sure—but with what enlightening glances into those fields you will be amazed to see) and you may not want to give time to a book of that sort.

I had a strange letter today from some German, a woman I think, who had seen some comment of mine on Goethe's so called last words—(I have forgot what I said or even that I had said anything). But this person told me that I had given perfectly what the spirit of his dying words had been!

The so-called last words "Mehr licht!" were the invention of some journalist. What Goethe really said was (to his little—but let me quote from the letter),

"Goethe's last words were spoken to Ottilie, his daughter-in-law. They were,

"Gib mir deine Kleine Pfote!"

approx. Let me hold your little paw!

The information comes by word through the following family channels:

Ottilie was a friend of Minchen Henzhel in Jena who was friend of my grandmother and her sister Sofie and Anna Kieser in Jena.

(end of quote)

O.K.?

Bill

[P]   [Rutherford]

Jan. 10, 1947

Dear Ken,

Criticism, like most intellectual exercises, had better be a full time profession; snippets of comment such as the stuff usually exhibited in the backs of magazines of which the comment on Reich's book, of which we have been speaking, as an example are seldom worth reading.[89] I don't think this one amounts to much.

A solid point against Reich's presumable position is made: when we attempt to enlarge on that which applies to the individual and try to apply that to the masses we are, definitely acting politically, it is in effect politics.

But, did Reich say otherwise? I doubt it. I haven't read his book (and I grant he may have slipped into such a statement as that credited to him, that all politics and politicians should be abolished) but I suspect that what he really said is that all politics as at present constituted should be abolished.

In any case I have not read the book in question and in all probability I'll never read it. The man may have fallen from grace. Even if he did come out against politicians in precisely the way it has been said against him I'd still feel that he was speaking as a clinician and that what he meant is that our ills are political in their essence and that we have in ourselves the cure, clinically speaking again, which if we would pay heed to it would lead us back to grace.

Now this is a theoretical position. But the theoretician, if his point be well taken, has a perfect right to use that as a fulcrum from which to pry apart or out of the way all heterodox opinions. From his standpoint Russia is headed straight for neurosis among its individuals which in turn leads to mass neurosis, which in turn leads to a reliance on "leadership," which in turn leads to war. He sees war from his partis-pris as the inevitable effect or affect of Russia's denial of his basic stand that uninhibited (<u>not</u> profligate) sex freedom is the <u>only</u> way in which neurosis can be eliminated.

Maybe he's wrong. But I'd rather (not having read his book) believe in him, since I know the man he is, rather than his stumpy reviewer.

Bill

[B]   [Andover]
January 30, 1947

Dear Bill,

Back from Babylon.

I'd love to take you up on that offer to let me look over the book on nookie by the imperial Reich.[90] Since you won't tell me what in the hell the guy says (or rather, since you seem to take back in par. 2 what you put forth in par. 1), I guess I'll have to see for myself.

Our trouble is, I suppose, what it always was. All your life you've been railing against philosophy. And all my life I've been saying: "Listen to that guy philosophizing. Every time I hear him, he's philosophizing. Like Roethke,[91] he thinks he's against philosophy; but all he's really against is good philosophy. He hands out bad philosophy by the barrel full."

From your last letters, I think I begin to see the point a little clearer. That is, your equating poetry and health. I used to think that your poetry was the rounding-out of your medicinating (sorta the grace atop nature). But now I think I see it all more accurately: poetry is for you the <u>antithesis</u> of your pills. That's why you have to shout, ever more urgently as ills creep up, "Poetry equals health."

Well, you worked out an economy. You are perfectly entitled to put poetry in the bin antithetical to your vocation. (In this you offer a variant of the vacation-vocation antithesis I mention in the <u>Grammar</u> with reference to Wallace Stevens.)[92] Anything goes, if it works, along the lines of these personal alignments. But that's just the equation for <u>you</u> (and <u>your</u> ilk). It's not the one and only. Poetry is also, or can also be, ye grande bellyache. (And thank God for that, says this poor gent, who wants some viaticum to help him on his way.) If I may quote myself: a person writes about that which most interests him, and few things interest us more than our burdens, hence poetry becomes the ritualistic unburdening of burdens. Doesn't have to. And there can be ways both direct and indirect (with the direct-guys hating the indirect, saying there's no room for them in this here one world, and v.v.).

Poetry equals health? Pedetter. It can also be a way of dying well. Too often today health means Miss California Fruit Growers Association. (Recently, have got interested in Virgil again; how much more mature his man-politics-nature line-up was than the many fragmentary things of that sort we get now.)

Must expression be antithetical? Can't it also be of a piece with one's conditions? Why can't poetry ail in proportion as the poet ails, etc.? Or is only philosophy allowed to do that?

Why not come around, some fine day, and let's haggle about it? I wrote answers to almost every sentence in your last couple of letters. But it seemed anticlimactic to type them out. So come around, and we'll say them.

Sincerely,

K.B.

[P]   [Rutherford]
#1
1/31/47

Dear Ken,

I have nothing to say about philosophy—except that it had better keep its hands off that which does not concern it—for to do otherwise leads only to confusion, <u>beside</u> our difficulties.

All (I hope) I have ever said about phil. is that I sense its interfering hand in the difficult art of getting said in verse that which can be said only by the closest attention to the exigencies of verse, the inventions which philosophy tends to prune away in its attempts to find "meaning." There just ain't no sense to that.

Never in my life have I tho't to equate poetry with health. All I said was that the tentacles of poetry are signs of a living tissue, perhaps comparable to the same thing in the <u>best</u> philosophy (i.e. the least interfering).

Bill

#2

1/31/47

It is impossible for me to contradict myself—except logically which means nothing.

W.

And surely there must be somewhere in philosophy a def 't which says: "Hands off!" It's to that that I appeal.

W.

#3

But I'd enjoy, perhaps benefit, by analogizing my wit as poet with your wit as philosopher—never articulating anywhere with you but laying the one thing by the other. By this exercise and no more (no closer articulation) something valuable in me—in pleasure, enlightenment might it, I hope will (as it has already happened between us), result.

W.

[B]   [Andover]
February 1, 1947

Dear Bill,

The patient's symptoms were very bewildering. Obviously, the most expert criticism was necessary. They called in the Great Diagnostician. Tell us, they asked.

The Great Diagnostician pondered, then spoke. In the first place, he said, the patient must be operated on immediately. In the second place, there is nothing wrong with him at all.

They were all a-fluster. But there happened to be a logic-chopper present. He didn't know an appendix from an appendage, but he could chop a logic any time. He spoke up to the Great Diagnostician, asking: Aren't your two statements contradictory?[93]

And was he promptly slain? He was. For the Great Diagnostician smacked him down thus (I quote his actual words, as written to me in a letter):

"It is impossible for me to contradict myself—except logically, which means nothing."

The G.D., I believe, did not deign to answer.

Otherwise, where were we? Our sudden flare-up of controversy vastly interests me, because it reveals to me the unexpected possibility of my finding a whole new set of lines (i.e., times when you and I, when talking about the same thing, draw the lines at strategically different places). I'm not just trying to make you grouchy-wouchy (though that's what I do seem to be doing). I'm trying to find just where you draw your lines. If "logic" meant to you what it means to me, for instance, your remark quoted above should strike terror in the hearts of all who depend upon you. Hence, it must mean something different. To you it must mean the <u>opposite</u> of the practical; to me it is the necessary aspect of a rational act.

Perhaps you had in mind the fact that an image, in a poem, can "contain opposites"? If a religious fanatic, for instance, burned for a woman whom his beliefs did not permit him to enjoy, he might, in dreaming of a fire which he had set and which "unintentionally" caused her death, both have her and prevent himself from having her, in one and the same symbol. Or an image of rain might be, simultaneously a weeping for the departed and a furtive symbolizing of fertile preparation for the New Love. Similarly, as per my lucubrations on the "paradox of substance," the simple either-or's of logic can become involved in dialectical switches. But such matters don't apply to the situation which we were suffering under, and which was thus:

The G.D. said that he greatly admired Reich's book.[94] The L.C. said to himself, "Here's a gent who knows his business, so let's ask him what's good about Reich's book." The L.C. asks. And, to his vast bepuzzlement, he receives from the G.D., not the clear bing-bing-bing answer he had expected, but first, a fog, and second an oath in the dark.

What I hoped to learn, in particular, was his way of lining up the love-war business. When a male animal is most a-loving, I grant, that's also the time when he's most a-fighting. And the female fights most over her beloved offspring. So I grant that the love-war entanglement is central. My own scheme (mentioned in passing on p. 286 of ye Grammaire, par. beginning "On the Symbolic level . . .") finds it necessary to worry over a trio, "love, war, work," with all the <u>conflicts of property</u> which, since property is necessary to love and work, are forever getting us into war.[95] There is a passage in Coleridge's "Religious Musings" which (if you can pardon its philosophic nature) suggests the pattern quite well:

> But soon Imagination conjured up
> An host of new desires; with busy aim,
> Each for himself, Earth's eager children toiled.
> So Property began, twy-streaming fount,
> Whence Vice and Virtue flow. . . .

Then follows a genealogy of invention and disease (quite in keeping with our interchange on the double aspect of poesy) . . . and then, finally, his reversal and apotheosis:

> From Avarice thus, from Luxury and War
> Sprang heavenly Science; and from Science Freedom.

'Tis a bit nineteenth-century, but it does well suggest the really rich (not Reich?) tie-up.

My own notion, reduced to its simplest form, would run like this: The individual, to be moral, social, communicative, etc., identifies himself with "property." Property may be of many sorts. Capitalist property, property in methods of working, property in wife and children, property in convictions, property in one's job, etc. Such properties lead to <u>conflict</u>, (as one man's area of integration encroaches upon another's). Under certain special conditions, such conflicts can lead to <u>war</u> (in the modern, imperialist sense). Important among such conflicts is the conflict over nookie (though not since Troy, I guess, has it directly led to war. A Marxist could show that it didn't then either, of course; but I was being gracile.) Petty bourgeois American women, equating the "higher standard of living" with perhaps the stupidest way of life known to the history of human decadence, fall into the tangles of this business in ways which show, clinically, purely and simply as sex neurosis. Hence, the clinician might tend to draw the whole difficulty from the sex source alone. But it is political, rather than purely sexual, in the sense that property is political. . . . The <u>Rhetoric</u>, if it turns out as planned, should show the many ramifications of property.[96] Theory is: maybe we can mitigate the imperialist itch, the ultimate frenzy of property, maybe not; but at least we must accurately contemplate the source of our fantastic ambitions. Property in sex is a major one of these, but in a familial rather than purely physical sense. The physical gratification is as essential, perhaps, as food (no; in the natural state, I guess sex doesn't become important until food allows for an extra?); but the physical gratification, as translated into terms of set social relations, involves property— and the big wars are wars of property.

As to Philosophy, and your demand that it keep "Hands off"[97] poetry: pick up the <u>NY Times</u>; read the hundreds of thousands of words of "news" and advertisements (another kind of news); then turn to the Editorial Page, and read the little poem for that day: twelve doggerel lines, a kind of rhymed editorial, the day's quota of poetry. There, in that proportion, the newspaper has spoken. It has put poetry "in its place." Then read that prime journalistic hack, J. Donald Adams,[98] asking himself where to place the blame. And where is the blame to be put? Echo answers: On philosophy. And from across the stinking swamps, the Billious Echo answers: On philosophy. Itshay, say I—and I'm speaking not figuratively, but literally.

There are many kinds of poetry. If I happen to like Lucretius, I am not forcing philosophy upon poetry; I am but recognizing and enjoying a kind of poetry that has actually been written, and well written. I also like Imagistic (Objectivist?) poetry. I recognize that it has its virtues and, naturally, its limitations, like any other kind. But if an Imagist (Objectivist?) poet wants to insist that <u>all</u> poetry should be of his kind (not even allowing for the many <u>ideas</u> in <u>dramatic poetry</u> as <u>traditionally existing</u>), then, say I, "Hands off." This theorist should keep hands off the other kinds. Yes, philosophy believes devoutly in the principle of hands off. In fact, Aristotle's whole method was built upon that principle, as he attempted to take into account the situation that the Greeks confronted in their day as we do in ours (though they confronted it much less drastically than we): the vast number of specialized disciplines, with the need for the autonomy of each, for principles and methods intrinsic to it alone. Kant, too, was directly concerned with the same problem of science (and in the Introduction to <u>Cr. of Pure Reason</u>, takes some cracks at the muddling of the disciplines). One may, however, be over-strict in defining the resources of his medium. Poetry, for instance, being in words, can handle ideas as easily as pie, if it wants to. There is at least no strain <u>on the medium</u> here. (Perhaps we must here distinguish between the nature of the medium, in the Lessing sense, and the aims of particular school or esthetic doctrine, which may even want to deny itself some intrinsic aspects of the medium while trying to get a percentage of music, architecture, the graphic, etc. more easily got in other mediums.)[99]

But maybe this is all offen the subjick. The trouble with letters is that one must carry out a direction without conversational hints when he is wrong. Maybe we're just in violent agreement?

K.B.

Addendum: Thought afterwards, how I must be on guard lest dialectical pressure get me into defending more than I would, or otherwise than I would. For instance, my primary interest is <u>linguistic</u> rather than <u>philosophical</u>. Or rather though my approach to the poet's expression may not be quite what the poet would have it be, the divergence is not flatly that btw. "poetry" and "philosophy" (which, though they have often been allied, and quite seem so to me, today seem generally at odds to most, who would perhaps allocate concepts to science, images to poetry, and ideas to philosophy—and the images, along Kantian lines, wd. be taken as nearer to science than to the ideas of philosophy, since they would involve "intuitions of sensibility," which Kant also includes, along with "concepts of the understanding," in the materials that form the basis of experience in empirical science; though the other day, reading an essay by Hazlitt, I came across "ideas of the imagination," which would draw the lines quite differently, nearer perhaps to the way Coleridge would have drawn them).[100]

However, coming up from that dive, let's get back to the simple beginning: whereas a <u>linguistic</u> interest in poetry may differ somewhat from the poet's own interest in it, such an interest does not attempt to find "meaning" in the restricted sense of the term. It begins with the poem as <u>act</u> rather than as a proposition; it recognizes that the image can <u>state an attitude</u> (hence, can be the lyrical substitute for an act); and, since ideas are also involved in action, in the practical or moral realm, it recognizes that an image may, in some roundabout way, <u>serve as substitute</u> for an idea. One of my main interests in Roethke's work, for instance, is in my lurking for things of this sort.[101] (The strongly tonal nature of his poems also encourages me to believe that I may legitimately look for unconscious puns, as were he to say "voices" for "vices," or at least have "vices" as a subsidiary meaning in "voices." The substitutions, of course, would be allowable only if they can better account for the entire development, or structure, which they sometimes do, I think.)

I am quite sympathetic with the aims here. They correspond, I think, to the way of teaching expression in dance: "Try to gesture good-bye without waving your hand," "Try to show anger without curling your lip," etc. But there are many other things going on here; and above all, there is the tendency to <u>make images as abstract as the ideas they are avoiding</u>. Sometimes this happens too. Blackmur wrote one really important piece: his analysis of the imagery in Cummings.[102] He was, as I understand him, there concerned with something of this sort.

As for the other problem: the problem of getting an expression that maturely encompasses the modern scene, and permits of sustained, organic development in the monumentalizing of such a statement, I can't see how it can be done in any way except along Virgilian lines. The esthetic of youth, or of dream-sincerity in its purity, etc., may be able to meet these tests <u>but at least it hasn't done so</u>. It is free to go and do so. Nobody is stopping it. I think it is being stopped, not by "philosophy," but by the fact that the esthetic itself does not, intrinsically, allow for such possibilities. But the proof is in the doing; poetry is as poetry does.

K.B.

[P]   [Rutherford]
Tuesday [February 4, 1947]
Hat and coat—and scarf on at my
desk (just took off my hat and
changed my glasses) all set to go
out on calls: 3.30 P.M.

Dear Ken,

I welcome <u>your</u> philosophy more than I could ever welcome philosophy.[103] One of my difficulties (generally speaking) is that I do not understand your terms since I am not skilled in them. BUT since I do not find it necessary to bother about your terms and have to do the best I can with you (and them) to keep up my end (and in my own defense) I throw them out the window.

But I think I can turn your own logic against you when I say that logically, Reich is unassailable.[104] It is only in the practical application of his principles that he can be attacked: in an illogical world all logic is suspect.

Your trilogy, with him, is a four-part affair: WORK, TENSION, ORGASM, RELAXATION. The function of the orgasm is not nookie, not pleasure but the (the words fail me) summatization, the recurring assertion of the psycho-somatic individual as one, as a whole. It resynthesizes (at its best) the at-loose-ends man into the individual. It also charges his organs with an equivalent of electrical energy in a very real manner.

It also as it "recreates" the man, theoretically makes him want to assume responsibility (since his world is completed in that cycle—that's what he knows).

In other words he does not have to <u>ask</u> someone else (the politician) to lend him something, to "grant" him equality with others. He does not need a Fuhrer, a Duce. Those bastards can only practice their arts on an incomplete man (robbed by the cute bankers, by the nifty systems by which men are always robbed) therefore no politicians.

HOWEVER I do see Coleridge's contention (that's all it is) that war does actually lead to science and science to freedom, etc., etc., round and round inside the cage.[105]

(Gotta go.)

Note: Stan Musial could talk easier with some champion of pelota, I think, than with some fifth rate ball player.[106] Aristotle must 'a bin good. I agree with him.

Note: All I say in this line sounds like crap to me, inexperienced babbling, fiddling with the keys of a piano when all I can do is play the violin—but if you want it . . . I don't know how to express myself well.

By the way I have been realizing recently that a man can think without words. I know perfectly well what I want to say but I don't have the words to say it. I have always felt that in an argument the expert has an unfair advantage over the unskilled. <u>Unfair</u> is the word that I want to emphasize.

––––––––––––––––––––

(to continue)

Thus as between logic and a poem that appeals to men (as a poet) as new, an innovation, an invention in my scheme of things, even tho' illogical (unacademic!) I take the poem.

Reich can say, in my scheme of things sexual completion removes the need for wars but <u>work</u> is essential.[107] That would answer Coleridge if "work" is taken for "war." But War, in Reich's sense, would be illogical, wasteful, a superfluity—pathological—a diversion of the sense.

The orgasm is (in Reich's scheme) however essential and he is planning to prove by quantitative measurements of the discharge, discharge of biologic energy quotients, an identity with the life process itself.

––––––––––––––––––––

(to go back to your letter)

Each of us by skill in technique wishes to gain himself freedom in his field and does do so to a limited extent. For myself I want to "escape" those who press too hard on me everywhere and I seek to develop my own resources, my own "property" of ability in poetry beyond the possibility of being overtaken by anyone else: as I believe.

Let me tell you a little story: Auden came to the party given by Bonnie Golightly for me last December.[108] He was very polite but quite friendly in his manner. He, quite unsolicited, even went so far as to give me his New York address. I was pleased since I recognize him to be skillful in his field—more skillful than I am though I feel not the slightest jealousy toward him (as I do toward Eliot whom I despise as a liar and a [successful] faker.) But to go on about Auden. I had an idea one morning shortly after our party, an idea concerning poetry in our day. It was this: that four or five men, "master" poets such as Auden and myself might profitably get together here, at my house, over a week-end to discuss the technical advances that had been made in the writing of poetry in modern times. I have several theories that seem sound to me and I believed that others, competent poets, had other theories or ideas to contribute.

I told Auden that, avoiding a discussion of technique, which is each man's private affair, but keeping ourselves to technical matters we might be in a position to advance the writing of poems twenty years in our time. My feeling was that by this we could avoid all the amateurishness of the usual poetry magazines, cut out the empty "criticism" that such magazines deal in (especially <u>Poetry</u>) completely sidetrack metaphysics, philosophy and all such side issues and get down to brass tacks, to the skillful making of poems. Reams of incompetencies could be wiped out in a day and some sort of basis for a true criticism of poems as technical constructions could be arrived at.

I suggested that we take five texts for study: Milton's "Agonistes" (because of the amazing technical skill with which his choruses are made there), one or more of Pound's <u>Cantos</u> (because of some technical phenomena I wanted to point out there), Eliot's <u>Quartets</u> (for technical reasons) and Breton's "Young Cherry trees Protected against Hares" (in French and English) to show how ideas, "advanced" ideas can be negated by formal poetic treatment—I have forgot the other text.[109]

Auden never replied. I wrote twice. No answer.

I thought of you as one of the group—even tho' you are a professional philosopher.

Chas. Abbot, when I told him about this said that Auden was probably scared out by my desire to have 5 men there. If I had offered to discuss the question alone with him he would probably have accepted the bid. Auden is covertly <u>very shy</u>, says Abbot. I can't understand it.

____

You see, we've got to step up our argument to a higher field if you and I are to agree, to a field where poetry and philosophy will merge. I don't think that field is logic, not ordinary logic which applies to a much smaller field. We've got to get up somewhere where "the life," not just life, is paramount. I can't bother with the internal arrangements of philosophy within its own sphere which are your bread and butter—and caviar. I am too deeply concerned with the field of poetry which, I believe, offers unguessed opportunities— opportunities such as Mozart realized in music. I think poetry has a technical future which old fumbling Bridges only "goosed."[110] It is blocked by ordinary thinking and by all metaphysics: Eliot to me is a traitor, a backslider, and a weakling who has evaded the really thrilling possibilities of the art or the science if you prefer.

With this in mind I don't give a damn what the philosophers say about my meaning, my "beautiful" or otherwise body of thought. I want to think as well as I can but that isn't the point: the point is HOW am I to embody that thought in the technical matrix of the poem, how NEW to embody ANY thought in the INVENTION of the poetical body alive! For only by invention IS the body of poetry kept alive.

By the way, we have a new 12 tube Magnavox Radio. It's a beauty. I made some records of my reading at the Library of Congress two years or more ago.[111] I wasn't prepared for it but did my best. When I heard the records at first I was sick, they have been on a shelf in a back room ever since. But on Sunday, urged by a friend, I brought them out and tried them on our new machine. They knocked me over. I have never heard such recordings. Not that I was good, I wasn't but these records on this new machine are extraordinary. You've got to hear them some time.

Well, Ken (I never did go back to your letter) come at me again—and again if you care to. I am interested and interested in what you want to know that I can help you with.

Reich does not touch morals, he specifically says he is not concerned with morals. Just recently I have seen in an English periodical an indirect reference to Reich's work. The critic or poet or whoever he was said that man might be generated by a spark from the sun (Reich's biological energy which he has recovered from sand and which, he says, makes the sky blue!) but that his responsibility, his moral responsibility, still remains to be explained.

No, you can't lay every dame who presents herself. But, Geezus! if you're not neurotic you won't (we hope) want to. And then, again, it may be that the dame will invite you. (We're not talking about the present day world, the present day world is almost entirely neurotic in its make-up; we're talking of a biologically functioning world in which relationships between the sexes are uninhibited by "property" let us say.)

Naturally I can see whole areas of disagreement cropping up in your mind. But, Ken, your world, the world from which your are arguing is, in Reich's sense, largely pathological.

AND FOR THE LOVE OF GOD DON'T MAKE ME OUT A PROPHET FOR REICH. I am merely presenting something that interested and satisfied something in me as best as I am able to present it. It rooted a neurotic slant of thought dealing with suicide clean out of my head. Suicide is not only a stupidity but a non-entity if you once realize what the new physical conception of the universe is likely to be. Life is so far more important, astronomically, than anything to me but poetry, that I am thoroughly humbled in one (personal) sense and raised to an infinity in another.

Yours,

Bill

P.S. As to the analogy between philosophy and the editorial page of the newspaper, that's crap. Philosophy is a serious adversary, on a serious (intellectual) basis, the newspaper editorial page is only serious in its practical effect, not intellectually. It is just a breakdown of the presses (figuratively), has no effect on the mind whereas philosophy teases and diverts the mind, the good mind, from the poetic problems, failures and successes.

Here, enclosed, is a letter received in the same mail with yours, also attacking my position (not me). It is from the boys, avowedly homosexual, at Cummington school.[112] I like them and approve of them but they both disliked, violently, my editorial printed in the Williams issue of the <u>Briarcliff Q.</u> which if you haven't seen it write at once to Normal Maccloud[113] and get it—it will be a rare item in a few months.

Please return the enclosed letter.

Bill

[P]   [Andover]
February 7, 1947

Dear Bill,

You're a hard guy to race with, for you start running before the gun goes off, and in any old direction. But at last methinks we're beginning to get somewhere (in the great problem: How to find out what Reich says in his wonderful book?).

You have now got down to four key terms. (That, incidentally, is what I always find myself looking for, in poets as well as peasants: key terms.) Work, tension, orgasm, relaxation. They are, I gather, a series, or cycle: Work leads to tension; tension leads to the need of orgasm; the orgasm, when it comes, brings relaxation; and relaxation is the condition for new work. Is that the line-up? Work might start getting more out of tension (effort is more stimulated by a condition of hunger quite as it requires a prior gratification to provide the energy).

I'd like to stop at that, saying no more until I get your answer: one move in each letter, like playing a game of chess by mail.

Or are they aligned, rather, in a proportion, thus: Work is to relaxation as tension is to orgasm. That is, might we really have but two terms here, operating on two different levels? For instance, if we thought of some generalized, formal process, like "building-up" and "letting down," might we say that human experience shuttles back and forth between these two, first "building-up" in either the reproductive order or the productive order, and then "letting-down" in either the reproductive order or the productive order. And if you don't properly complete this process on the one level, (the physical or "reproductive" level) you are not "freed" to complete it on the symbolic level (the "productive" level).

Or is there still some other arrangement among the terms? Or does the arrangement shift in the course of the book (a dialectical resource that is often resorted to, consciously or unconsciously).

So, how about, for our next step, you're telling me just what the relation among the four terms is? And then also, what the relation btw. <u>work and property</u> is? And then, finally, how the <u>division</u> of labor (making for fragmentary jobs rather than complete jobs) lines up with the ideal of relaxation. I had assumed myself that modern man usually sought relaxation vicariously, via the "amusement industry," because the work itself was not a complete act, hence would not allow for gratification in its own terms. And I took the great stress upon sex ("Love Among the Machines") to be a <u>compensatory</u> striving, an attempt, albeit a frustrated attempt, to find in the sexual orgasm the kinds of fulfillment that could not possibly be got in typical modern work (on the assembly line) or typical modern leisure (subsidized unemployment).

As for the place of politicians in this line-up: I took them to be a <u>necessary adjunct of this same specialization, or extreme division of labor</u>. Specialists in political coordination are an integral part of a specialized culture. I took this for granted. But of course the whole business might be lined up differently. I then merely ask: How?

My own notion is that liberalism (which grows out of <u>specialization</u> as well as out of <u>money</u>), must always <u>stumble upon</u> the principle of interference (which, however it may be <u>in itself</u> the cause of neurosis, is necessary to the world as a going concern, hence also helps to prevent neurosis). And since this principle is usually, in our society, or in any society for that matter, strongly embodied in <u>political government</u>, the politico takes the rap for a lot that is not his fault at all. And, ironically, the entire misunderstanding of his place in a dislocated business structure can in itself be a major cause of his corruption. As even Thurman Arnold pointed out, many <u>normal necessities</u> of administration in our society are still defined only in terms of <u>corruption</u>.[114] "Horse-trading," for instance, is a <u>political necessity</u> in our society, yet is looked upon as something that a truly honest man would not descend to. Think of how much finagling, in the privacy of his study, the poet does with his text; this is taken as normal and proper; yet when the politician, in a goldfish bowl, shifts his opinions, alliances, tactics (in other words, does in the <u>political</u> medium the same kind of revision that the poet does in the <u>literary</u> medium) his ways are treated as mere shiftiness, corruption, lack of principle, etc. God knows, there is a lot of corruption in politics; but part of the blame can be laid to the naively anarchistic frame in which haphazard liberalism (a la down-with-philosophy, up with mood-fellow stuff) considers this entire problem. I can't say that I know a great deal about medieval philosophers; but what I do know makes me realize how much more civilized they were than their detractors. They <u>began by recognizing</u> the sort of necessities it takes to run a world. (And some of the most "intellectualistic" of them, incidentally, could write powerful poetry.)

. . . our interest in Reich—as aspect of criticism, or philosophy (a terminology of motives). My interest in medicine generally is of this sort . . . his clinical views as aspect of <u>criticism</u>. Also, as aspect of <u>dialectic</u> (as all philosophy of criticism or terminology is). Hence, our interest in his key terms, and their relations, and the resources and embarrassments indigenous to them.

Our idea of teaching philosophy:

Get key terms, then speculate as to the various ways they may be manipulated. This along with noting the particular way in which the given writer manipulates them. This method (a) enables one to call the plays, (b) enables one to see limitations of a given use, (c) enables one to see how other terms shd. be spawned and spun (or are spawned and spun).

[P]   [Rutherford]
2/7/47

Dear Ken,

The trouble as between me and the "placed" critics is that they think I am fooling or rambling or at best uninformed. To put it in its "academic" light: ignorant. I <u>am</u> ignorant but only of unessentials, I haven't had time in my life to bother too much with them.

But I am neither uninformed nor unguided in the essential matters that concern me as a poet. Rather the others are infants to me and the more so because of their "training," their learning (which has taken so much of their time).

To me they are freshmen who because of irrelevant learning think themselves competent to write a poem. They know very little of the difficulties involved, deal only crudely with the materials and have let themselves be led astray by their faulty approach to a very difficult subject.

Not that the approaches are difficult to me. As between a squirrel and a fox-hound the matter of trees as compared with fields presents, to each, diametrically opposed facets: a dog cannot run up and down a tree. But to the squirrel it is very easy. It is my one "natural" field of endeavor, I do not overlook the modes of approach, the cylindrical and perpendicular nature of my racetrack. At least it is all the safety I have, they are unlikely to catch me there—from what I have observed.

Here's more "logic": The skilled physician examines his patient very carefully. Every sign indicates an acutely inflamed appendix. Does he refuse to operate? Certainly not. He follows the logic of the matter and opens the patient up. The appendix is normal. So what, so what for logic—in the field in which we are investigating? In a vacuum he acts logically. Actually he acts illogically.

W.

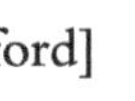

[P]   [Rutherford]
[1947]

Dear Ken,

We seem to get on much better by the indirect rather than the direct approach. What you reveal in your letter over the Reich book is to me thrilling in the extreme, it seems to state or does state what seems to be the basic reason for our interest, our sustained interest in each other which has never been explicit—a desire on both our parts to find some basis for avoiding the tyranny of the symbolic without sacrificing fullness of imagery.

You know the dead serious sort who know nothing of the symbolic. Or is there such a sort which does not postpone its heaven to another world— the deadliest symbolism of all?

My whole intent, in my life, has been as with you to find a basis (in poetry, in my case) for the actual. It isn't a difficult problem to solve theoretically. All one has to do is to discover new laws of the metric and use them. That's objective enough and little different from the practical deductions of an Edison. The difficulty lies in the practice.

For myself I reject almost all poetry as at present written, including my own. I see tendencies, nodes of activity [obviously intentional], here and there but no clear synthesis. I am trying in <u>Paterson</u> to work out the problems of a new prosody—but I am doing it by writing poetry rather than by "logic" which might castrate me since I have no ability in that medium (of logic).[115] There is no reason, besides, why I should do otherwise than I am doing. That is, if I succeed, the effect will be the same no matter what the approach.

Well, I'm glad you can use the Reich material. Best of luck to you—your letter was a revelation.

Sincerely,

Bill

[P]   [Andover]
February 14, 1947.

Dear Bill,

Dawlink, be my valentine.

Came home from Babylon yesterday (where I had two teeth gouged out, and I mean gouged), to find your cry from the desert.[116] All night long, half asleep, half awake, while the outraged jaw growled, I kept answering you. So now, alas, by the accidents of history, your letter has become equated, for me, with an irritating pain in the pain-receiver.

But by all means, let's consider the Reich case settled, or at least indefinitely postponed. Since you refuse to tell me what Reich says, and refuse to lend me the book, there's nothing to do but wait until I get a less ill-starred opportunity to improve the mind on this sumjick.

Having been signed up to give a talk on "Ideology and Myth" at school next term, and having become more and more interested in the notion that

Virgil (rather than the Greeks or the various primitives) might be nearest prototype to our situation in past poesy, I used some of my time, before the brutal professional attack, to go through J. W. Mackail's little book ("Virgil and His meaning for the World of Today").[117] If you ever happen to see it, I wish you'd take a glance at pages 74–76, and tell me how they struck you. He here lists twelve important "motives" (Mackail's term) which figured in the <u>Aeneid</u> (presenting them, not so much as accomplishments, but rather as problems-to-be-met, though the assumption is that the problems were met handsomely). His chapters on the Bucolics and Georgics are also worth looking at, particularly if you can imagine the academic idiom translated into a somewhat nimbler equivalent. My point about Excavation Man is treated, with regard to the strong <u>archaeological</u> interest, derived from the Alexandrian schools. (Virgil's treatment of the gods is interesting because, like the typical educated Roman, he did not literally believe in them, yet they had a <u>positive</u> stylistic function.) The <u>political</u> <u>rhetorical</u> awareness was highly developed, along with the pure poetry of man and nature. All told, a combination considering—and it is, of course, the sort of thing I immediately think of, when you would scare me with that "hands off!" admonition, warning villainous me to unhand the naive virgin. The Georgics were actually written, among other things, to popularize a back-to-the-land movement among the upper classes. To be reminded of such things is especially good for me this year, this being Rhetoric Year in my project.[118]

My one real disgruntlement with you is this: You seem to assume that my method of analyzing books is "academic." I can agree with this only if you will, at the same time, be willing to recognize that our schools now are <u>not</u> academic.

You made a confession about the Reich book; I'll make one about my own method. Some years ago, I suffered from a most damnable symptom. When I read certain words, I would "hear" totally different words. I recognized the word as it was, but at the same time I "heard" this other one. And apparently this outlaw word would always be the same. (Though I know I had something here, I was really too frightened to encourage the dislocation by taking notes on it. Rather "waste" it, I thought, and try to kill it, than "cultivate" it, perhaps to my permanent confusion. But I do, in spite of my resolve, remember one such outlawry, such dissociate association: every time, in the newspaper, I read "industry," along with this word, I heard "insanity," just as clearly as though it had symptoms of the same sort: I would wake up in the night, for instance with the suddenness of a shot; some word had been spoken, and this word awoke me. And then something would occur which I can best suggest by calling it a zigzag flash of lightning. For of a sudden, spontaneously, I would remember a whole series of "connected" things (things that I had never before thought of as connected, or often things that I had not remembered at all, but that seemed "connected" from the standpoint of this "key" word that had awakened me). The zigzag might connect, for instance, something that had happened yesterday, something I had written in a review, something I had said in an argument or as a wisecrack, some hitherto unexplained response to another person, something out of my novel, something out of my childhood, etc. On these, too, I started to take notes; and then I quit, because the symptom was increasing—so for months I resolutely refused to take a single note that thus occurred to me spontaneously, aside from the hours that I had deliberately assigned for my work.

Eventually, I got my life and myself straightened out somewhat. And finally I got far enough along to dare looking back at this period and studying it somewhat glancingly (like looking at the Gorgon's head, I found that I could look, without being turned to stone, so long as I looked <u>indirectly</u>, watching the process as <u>reflected</u> through the study of others' works, etc). So I developed a new modus vivendi (I am convinced that my high blood pressure had its psychogenic origins in the kinds of repression I had to use, or thought I had to use—but hell, an out-an-out physical symptom is so <u>consolingly real</u>, as compared with that damned jumpiness, that I could even make peace with it, use it, one might say, as a motive that helped me to a kind of resignation, or better let us say a cult of resignation, for it takes all the cult of resignation I can muster to keep me fairly even).

Anyhow, for better or worse, there was the start, <u>in personal experience</u> of all my concern with "equations," "clusters" of "key" terms, etc. (De Gourmont's essay on "The Dissociation of Ideas," which I had read many years before, was probably the start, so far as critical method is concerned.)[119] To build out the whole works, I have done what I could to develop an understanding of the purely formal, or dialectical, aspects of terms, as well. For a book is, <u>at the very least</u>, a set of <u>words</u>. And according to my notions, to understand it properly we must, <u>at the very least</u>, know what it is doing <u>just as</u> <u>word</u>. This accounts for my notion that, in order to call the plays in a given set of terms, we should first have clear ideas about the resources of these terms <u>in general</u>. Such knowledge, I feel, can help us better to place their use <u>in particular</u>. To study the particulars, one must trail through the zigzags (someday I shall publish my notes on Coleridge, showing how much zigzagging I did in the preparatory reading of his books).[120] But at the same time, there are formal principles which these zigzags are embodying, so one tries to place the particulars with reference to these generalizations too.

For better or worse, I guess that is all I know. Perhaps I am a crank on this subject. But I believe that all our unnecessary turmoils are rooted in spontaneous "equations" that happen to draw the lines at the wrong place. You, for instance, seem to need to deny yourself certain areas of civilized literature which, whatever their excesses, can also be amenities (and with others who draw the lines differently, can be assimilated without distress). And you seem to need to call certain things "illogical" which are not illogical at all. That example you gave about the physician who read the signs wrong, for instance, was no example of an illogical act. He was certainly being logical in interpreting the signs as he did; so much so that, if any sharper observer were able to draw a new line in one of the symptoms, showing how to distinguish between this symptom when it meant appendicitis and the slight modification of it when it didn't, this same diagnostician would have no difficulty at all (if the distinction were clear, methodical, and implemented) in adding it to his diagnostic methods. To read the signs in accordance with the best known methods for reading the signs is quite logical; it is also quite logical to be ready to recognize that we may not, for all situations, have all the distinctions necessary for the proper reading of the signs. It is beyond me to understand what cock-eyed mental medicine it is to you, to place such a matter in terms of the "illogical." An "illogical" element would enter, I think, if someone were able to propose the subtler discernment here, and to offer his demonstrations for it, and the physician were to refuse to listen, insisting upon his rights as a master of intuition, and denying that the mistaken diagnosis should be more closely studied at all.

My notion is that, if life is worth living, it is worth being meditated upon. That is, it is worth having "key terms" for all the important motives in it (such as love, poetry, property, dreams, war, work and its problems, etc.). It is worth our asking ourselves how all these things are or should be related to one another. And since such a line-up must be done by words, for both appreciative and admonitory purposes we should want to know how the <u>nature of the words themselves</u> may both favorably and unfavorably affect the line-up. I see no reason why anybody should, in principle at least, feel insulted or confined or sullied by even the mere <u>attempt</u> to study such matters.

As for poetry: in such an approach, I grant you, poetry would be but one department. (It would figure, not as poetry, but as poetics.)

And I further grant you that, in the last analysis, the test of poetry is in the writing. Poetry is as poetry does. In this sense, nobody has his foul hands on the pure virgin of poesy. You are free to write what you want. No critic can prevent the poet from writing the greatest poem in the world. All he has to do is write it. And that's his answer.

Hence, insofar as the poet wants to write poetry, there is no issue.

But suppose the poet begins to theorize about poetry? Suppose he wants to write about writing poetry? At that point, he falls into a new department. And suppose that (like Wallace Stevens in his <u>Sewanee</u> essay)[121] his writing about poetry happens, some 150 late, to have put forward <u>strongly Kantian</u> theories of poetry (as the entire Imagist movement is saturated with post-Kantian thought, I am coming to see with greater and greater clarity). Can the poet himself consciously or unconsciously build upon a <u>philosopher's aesthetic</u>, and then yipe "Hands off!" the moment one wants to discuss this statement as a <u>philosophy of poetry</u>?

But we could run around and around in this circle forever. So let's give it up, as hopeless. My conviction is that you are still trying to think of poetry, like Stevens, as a "virile young man," whereas you should now think of poetry as a "mellow old man." If you won't do this, you're just painting your face, like Von Aschenbach.[122] And making yourself unnecessarily miserable, while denying us all the advantages of your own mature experiences. True, you're not as old as I am, by far.[123] Working at a girls' school makes one feel as ancient as the Alleghenies (and as worn down). Yet you are surely confronting the same situation "in principle."

If you ever get a chance to look at those three pages on Virgil, please do. And please tell me how they struck you. Among other things, your reaction to them might help enliven my scheduled talk.

Meanwhile, best greetings, good luck,

Sincerely,

K.B.

[P]   [Rutherford]
Feb. 25, 1947

Dear Ken,

At least we are in perfect agreement—or almost. I don't want to have to call you the philosopher of Andover but that aside nothing remains as an obstruction between us.

You see, the moment you drop logic, as an incentive, at least, to action, you become convincing. Instinctively you sent me the summary of Virgil's plan (an instinctive plan, no doubt) for the composition of a long poem. I am delighted, not to say thrilled by both the summary as you copied it out and your thoughtfulness in doing so and sending it to me.

But when, logically I suppose, you think I will be furious over the matter, plan and action, you are absurd.

I do not believe you think Virgil formulated any such preliminary plan as this before beginning composition in the <u>Aeneid</u>. He was an alert and intelligent citizen of his times and besides a gifted poet; he saw a need (he also saw words) and must have felt a tremendous pleasure of anticipation. In composing the poem he felt an undoubted pleasure—of various sorts: sensual, sociological, historical identifications and so forth. He may at an outside guess have indulged in a bit of logical philandering—if he found the time for it in a dull moment! But that he set down a primary scheme and followed it I can't for a moment believe.

The thing is, Ken, and in this I am sure we perfectly agree, there are not many things we poor human bastards can do. Or shall I say there are not many approaches we have to our satisfactions and not one of them all is of any more worth than the other. We each of us do what we can. My approach, as a poet, is just as valid as your approach as a philosopher to whatever mass of material is presented to us to work with.

Now, Virgil having written a poem, someone comes along later (it could just as well be himself after the work is completed) and fools around in it like a squirrel in a box of birdseed for something he can use in his own economy. That's fine granted the beast knows that the seed was not put there for him— or he might get shot—oh well, let that pass. I only object to the philosopher when he tries in the making of poems to insert his dictum before the poet composes and would reject the poem before it is a poem, of words. His function, to the poet, except in a very general way (important as it often is) comes after the poetic deed. For if the poet allows himself to fall into that trap (of listening too early to the philosopher) he will inevitably be of little use to the very philosopher himself as a field of investigation after he, as a poet, has completed his maneuvers.

The nascent instincts are the feelers into new territory—even Einstein has recently acknowledged or stated that. Deductive reasoning is in the main useless to us today or if not useless at least secondary in value.

Yes, words. I accept your differentiation between a fact and a book or train of reasoning about those facts. The book is only a defense or reasoning in support of the findings. I know all that and as you must realize (having lived in the age of Gertrude Stein and Joyce) all that is primary to me also.

We, you and I, have nothing to quarrel about once we get by the simple beginnings (the universal activity of the mind—analysis is merely an adjunct to that). At that point we may begin to use each other at will—or perforce if you prefer. My whole contention, so far is that we keep separate in order to be of as much use to each other as possible—to penetrate separately into the jungle, each by his own modes, calling back and forth as we can in order to keep in touch for better uniting of our forces.

Do you know the story of the two French military officers conducting a column of infantry through the desert? It was a hell of a three-day march in the broiling heat, with rebellious troops and heavy work to be done. One of the two officers in charge asked the other at daybreak of the third day: Are you going to march in the van today or the rear? I intend to take the opposite post or else I'll murder you.

Bill

Many thanks, really, for the bit you copied out for me. I may use it in the part of the <u>Paterson</u> I am working on now.[124] Very helpful.

Re: Medicine vs. logic or poetry x logic, the same—

All I mean is that your logic has not "worked" in that particular medical instance mentioned. I do not say that the conditions must be reexamined, rather I insist that they should be reexamined. But I still have no central interest in the logic (not my province) but in the medical effort of that particular logical sequence which led me astray: you take the logic, I'll keep the case.

I'm aware that I am not answering your questions. It would be irrelevant for me to take time (if I were able) to do so.

Reich's terms mean nothing as compared with his work. Logic may, if it wishes to, transpose his terms, create a different or "key" dialectic, which as far as I can tell is the definition of philosophy, but all that [****] concerns philosophy and in no way psycho-pathology. Of course phil. may look anywhere it pleases for its material and discover it in poetry if it can, but at that point beware a typical and fatal blunder: keep off!

As for Reich and his book: I never refused to send it to you. I did not send it because after you protested against the man, it was logical to conclude that you wanted no more than the smell of him, which I tried as best I was able to give you. (I'll send the book as soon as it is returned to me by the last borrower.)

Poetry has a right, I say, to choose its own logic as it pleases. Ain't that fair enough for the poor virgin? Or do you want to force her?

[B]   **[Andover]**

Dear Bill,

Glad you liked the cite.[125] But I'd be vastly grateful if you could hand on to me any remarks about the ways wherein you wd. accept, modify, or flatly reject its various clauses, as regards any analogous recipe for today. (I mean: assuming that a poet could do just exactly what he decided to do, what sort of corresponding "ideal pattern" might he set for himself now? Though I grant you that, in the working out, new things can be expected to turn up. "On s'engage, puis on voit.")

Fact is that I'm preparing a talk on Ideology and Myth.[126] And I sent copies of the recipe to various types of correspondents. And am getting some interesting replies, which I intend to discuss somewhat in my talk. Anything you wanted to say (on ways in which the 12 points, ideally considered, would be a fit or a misfit with present conditions, the local scene) would be discussed either explicitly as statement by you, or anon., as you preferred.

At moment, am wondering what Caesar Augustus Tr-m-n[127] is going to say to the Congress at one o'clock. In behalf of the pox Americana. Meanwhile, as ever, yours for the non-aggressive and non-expanding extension of the Monroe Doctrine to the Mediterranean, the Pacific, the North and South Poles, Iran, China, Korea, the Near East, the Moon, Jupiter, and Hell.

Sincerely,

K.B.

[P]   **[Rutherford]**
March 21, 1947

Dear Ken,

Exhibits 1 and 2. The oil pamphlet was an afterthought. The original intent was to have you see the <u>Reflections on Poetry</u> by Thomas Good.[128] My own poems in the issue are incidental. Please <u>return</u> the <u>Poetry</u> issue—the other you may chuck.

Also a justified criticism of Aiken's work by Julian Symons,[129] something long overdue. The English do, at best, use their English well. But they also use it in the most atrocious manner ever permitted by God to an atresic world. They use the language to tie themselves into constipated knots in a way no

American would ever fall into. It must be "convention" and much bastard reading (reading to avoid all freshness) that does that. Perhaps it is the uncompleted university product abetted by renegade Americans which causes that. Horrible, the rigors of death long overdue.

But the Thomas Good thing is well worthwhile pondering. I thought it might be of assistance to you.

Bill

[B]   [Andover]
June 11, 1947

Dear Bill,

Oof! Have been super-commuting.[130] Schedule still calls for one more month of same. So I shall go on word-slinging, somehow. But wd. like to crawl into a hole with my notes for the <u>Rhetoric</u>, and grouch and glum them to completion, otherwise saying nothing but please pass the please pass the.

I have a gazette of yours, England's <u>Poesy</u>, which I shall send to you as soon as I get the proper sized envelope. Have been trying to send it back to you for something like four months now—and by God, I'll do it yet.

If you ever feel like sauntering out this way, do. Shall be here the rest of this week. Then schedule calls for return to Bennington until Friday (i.e., trekking thither next Monday, and back thither the following Friday, to be hic et nunc until the Monday thereafter).

Yours in behalf of all the new diseases.

Sincerely,
K.B.

[P]   [Rutherford]
June 20, 1947

Dear Ken,

Going, next Saturday, to Utah, probably by Buick (1940), as hero of Writers Conference: or so the prospectus seems to indicate.[131]

If I return (or even get there) you may expect a report in August or later.

Meanwhile <u>Paterson II</u> has been completed—more or less—and sent to Laughlin for the printer. It contains the "prayer" you wanted me to write. Now you'll have to wait to see it—unless you want it before publication.

Life isn't sweet anymore but at times the garden is—especially in the early morning: sometimes too in the evening when the nicotianas are breathing hard.

Have been reading Saintsbury's <u>Manual of English Prosody</u> in preparation for bouts with Tate who will be also at Utah—so's not to be caught with my pants too far down on technical matters. It is a superb piece of work—and amazingly revolutionary in implication viz a viz our plight today following Whitman.

Yrs,

Bill

[P]   [Rutherford]
Nov. 4/47

Dear Ken,

Love to come! for lunch. How about Friday the 14th? We'll get there by 11. Natch if it storms too violently we'll let Jove have his way and duck it. But you can pretty well count on it for all that. Say the word.

Last Friday, by the way, we drove out to Erwinna, Pa to see Josephine Herbst in her colonial house there.[132] You know her? She's one of the best, has an old brownstone, sandstone farmhouse of the colonial period situated up a narrow valley just west of the Delaware. The rich have bought in all around her but she has been able to stick it out for one unknown reason or another.

Jesus how it rained that day!

More when we see you.

Glad you wrote,

Bill

[P]   [Rutherford]
November 7, 1947

Dear Ken,

Floss says, following the receipt of Libbie's card: Why not Sunday?

Sooo! Sunday let it be—especially since I find that next Friday is taken. We'll try to get there by 11.30 at the latest.

Unfortunately I am in all probability too late for you to receive this before Monday. Thus, assuming it is now Monday. We really had a nice visit. It was a pleasure to discuss the personal, national and international situation with you and to hear your views on the relationship between abstract ideas and practical affairs which so often appear to be quite unrelated as the raccoon washes its hands. The parallelism between poems and philosophy, as you said, is more fancied than real and lucky the man who realizes it before too late in his career. For as Pope objected in his First Epistle Shakespeare is reprehensible in that he wrote for mercenary reasons and there's no use being too bedazzled by his, by either his fame or his accomplishments.[133]

But assuming that this letter has arrived on Saturday as I hoped, we'll see you tomorrow. They say some person by the name of Morgan has besmeared me in the <u>Sewanee Review</u>.[134] Now ain't that too bad for Mr. Morgan, what a chance he missed to get in on the ground floor and praise me while yet there was time. St, st, st, st, st, st!

I hope that red headed woodpecker will be flinging himself back and forth from tree to tree on the approach to your farm as he was doing last year.

Sincerely,

Bill

[P]   [Rutherford]
Monday [November 10, 1947]

Boy! Here's one for a philosopher. See if you can follow it.

Yester was a bitch of a day—but contained its own cure (in the enclosed letter's delay).

Bill

[P]   [Rutherford]
November 9/47

11 A.M.

Dear Ken,

After fierce preparations "the work" and no car finally licked me. I presume that I am not as yet (if I shall ever be) inactive enough to command my own time and engines. The worst of it is I doubt that I can get away next Friday— and this is such a day that nothing would have pleased me more than to be out in the country visiting you and yours.

A maternity case, after I have sworn that I will take no more of them (but the human plea was too much for me) has had me on edge for three days. I love the woman and her Catholicism which I would not betray for any devil, so that I could not leave her in the middle of her 5th labor—a long drawn out inconclusive sort of process which had me puzzled.

12 Noon

The mechanic came in the middle of the last sentence. I had left my car on the curb (it cannot be geared in reverse) we started it in second, got it to his shop and found the shift-lever to be snapped off short. I could have used the car but with a loose piece of metal wobbling in my hand I didn't feel secure enough to take the chance. As soon as tomorrow comes he'll get me another lever, slip it in place and I'll be on the road again.

By the way, a use for a novel mechanical principle came up in the discussion: I asked him how he was going to get the loose end of the lever out from the housing where it lies. It's loose in there, he replied, we'll use a magnet. Thus sometimes in composition a little used means must be employed.

Next Friday Robert Lowell is coming up from Washington for a visit, he'll stay until Sunday when other guests also will arrive from New York.[135] The following Sunday will be the 22nd. Would you be at home that day? For if you plan to be home that day I'd like to come then. And if we come it might be that I'd have my son and grandson with me instead of Floss or in addition to Floss.

I'm getting the records I made in Washington, so says Lowell, this week. You have a machine for them haven't you? When I finally come I'll bring them along. It is said that they are good, something of <u>Paterson I</u> as well as a section from the as yet unpublished <u>Paterson II</u>—which should be along pretty soon, they say the galleys will be returned to me or sent to me before Thanksgiving.

Thus ends another happy dream, I would so much have liked to have got out to see you today.

Any walnuts or butternuts lying around going to waste on the ground up there these days? Tell the kids to pick me up a peck of them and I'll pay the usual market price or the prevalent market price for them.

Sincerely,

Bill

O yes, the baby, named Monaham, arrived very normally at 9.30 this morning. So that, after all my apprehensions of hydrocephalus or the necessity for an immediate transfusion, nothing happened but the tensions within myself. I could even have kept my date with you had it not been for the disabled car.

[P]   [Rutherford]
May 10, 1948

Dear Ken,

Various things have happened since you were south, among them an illness, a prize and an engagement to attend a literary conference this July in Seattle.[136]

For the latter I've prepared a ponderous essay which if you care to have it so I'd like to consult you about.[137] No need to feel obligated in any way: if it would amuse or interest you to glance over my fumblings, well and good; if not—the top o' the marnin' to ye. I could mail you the carbons, running to about 50 pages, then, at your convenience, drive down or up to see you for a pow wow.

What I should like, specifically, would be to have you line up my echelons a little better than I have them, make a sharper line between my strategy and my tactics and—blue pencil the script up as you may see fit. In other words, as the seniors at various colleges continue to write to me, <u>you</u> write my thesis.

Por favor.

My ticker gave out.[138] I was on my back for 5 weeks—wondering, much of the time, whether the cobweb above me contained a live or dead spider. I found, as soon as I could wield a broom-handle that the speck I was looking at was a dead mosquito, a Tu-an-kamen of his world. I insisted that he be not removed until I was well enough to investigate his state in person.

The prize, which is to be bestowed upon me the 21st by the Institute of Arts and Letters is the Loines Award or, as Allen Tate puts it, 1000 dollars.[139]

I attacked your <u>Grammar of Motives</u> again while in bed and made some progress but have not yet finished it. I look to it, however, as a guide where it sits enthroned in my thoughts—literally. I hope the winter in the south was fruitful for you, the winter here was unspeakable—no doubt it was the direct cause of my downfall. I'm better.

A book of new poems (containing—"At Kenneth Burke's Place") is being set.up by Wells College and Cummington Press jointly.[140] It should be out by early fall—or sooner. Other things are on the road, <u>Paterson III</u> among them. The last play is being printed (not performed, alas!).[141]

Best all around,

Bill

[P]   [Rutherford]
May 13, 1948

Dear Ken,

No use pretending I can go south next winter.[142] I gotta work—unless I should break down again which I hope won't take place. Or if I go south it will be for no more than a couple of weeks during the worst of the snow— which finished me this time. But I believe, with Bill here, I'll be able to go along working for awhile yet or until he gets well established.[143] But next winter won't be the time for me to quit.

My "discourse" enclosed. Maybe you can "think out" some of my leads and help me align them better than I have been able to do by myself—unless you want to junk the whole business.[144] Don't do that!!!

We'll take a run up for a dose of pertinent questions after another couple of weeks.

You are quoted more and more as time goes on—present by Bentley, by Fergusson and others.[145] More power to you. I'll get this famous book read before the other is out and then go on to that.

My profound admiration is yours for what you have done and are doing. Please do not let vague if virulent doubts (and certainties) as to the brains of newspapermen and their bosses spoil your sleep.

I go on writing. I'll bring <u>Paterson II</u> with me when I come.

Best,
Bill

[P]   [Rutherford]
May 27, 1948

> If rain there be
> > Think not of me
>
> But day be fine
> > We'll come to dine
>
> Most happy we
> > For such a spree
> >
> > > [From Williams]

⌒

[P]   [Rutherford]
May 30, [1948]

Dear Ken,

11 A.M., our theoretical starting time: it's raining so the trip is out. Is there any particular moment more favorable than another for me to see you next week? What about next Friday, if other day lacks?

(That's as far as I got. For the rain stopped, we had lunch and at the last moment Bill and I decided to chance the trip—as you know.)[146]

It was nice to see you all again and to sit and talk. After Bill gets through with his State Board exams we'll have to drop in on you for another set to.

Thanks for looking over the script of my talk.[147] You didn't have a great deal to say about it but I presume that to be more or less approval, that is, general approval of the writing as something that could be listened to without embarrassment. That in fact is what you implied. I propose then to start at the beginning and let fly. When I feel that the moment has come for a pause I'll pause —watching the clock. At the end of an hour I'll blow the whistle and stop.

It was a pleasure to talk with Mrs. ? "Granny," your wife's mother. Do they make women like that any more? Or do they get that way only with time, especially after their husbands, God pity them! have died? I liked your unmarried daughter too. And the turtle!

How many lovely things that bomb is going to blast!

Bill

⌒

[P]   June 1, 1948

Humphrey Clinker down and is the novel whose name I couldn't recall. Now I'll take on Moll Flanders.

Bill

⌒

[B]   [Andover]
June 9, 1948

Dear Bill,

I guess it's my age. Some years ago, I'd have told you how to write your poems. Now I even hesitate to neb in a gent's work when he's more or less muscling in on my own racket. I tend to say to my honorable self: Hell, he's getting something said his way; if you persuade him to bring in other things, maybe he'll just be neutralized and get nothing said.

Your essay sounded like a good act. I could even see where you cunningly laid plans for some of your most winsome spontaneous boyish effects. (Spontaneous! You old whore!)

Main thing that bothered me, only thing in fact, was this:

You seem to put it all down too much to a matter of Rhythm. For the whole story, I'd like to see you decide just how many ingredients there are in the recipe for a poem. (As Old Ipse Dixit picked the Plot, Character, Thought, Diction, Spectacle, Melody batch to name the elements of Tragedy.)[148] When you talk of the Foot, you obviously mean a lot more than the book on versification does (including, I suspect, some double entendres that might best be revealed by psychoanalysis on the foot as phallus). For a complete critical job, I'd like to see you separate out all the components lurking in your term, and discuss each in turn.

On the other hand, your method is more like one of your own poems. You talk about one thing, leaving other unmentioned things flitting about the edges, to provide resonance. The method works. So what the hell? But to me, your essay was closer to an imagistic poem than to "total" criticism.

You know what I wish you'd do, at least for heuristic purposes? I wish you'd try writing a poem, as fast as you can, on Rhythm and the Foot. Or the New Rhythm, the New Foot, etc. Including your doctrine of the stress upon Change. Knock it off at top speed. And send me a copy of it. I'd really be tremendously interested in seeing it. (For I still hope to do a really thorough analysis of your work, from the standpoint of my lucubrations on Motives. As soon as I get through the <u>Rhetoric</u>, I shall then be free to concern myself wholly with the Poetic and Symbolic matters that delight me most—the stuff for Vol. III—and my thoughts on the Rutherford Cricket-eater should go there, along with, among other things, my notes on Ted Roethke, who is, at the moment, I suppose, sulking in his tent because I haven't yet written on his new book.)[149] My notion is that, if you slapped down such a poem, and then began to take it apart, you'd find very quickly what other elements besides feet, in the versifier's sense, are in the same package with your ideas on Rhythm.

Meanwhile, I am much interested in your project for a list of poetic "Devices." (At the moment, in my <u>Rhetoric</u>, I am writing a list of what I call <u>rhetorical</u> "Devices," with illustrations of each—a kind of "post-Aristotelian" list, for God knows his batch in his <u>Rhetoric</u> certainly cleaned up all the metropolitan districts, leaving only marginal farms for us.)[150] Don't you think that Yvor Winters (the stinker) proposes a few of them in that essay of his written atop my theory of form in <u>Counter-Statement</u>? (The Winters' essay is reprinted in Schorer-Miles <u>Anthology of Criticism</u> recently published by Harcourt-Brace.)[151] At least, you might look at those, and if you don't agree that they are Devices in your sense, you could get some added precision by deciding just exactly why they are not. (The great trick in our racket is that you can use anything, if you merely learn to shift among "therefore," "and," and "however.")

Glad you turned up. Sorry you didn't turn up for longer. Hope you'll turn up again.

Meanwhile, back to the grind.

Sincerely,
K.B.

[P]   [Rutherford]
August 9, 1948

Dear Libbie,

I don't know whether or not I wrote you last week. If I did then this will be a second letter—to say the same thing. But I do want you to get one or both of the letters.

We couldn't come that Sunday. I had just returned from Seattle and what with the office a shambles, the carpenters, painters, plumbers having done their worst—Bill at the hospital working up his future duties there.

I don't know when we'll be able to come. Paul and his family are on vacation visiting in New England (costs less to visit than to do something else).

The trip west by train was an eye opener—saw much that this beast, man, has devastated.[152] The brainlessness of the entrepreneur was never so forcibly jammed down my gullet. He is no different today, he merely has better lawyers (tell that to Kenneth—that the lawyers will be the main ones to read his works to turn them against the public. That ought to put him into the abyss for years on end).

All that remains to us is the barren mountains, the sea the sky and—lots of weather.

So there you are. Best (what's best) to all.

Bill

[P]   [Rutherford]
Feb. 15, 1949

Dear Ken,

Your last letter went unanswered—for no particular reason except that I intended to answer it. I was bogged down with this, that and the other. <u>Paterson III</u> has had me on its hip.[153]

Now that that has been thrown I come up for air.

If the snow isn't too deep on Sunday we'll make a try at Princeton. I'd like to go as would Floss and with Bill here to take over it shouldn't be too difficult for us to get away. But the thermometer being 76 on our back porch right now I foresee a vicious blizzard for Sunday.

Nothing new except that Ez writes me from the hospital that his gums are receding[154] and J. Laughlin is going to Switzerland to ski for a month. The rest of the world lies between.

See my pitcher in <u>Vogue</u> for February?[155] Borrow one and look page 213. Floss sez that's what I get for sticking my long nose in among ladies underwear.

It's been wonderful to have Bill here with me beginning to take things over. Best all around.

As ever,

Bill

Will phone if we're coming.

[P]   [Rutherford]
[July 8, 1949]

At <u>Hudson Guild Playhouse</u>, July 19 for 2 weeks (perhaps) a play of mine, <u>Loves Labors Aborted</u> (sic) by a group of youngsters ("We Present" professionals): 430W27 CHickering 4–0795 (for 1st night at least)—wish I could send some passes, I'll try later but since no gravy, no meat.[156] I ought to be at least amusing and so the world pisses and passes. We'll see you later in the summer if we survive it.

Best,

Bill

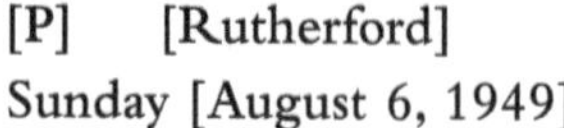

[P]   [Rutherford]
Sunday [August 6, 1949]

Dear Ken,

Just finished reading your translation of <u>Death in Venice</u>. But I don't want to write like that.

We're here at Chas. Abbott's—in the country near Buffalo (corruption of Beau Fleuve) trying to recover our wasted strength—it can't be done.[157] After reading that story I had a bad night. More and more as I grow older I have "bad nights" after my reading. Is it the reading or is it the man? Hard to say. Or is it hard after all? For as there grows to be less and less of the man, the reading grows more and more powerful and the man succumbs.

What a beautiful place this is and without pretense, without fake of any sort yet with about it an aura of culture well corrected by chickens, ducks and prize sheep.

All I wanted to say was that I had read your translation.

Best,

Bill

[B]   [Andover]
August 16, 1949

Dear Bill,

Why not write like <u>Death in Venice</u>? What's the sin of same? Spick.

Incidentally, Francis Golffing, whose poesies were recently published by the Cummington lassies, has written saying that he will be passing this way next Sunday.[158] Also his wife, Barbara Gibbs. Any chance that you and Florence might care to be about? We could feed you too, if you said definitively when.

Dint get into NY to see your play.[159] Have been a-glumming and a-ailing. (I promise not to ask you for free medical advice, having decided that doctors, like philosophers, are merely to help one die well).

How about this: He might think of heaven, but objectively, in terms of clouds. The clouds would be seen not by looking up, but as reflected in a puddle. His pudency might carry him even a step further, as were the puddle under a horse. Can you guess who is it?[160] And do you sanction the formula?

Spick.

Sincerely,

K.B.

Sanction it—just for a first rough approximate? Or do you say neigh?

[P]   [Rutherford]
Wednesday [August 17, 1949]

Dear Ken,

Not this Sunday or any Sunday—without a foot of snow on the ground to slow up traffic. Sundays are impossible on the road. In the fall, on a Friday we'd enjoy seeing you again, sez Floss.

"Heaven" is a bad word, it has too many connotations of inaccurate meaning to be well used in a sentence such as you propose.[161] The moral implications prevent any possibility of objectivity of perception. A cloud isn't heaven and can never be for a Christian, even such a Christian as I am (not). But if you say, objectively, "sky," then your sentence becomes nonsense. I don't know whom you mean—certainly not Mr. Cowley![162] He wouldn't recognize down from up. And don't tell me you mean yourself. Freud perhaps. Hoss piss ain't no different from any other liquid when it comes to reflecting the sky; where's your physics, Mister?

Doctors and chicken broth, Sir, are both means to help a man to die well and—later. What the hell do you want? You want to be "cured." Why you're just an infant, nobody is cured, not even by philosophy. Not even by Christ, by Christ. Only Mr. Eliot has been cured (nutted).[163] Or did Christ do that? Or the stuttering King or the Archbishop? Shit.

Go jump in the lake.

Best,

Bill

[B]   [Gambier, Ohio]
June 30, 1950

Dear Bill,

Greetings from old Gastric Juice (who somehow or other keeps repeating).

Am here, peddling my wares for six weeks, maintaining, in these days of not-at-war, that what the world needs is to buy more of my books.[164]

As for you, jeez, I can't open a litry society-column any more without reading of your doings, and your very well-deserved successes. (Proudly, as regards the infamous Pound-controversy, wd. say that, from the start, I avowed the prize should have gone to you: for your humanity, as vs. his inhumanity.[165] Part of Pound's glory was developed, I think, thus: Eliot avidly proclaimed Pound to be the Great Forerunner, a delicate diplomatic maneuver for suggesting that he himself was the flowering of all that Pound presented in its incomplete stage. By making Pound into a John the Baptist, Eliot suggested that he himself must be . . . but you get the point. You're an intuitive baystard.)

I wonder if you would have any person to suggest who might help me out of this difficulty: It turns out that my son, Butchie has a slight hernia. We have been told that only an operation can remedy such a condition. And I wondered if you could suggest someone, in NJ or NY, (preferably NJ if he was as satisfactory) whom we might consult, and who would do the operation if it is necessary. (I always dare hope for some other way out.)

If you do have any suggestions, I'd be vastly grateful to you for them. (Hope to come home for a few days in the middle of my term here. And thought the operation, if necessary, might be done then. So, to save time, if you do have any suggestions, wd. you please send them direct to Shorty, at Andover, N.J., so that she could start negotiations forthwith?)

This is a hell of a way to pipe up. (I seem to turn up thus, every once in awhile, with a burden which I would plague you with. But I dared hope that 'twould require only a line or two of your time, e'en while drawing upon all your expertise.)

Meanwhile, best greetings. And you really ought to flit out our way once in awhile. (Blackmur and the Fergussons were up from Princeton, just before I trekked hither.)[166]

Sincerely,

K.B.

[P]   [Rutherford]
July 3 [1950]

Dear Ken,

I aim to be useful. Your best bet would be DeBell in Passaic, the same who chiseled the excrescence off your hard palate. He's good and at the same time reasonable in his charges. 3 days at the Passaic General Hospital, semi-private, would do it. It's the only answer—if you don't want him to be a Henry James for life—to boast about it as a great injury, something to be mortally ashamed of like piles. Or shit to the literary profession.

Yes, I ought to meet Blackmur, I dislike him enough to make it almost obligatory.[167]

Sorry the newspapers and their diseases have to speak of me. It wasn't my fault.

Best,

Bill

[P]   [Saratoga, N.Y.]
Monday
Aug. 1, 1950

Dear Ken,

Here at Yaddo, with Floss (Guests of the Corporation) for two weeks—almost over—working on <u>Paterson IV</u> which I have lined up and almost finished; a very profitable occasion.[168] Ted Roethke is here also and several others, writers, painters and musicians—good crowd, male and female—the females nearly all deaf for some inscrutable reason.

The <u>Sewanee Review</u> (Winter, 1950) which had hitherto escaped my notice I found here also and read (am reading) your stuff on Ted and his poems.[169] Very illuminating on the first part and beautiful on the second. These are two exhibits I am glad I didn't miss.

This has been a rewarding experience for me inasmuch as I have never, you might say, in my life had any leisure for writing. I quit practice, hopped in my car, drove up here and immediately plunged into the work. At first I thought I was dying! My back ached from sitting in one spot for hours at a time, my asshole bulged, my eyes began to drop from their sockets and my stomach felt as though it had swallowed a decayed rat. Age, sex I to myself, has at last got me. I'm through. All the fakery I practice now that it has the full light of day upon it is being revealed to me for all the shoddy that it really consists of. I was in agony of mind and the rest of it.

But, after finding that mornings are the best time for me, and not trying to push myself too hard after noon, I have done very well, in my own opinion. At least I have destroyed a lot of paper. We do what we are able to do. Day after tomorrow we go on to other fields. Back home by August 16.

I suppose you know something of this place and its history; very impressive. Did you know, for instance, that Poe completed his Raven here—not that that is anything devastating but it's amusing?[170]

All I wanted to say is that I was impressed with your analysis of Roethke's work. He's getting to be one of the best—a tremendous improvement, in my opinion, over his earlier work. He seems stable enough here though last winter, as you may know also, he had a severe bust up.

Regards to wife and kids—did you do anything about seeing DeBell? Try my damnedest to reach you up there either in August or early September. I never seem to shake myself loose once I arrive home, I have to go nearly to Canada to untangle my legs.

Best,
Bill

[B]   [Andover]
August 24, 1950

Dear Bill,

Two words, to thank you very much for expert advice anent Butchie. All seems to be going quite to perfection. And I think that to-morrow (Friday) we can bring him home, all ready for the Next Phase.

Incidentally, if you do feel like flitting out this way, do let us know. Or even, if you're willing to take potluck on meals, don't bother to let us know. Main thing is that, after Sept. 6th, I resume my treks to Bennington, which means that every other week I'm absent from Monday to Friday. But, except possibly for the first weekend, I'm scheduled to be here every week-end.

What a year! 'Twas supposed to be my year off—but I never worked harder in my life. Every once in a while (as regards the ailments), I discover that I'm a breath behind. So far, each time, I've been lucky: I manage, by a quick intake, to catch up again—but every once in a while it seems as though I just did make it. So, hurrying on, I casually wonder: what if, just once in all the while, I didn't quite make it. (Hurry, hurry.)

You were right to vanish presto, when I got on the sumjick of the politico-military. Medicine and poesy maybe; but medicine and _that_, oof! Or anything and _that_! Or even just _that_! So much, oofitude.

Glad you liked the Roethke article. It's the honest-to-God's truth, Bill, that I want to do one of those on you; I've wanted to for years; and all the more so, as I begin to see how rare humanity is and how much of it there is in your work. I'm disgusted, because I have, on the side, been plugging for you quite zestfully, quite along those lines (also including your skills)—but if and when I get my article done, all I'll seem to be doing is to some lumbering up in the rear. My scheme has been to do three of them, as a set (Marianne Moore, whose work I did deal with somewhat in an article reprinted in my <u>Grammar</u>; Wallace Stevens; and YOU).[171] But there are a lot of accidents in this business—and as a result of them, certain things get done and other things don't get done. But, if I continue to catch that almost uncaught breath, I'll finish that article, bejeez: I owe it to myself. (This sounds like a high-jacking proposition: If WCW the doctor can keep Ignatius Burpius alive, Ignatius Burpius will in his ignatian-burpian way sing of WCW the poet. To say as much is to realize that I'm in danger of getting an overdose of arsenic. What a chance you fellows have! For perfect self-expression.)

Where were we? (To be exact, we were at the second glass of port, before lunch, a time when I—parsimony-minded always—have learned that one can get the maximum befuddlement—or, in other words, clarity—at the minimum cost.)

But, the postim is due. So I desistee-wistee. Best greetings, to one and all. And do, if you feel so inclined, venture hither.

(Incidentally, if you want to do it all in an organized way: later, the Cowleys are coming over from Cuntcunticunt and the Tates are coming up from Princeton. And if you were interested in a general gatherum omnium, we might arrange to have some others also at the same time from Princeton. But all that would involve negotiations that at the earliest moved us into late Sept., since Cowley can't come before the 12th. We could do all that anyhow. And, in the interim, if you were trek-minded . . . etc.)

Sincerely,

K.B.

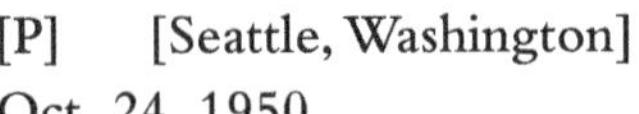

[P]   [Seattle, Washington]
Oct. 24, 1950

Dear Ken,

Don't be so god damned coy. They're mad to have you come out here and talk to them, for a day, a week, a month or longer.[172] They tell me you won't do it.

Now listen to me and come. You can get a week off from your present assignment during an interval of one sort or another. These people pay well. Say yes, to them. They deserve it more than most of the slippery guys from down our way, believe me.

Or maybe you <u>won't</u> believe me. Go on knocking your brains out for pimps, then, if that's what you like. Or maybe we're all aping the great monsters of our time, just that. It's possible. Come on out and tell 'em about it. You must have the address around because I've been told that you know the score.

I wouldn't be a professor for anything on this earth but since you are one, come on out and profess. They <u>need</u> you.

Love & kisses,
Bill Williams
of Rutherford, N.J.

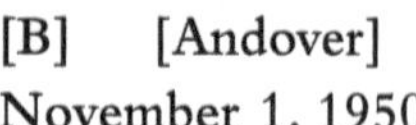

[B]   [Andover]
November 1, 1950

Dear Bill,

So that's where you are, dawlink.

But this winter, I simply must hole up (in what I graciously call, I mean dub, "self-imposed heart-conscious house-arrest").

I must besick myself monument-wise. I must get it all smacked into shape. Uddawise, I'll splatter like a cow-flop.

All last year, I was supposed to take off. And one thing or another turned up, and lo!—all my papers got into more and more of a blown-about condition. And when my papers are that way, how can I, a word-slinger, have a character left? I mean: integrity.

Hence, I must stay home and cultivate my ailments. Gulp, gasp, gag myself into a document Towards Health (on paper).

How about a dialogue between Ab Ovo and De Novo? How about (since I am buying a tape recorder) a series of imaginary now-it-can-be-told monologues addressed to various Ones I have known? (This just on the side, for setting-up exercises, while continuing to codify our bellyache on Man As Symbol-Using Animal? And our lore now on Catharsis wd. put a leading Chain Drug Store to shame.)

I see you say c/o Rutherford. So I send it thus. When back? And let me know if you feel like sauntering hither some time. (The one day the damned machine worked, I had an ecstatic time. Then the thing collapsed; and ever since, I've been in such frustration as no Freudian psychologue could ever conceive of.)

More anon. Please give my very best greetings to fellow-thinkers thereabouts. I do hope some time to be able to join in the enterprises there. Apparently 'twould be vastly pleasant. But this year, must linger here.

Sincerely,
K.B.

Incidentally, if you know anyone who is looking for a copy of my <u>Philosophy of Litry Form</u>, do please pass along word that the L.S.U. Press found 750 unbound copies, and is issuing them soon.

[P]   [Rutherford]
December 20, 1950

Dear Libbie,

No rough stories this time, I don't want to be injured!

Glad Ken's to be home. We often think and talk of you. Some fine day we will make the trip, try out my new (954 miles) Dodge. (I was surprised when Doc took that light car, I thought he'd go for a deluxe model.)

Tomorrow's the shortest day in the year. Let's not blaspheme but it can't be short enough for some of the things we're facing (hope not).

What's this new (?) mood I've got myself into?

Glad you like the stories. I'll bring you a book of the poems when I get there—tho' I did want Laughlin to send you a graft copy of them first.[173] We'll see.

I prefer it here to any place on the West Coast except Seattle. The rest of that climate (maybe you could except San Francisco) breeds dopes and Hearsts, i.e. a dope is not vicious. But the crackpots, the religious nit-wits that come up for "visiting poets" in his fan mail must come from SOMEwhere. Why not, then, the climate, the fact that there is no winter, no cold, no stiffening to the mood, to the intelligence? The flabby wishers are not killed off, the coddling pleasantness of the nights flatters them, it is just as one finds in the phenomenon of Christian Scientists going on breathing solely because of the sanitary laws which forbid yellow fever, plague, cholera, typhoid and scarlet fever. It becomes a business. It becomes a, passion, their only passion: to go on breathing. The male must squirt his sperm over the eggs in some warm metaphysical river where they breed, for it is not known that they cohabitate.

Be seein' yuh. Greeting to Pop and the kids.

Yours,
Bill

[P]   [Rutherford]
Dec 29/50

Dear Ken,

That's a heluvathing to say to a poet, that he makes what ain't there seem real, i.e. the "spirit." But I've always suspected these metaphysicians. Damn site rather be a physician and get my hands on it even if it ain't for me. It's a nice feelin' no matter how many times removed, a vurry nice feeling, a vurry comforting feelin,' makes you feel good to know it's there, anyway, and no foolin' about it. That ain't my understanding of what a poet is, let alone being' a physikan.

I'd like to see what you got to say. Wanna be in my autobiography? I'm writing it now. Save a place for you if you're going south this year.

Certainly let your mother come to me. How about some Saturday afternoon around 2 P.M. Call me up first so I won't sneak out on you. What I'll probably do after I look at her is to send her to my close friend in Passaic, Dr. Albert Jahn. He's an X-ray man but he's also got sense and decency and is a top diagnostician. From there on we'll take off as we find it necessary or not to go further.

Happy New Year and don't let nothin get you down. I hear T. S. E. will be teaching at Chicago U. next spring or fall or something.[174] Geezes! Or maybe it ain't as bad as that. What some men will do! And what others will let them do!!

Best,
Bill

[P]   [Rutherford]
January 4, 1951

Dear Ken,

Your mother and father were here today. She's marvelous and beautiful too,

I fell immediately in love with her—and he's as straight about it and as thoughtful of her as any man could well be about a woman. A very moving pair.

I got the story from the beginning. It looks as though she may possibly never have had any malignancy in the jaw at any time but a benign bone cyst. I don't say this is absolutely so but it is a possibility. Dr. Pool's report, if what your father says is accurate, seems to say that there is no malignancy there now. This, of course, I shall have to check with Pool himself which I intend to do before Monday afternoon when your father will call me for my report on that detail. Much will depend on what Pool says or what I can get out of him.

If the cyst which your mother now undoubtedly has on the jaw is benign the question then arises, what is to be done about it? Shall we leave it alone or remove it—for aesthetic reasons. If in spite of what appears to have been said Pool thinks it IS malignant—though I don't see how he can believe such a thing in view of the reported findings—another course must be followed. An extremely favorable thing is that in 7 years there is no discoverable metastasis.

I asked your mother about her eyes. They seem to be normal for her age. I asked her about her hearing. She said that on the left side her hearing had deteriorated very greatly during the past year and that she had a heavy feeling in her head—that, in fact, bothers her more than anything else. It seemed to be that which had begun most to discourage her. I examined both her ears. The right drum looked normal but I could not see the left because of the inspissated wax filling the canal.

So I decided to remove the wax. It was very dry showing it had been there a long time. With syringing with hot water, I loosened it and finally drew it out in one piece with a small pair of forceps. You'd be surprised. It was like a rock with all sorts of crumbly looking stuff behind it. Her hearing immediately returned and the "dull" feeling in her head disappeared forthwith. It may be all that, in that quarter, is the matter with her. Your father said she looked 3 years younger than when she had come into the office. I hope her symptoms were due to something as simple as that. Isn't it strange that no one looked into her ear. It's an old story.

As I have warned you the ultimate outcome of the case may not be as sunny as I am saying it looks now to be. There is an undoubted lump under the woman's jaw. It has not been proven to be benign even though Pool is reported to have said it is so. We've got to do more work on the case before I for one shall feel safe, but at the moment the favorable symptoms outweigh the others. Your mother weighs 112 pounds, has not lost weight in several years; her color is fine. We'll go ahead with her on that basis.

If you see <u>Sewanee Review</u>, next issue, look for my paper in it on Ford Madox Ford's <u>Parade's End</u>.[175] I'm real proud of it.

More when I know more. Best luck all around.

Sincerely,
Bill

[P]   [Rutherford]
Sat. 6 January, 1951

Dear Ken,

The revised report is this. I called Pool in New York as I told you, he replied by phone yesterday. He was extremely prompt in this and when I got talking with him I found him to be extremely interested and wanting to be helpful. Sounded like a swell guy.

He told me, first, that he hadn't seen your mother since last March, which was a surprise—I understood that she had gone to him only a few weeks ago but, of course, I was mistaken. In reply to my questions he said that undoubtedly your mother had had a malignant growth on the jaw but that it had been either cured or arrested by the X-ray treatment. The present lump has nothing to do with the original lesion but is due to blocking of the salivary duct by the X-ray treatment of if not of the salivary duct itself then of some other structure of similar nature. It is not malignant.

The only question now is: will the cancer recur? It is a possibility that must be guarded against by occasional reexamination which HE will make under my supervision. That's the way things have been left. There appears to be nothing to do now except, following that plan, other than to send her to him, to Pool, at her earliest convenience. This she should do, to his private 54th (St) office with which she is familiar.

The gal may not want to do this but if you will explain to her that I am not surrendering the case to Pool but will continue to see her from time to time as she may wish to have me follow her I think she will submit. Get after her and make her behave for Pool is keenly interested and seems to be a very reliable and understanding guy.

So there we are. Your father is going to call me on
Monday when I shall tell him exactly what I have written here for you.
Are we living or dead, any of us?

Yours,
Bill

(among the quasi-living)
My grandson just chopped down 4 of his father's young fruit trees. What does
that make him, a criminal or 4 times a hero?

[P]   [Rutherford]
Jan. 20, 1951

> Dear Ken
> here we are again
> women won't be women
> till men become men

I was much excited by Blackmur's recent <u>Hudson Review</u> thesis, "The Lion
and the Honeycomb" (which is the only unclear portion of the whole; a bum
title).[176] I very much enjoyed the work and felt myself elevated by it to a level
of understanding heretofore unattained in the area he covered.

> And when will men
> seizing pen
> expound a world fitting
> for the intelligen-
> ce to live in, then
> go out and
> build it?
> The answer is beyond our ken.

The enclosed letter from Doc Pool sounds good to me. File it or send it
to your Dad as you think best.

The autobiography is up to 1119 pages of longhand script. Hope to get a
book out of it by March 1st. It's wonderful to live without brains!

Sincerely,

Bill

Fine summer day! Wish I wuz up visiting you. New York bound.
    W.

[P]   [Rutherford]
January 24, 1951

Dear Ken,

The reason I haven't been seeing anyone recently is, as I may have told you, that I'm doing my autobiography. March 1st is the deadline. It's been a battle.

If you know Blackmur well enough for it, ask him to send you my two-page letter to him written last week following my reading of his paper.[177] Tell him the circumstances, of your having written me, etc. My letter to you wasn't intended to be informative.

But if you must have a direct answer: with my feeble brain he gave me something at least that I could follow. For the first time I clearly understood the difference between criticism and scholarship—a trivial matter, no doubt, but one that appealed to me. Then, following his major theme, I was glad to have someone that I could understand point out for me a possible analogy between a presumable correlation among the Greeks between criticism, scholarship and rhetoric, a balanced relationship, and our mind-destroying incoherence among these parts of a presumptive whole; he at least let it be known that SOME sort of relationship is desirable—a thing no one seems to remember in our day. It is all elementary to you but to me it needed saying in a broadly comprehensive manner, like the names Europe, Asia, Africa on the map. It may be window-dressing but I liked it.

Finally, I have just discovered, within the last two years the significance of Aristotle's use of the word "imitation." It has overwhelming importance to the writer and to the artist generally and is for us a "new" word. The imagination has to imitate nature, not to copy it—as the famous speech in Hamlet has led us to believe, there is a world of difference there. The whole dynamic of the art approach is involved, to imitate invokes the verb, to copy invoked nothing but imbecility. It is the very essence of the difference between realism and cubism with everything in favor of the latter.

And, Blackmur used one specific word, iamb, at the beginning of his paper and never clarified the reference further. I was seized by his reference to the iamb and furious at his neglect to make clear what he meant in that case—I wonder if he knew what he was saying and how drastically important it is for him to go on. He didn't. Does he know what he inferred? I wonder and I asked him to go further on the chance that he might bring light into an area where I am looking for instruction.

I read, last night, the stenographic record of your discussion of the New Criticism.[178] I particularly noted your part in the discussion which interests me as much as anything else stated there. You lifted all that was said to the dignity, the unconscious dignity, of a seriousness which otherwise was largely lacking. I particularly noted the silence which followed at one point of your remarks. I want to read the second part of the discussion, please send it to me when it appears. Your contribution was not pacifying but peace giving to the whole, I went out into an open place—a freshly "discovered" place where the mind could exist without restrictions placed upon it by outside circumstances, not its own necessary ones.

You see you stopped short as you yourself were well aware of doing— space! was what you needed to bring the ends of the discussion together in your "hierarchy" of meaning. I'd like to see you do it.

When you do, my feeling is that Davis,[179] in spite of his unbalanced statements, will have sustained his point as against the others—his persistence of staying within his references while the others tried their best to route him out was a high point in the whole display of wits. Some good points were developed, quite apart from the rhetoric of the discussion at large, for the casual reader.

Blackmur did get off some pretty bad writing in his piece, I acknowledge that. I merely skipped that sort of thing. What the hell else can you expect of a philosopher?

Best,

Bill

P.S. Had a small talk in N.Y.C. an evening last week over the Blackmur thing with a Prof. Thompson[180] English, at Columbia and R. Penn Warren—who also, both of them, tended to slight Blackmur on the "religious" tone of his paper. Why not go whole hog like, you know, what the hell's his name? the <u>German</u> guy, the Englishman and, for that matter, T. S. Eliot. They at least took a definite (false?) stand in favor of religion as the literary butt. etc. etc., instead of pussy footing around coyly with it. O well. "Sacred books" etc., phooey, they said.

[P]   [Rutherford]
June 23, 1951

Dear Ken,

What you've done in the Roethke criticism is what you do in all you accomplish: make the elements of a criticism, a possible "new" criticism, articulate, in that you give it terms to work with.[181] It is a heroic accomplishment (not a fight to make, etc., but a "made"). It is a laying out of terms that can be worked with.

In that way and in a sense you don't say anything about Roethke's poems, you are interested in correlating them with a comprehensive purpose into which they will fit as an integer. That is a laying of the foundation in a critique which has not yet got to a stage which appears above ground.

I wonder what you'd do with some of the buildings of a Frank Lloyd Wright? His buildings are ONLY that which appears above ground. You never think of his foundations. My brother,[182] for instance, thinks him a fake. He <u>has</u> no foundations, physically or ideally, he is all "show."

So when you go at Roethke you go at the reasons and you clarify. You clarify by relating him, his imagery, to past ideas, you anchor him to the past (Dante, Kant, Lawrence). IT is a generous gesture as from you to him, it is a liberating gesture in that you PUT a foundation under him, you buttress him, give him confidence in that you discover the old in his new.

That, at the same time, clarifies the old by showing it still active in new forms.

The thing you leave out is the shape of the language: the thing which has made your revaluation necessary. Naturally, you don't leave it out since you choose the instance of Roethke as important enough to comment, but you don't treat it directly.

In other words, the CONJUNCTION of the poems WITH what you are doing <u>is</u> the future (the present). It behooves us to stick together against regression: against, against—isn't it a shame we have to say "against" and not "To!"

(Poor old Longfellow with his banner sadly proclaiming his slogan for shaved wood furniture stuffing: Excelsior!)

An excellent piece, full of cheer, hard as a rock and as warm as a firm breast.

My fingers hit the wrong keys, sorry.

Bill

P.S. Louis Zukofsky has recently sent me a letter and a piece of writing which you may like to see.[183] Return them both with any comment you care to make.

These two specimens represent the opposite, complementary, facet from your writing—or what I take to be the completion of what you say: the whole which makes us necessary to each other; the full "act."

It was a good session on Thursday. I took the poem out there to get a little confidence from you, if possible, on which to go on working, to move ahead on. You see all my problems at the present time are technical.

Zukofsky wants me to summarize the technical advances made and to be made—even an extension of Aristotle is needed. We have suffered in our instruction from the fact that Aristotle was cut short (by the accidents of time) from commenting on dithyrambic poetry. His record is terribly incomplete, maimingly so. He also spoke of the various meters as "natural" to certain kinds of verse. That is not scientific, it is mere instinct. It is his failure to go on, as Aeschylus, if he had written a technical instruction book for some of his apprentices, might have done that has stalled us in the accomplishment of a FULL prosody.

It is on that phase AND ALL THE DIRECT IMPLICATIONS TO THE KIND OF THOUGHT WE FOLLOW which is my principal care. The <u>thought</u> will be liberated by the technical, the thought which is stalled in our <u>inability</u> to find the means with which to think (in a poem) which makes me stress structure. By structure I mean the thing with which we think is missing. It is to invent that that I engage myself. You show us how to think, I want to supply the material to think <u>with</u>. It isn't ever the terms, the terms can be ambiguous as there may be two kinds of terms, it is the shape, the context of the terms that engages me not their "meaning" as such.

After all you ARE able to differentiate such things and you are willing, generous, toward their study. You WANT to join with another to elucidate such interests. Most don't even know what you are talking about but get stalled on primary considerations or bile or are lost in the phase, never standing back to see how one phase meets another to complete the "thing" which is beyond any one capability.

Bill

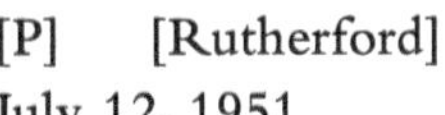

[P]   [Rutherford]
July 12, 1951

There's only one thing better than a lot of talk and that's a lot of fishing. But some pretty good boys never did anything else but talk (never wrote a word) didn't they? And people still talk about them. I often think I'll never say anything again, just write my piece, make it as tough as I possibly can (no explanation) and when I meet a friend spend my time talking about something else. We're going off for a couple of weeks at the shore. The good old salt water, makes a noise at that. A good obscure noise. No explanation. Best luck.

Bill

[B]   [Andover]
August 25, 1951

Dear Bill,

Bulletin: Chapters 43–44, superb summings-up on Motivation.[184]

P. 288, on "perfections" would neatly serve some purposes of mine. (My notions as to what Aristotle meant by the "entelechy," which I assert is a necessary element in his view of "imitation." Cf. paragraph marked on p.7 of the item enclosed herewith.

So, should like to lift paragraph three, for use in the Poetics section of the Symbolic.[185]

All told, I find the litry gossip entertaining; but the Fitzgerald-peddlers can do it better. But always, the medico-angle is a wow. At end of Chapter 44, bejeez, I wept with delight.[186]

End of bulletin.

K.B.

[B]   [Andover]
September 19, 1951

Dear Bill,

Holla!

Jeez. In my study alone, all is more of turmoil than if all the hospitals of Greater NY were suddenly scrambled into a hash. How do you do it!

(We have added the hospital angle, too. My mother, when visiting here, had hemorrhages—and since then many further upheavals have been in order. She seems to be convalescing OK now. But the normal chorefulness of this prehistorically accoutered outfit is further augmented consid.)

Writing this to say that, natheless, somehow, I've dug down among my booksnpapers to the Wms. layer—and it's testify or bust. (Recd. autobiograph. from publisher recently—and shall include references to that also.)[187]

Best greetings. More anon.

Sincerely,

K.B.

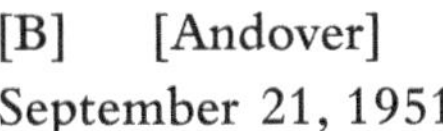

[B]   [Andover]
September 21, 1951

Dear Bill,

Am finding many interesting moments in your autobiography.

But I'm a slow, note-taking son of a bitch, who has never learned how to read fast (not even a book as fast-reading as yours), so I'm only on p. 222.

Your song-and-dance anent the chastity of profligacy (p. 221), however, filled me of a sudden with one last flutter of hope.[188] "Maybe I can get that guy to see what sorta thing I'm puzzling over, after all," I whisper to self. So I enclose the relevant document, asking only that you read the passage marked on p. 224. Here's what I mean by the twists and turns of the "hierarchal" motive, dawling, as considered in my <u>Rhetoric</u>. (As for document itself, use once and throw away. We must be hygienic.)[189]

Incidentally, top of 164: quite wrong. Marianne Moore did for a while get me to fill in for her, while she was on vacation.[190] But she was the last editor of <u>The Dial</u>; and never, throughout the history of the gazette, did the name of Kennel Bark ever fly from the masthead. (At an earlier period, I substituted for Seldes.[191] Indeed, over the years, I did all sorts of substitution jobs, even at one period doing sheerly secretarial work for M.M.—typing letters and returning MS.)

Best greetings,

Sincerely,

K.B.

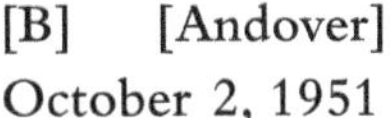

[B]   [Andover]
October 2, 1951

Dear Bill,

Sorry to be plying you so with brief sporadic bits. But since I'm working on your stuff now, I sorta somehow have you on my mind.

Would you, on the enclosed card, tell me when the <u>Collected Earlier Poems</u> is likely to appear?

Incidentally, in the course of my indexing the <u>Autobiog.</u>, I find on p. 270: "o, shades of Kenneth Burke."[192] And on p. 97: "Oh, shades of old Krumwiede!" Well, I'll be damned.

And do you, by any chance, know (off-hand) whether you anywhere use "rhyme" as a verb, literally or figuratively (as were you to say that one person or idea rhymes with another)? If so, it would be grateful for the info.

Here are some puzzlements I find quite interesting (in my zest for trying to discover the correlations within a given poet's terminology):

When speculating on your title, "Make Light of It," I naturally noticed that on pages 45 and 54 of the <u>Later Poems</u> you have other titles containing "It."[193] (These are the only ones I found, though I haven't yet looked among the various of your earlier poems I have.) I noticed also that both these poems have rhymes. (A rhyme in one of your poems is about as hard to spot as a right to the jaw.) Then, lo! on p. 79, the old baystard doth inform us (in a poem with a rhyme that practically steps on itself, it comes so close): "When Structure Fails / Rhyme Attempts to Come to the Rescue."[194]

Incidentally, I asked Butchie what "Make Light of It" means. He apparently didn't know the idiomatic usage, and said: "It means to explain it, to make it clear."

All told, then, we so far have three meanings: (1) as per the idiom; (2) illumination; (3) the ambiguities of "it"—whereat we are reminded, lo! that the old hoss, on p. 37 of <u>Later</u>, doth trip forth beauteously: ". . .enormous night / that makes / of light and fruit." Makes light a fruit. Makes light af (ru)it.[195]

I doan no. And naturally, I ain't after saying that that's litry criticism, not old style at least. But I find it engrossing to trail such correlations down, when one is dealing with a person who selects his words scrupulously, in keeping with his own (mostly intuitive) canons of judgment. Maybe I won't even use any of this in the final article. But I thought you might find it of some interest.

Incidentally, bejeez, the other day (or rather, two successive nights, while insomniac), I made me a Gedicht auf Deutsch. And I copy it out herewith. N.B. "Faust's fist," which is my contribution to the lore of the reflexive. (Greenberg was here yesterday; and I sprung this conceit on him when he was a bit under the infloonce—whereat he did avow that I had in that formula summed up the essence of 50 years of Faust-criticism.)

Faustkunde[196]

Wenn ein Mensch in seinem Bette liegt,

So denkt er an sehr fürchterliche Dinge;

Fragt sich ob grosses Unglück ihn umbringe,
Während in den Wogen der Ewigkeit er wiegt.

Wenn ein Mensch auf seinen Füssen steht,
So denkt er an fast irgend etwas nicht.
Lächelnd nennt er sich einen Bösewicht,
Während Galgenweg entlang er fröhlich geht.

Was mich betrifft: Seitdem ich Älter bin,
Beim Sitzen denk' ich, wie in Jugendtagen
Mit grossem Jammer und viel Unbehagen
Ich Faust's Faust war, die eigene Verführerin.
"Faust's fist, seductress of the self!" Vive la Faustkunde—and
naturally, all other kinds o kunden.

Yours for the Neck's Faze,
K.B.

[B]   [Andover]
October 15, 1951

Dear Bill,
    Bulletin Bulletin Bulletin
    While working on your poems, I caught, I think, summat of your accents.
As to wit namely this:

Mercy Killing

Faithfully
We had covered the nasturtiums
Keeping them beyond
Their season

Until, farewell-minded,
Thinking of age and ailments,
And noting the lack of luster,
I said:

"They want to die;
We should let the flowers die."

That night
With a biting clear full moon
They lay exposed.

In the morning,
Still shaded
While the sun's line
Crawled towards them from the northwest,
Under a skin of ice
They were at peace.

I know, Prima Donna Dawlink, you're mad at me. But, natheless, I'm first of all for accuracy—and to heck with the rest.

So, I wondered, thus:

If, on looking over that poem, you have any notions (spontaneously) as to where in your opinion it's not in your groove, and how you would tinker with it, to make it more along your lines, bejeez I could I'm sure get some angles by your saying so.

So I send this, just in case.

Sincerely,
K.B.

Here's one, by the way, in a different groove:

Night Piece

O pulsant autumnal jungle
Restore me to thy rhythm
Teach me to the knack.

I have stood on the edge of the jumping-off place
Waiting.

Have looked down
To see still stars at the bottom of a lake;
Looked out
Upon dark riddle within.

O mad, dreaming, absolute City
O Nature's Babylon
Make me of thy rhythm

Make me of thy pageantry.
Scene: two o'clock at night. Papa pickled, alone. All decent citizens in bed. Stands by shore of pond listening to the insect-roar from without, and the Alky-roar within.

[B]   [Andover]
November 15, 1951

Dear Bill,

Helndamnaysh. I swore I'd bother you no more about my troubles, knowing that you had enough of your own.

But bejeez, this situation with regard to my mother is becoming gruesome. And I wondered whether you could tell me if you have any notions at all as to where I should turn.

She has had a series of hemorrhages that are bleeding her white. And financially, they are bleeding me white.

Just this much, then: Do you have any notion how I should go about it to get the maximum easing for her, with the minimum financial drain upon myself?

The little I have laid aside, against the needs of sending the boys to college, has already (has it not?) been cut by a capital levy of about 50% (inflation being the delicate capitalist, free enterprise way of doing what otherwise must be done by blunt socialist confiscation).

The last step: We went to Pool.[197] Pool suggested Memorial. I said yes— and lo! I am finally informed that arrangements have been made for a room at Doctors' Hospital. They all sounded alike to me. And lo! there we are, with a room with private bath and all the swankeroo of the Hotel Pierre—and me each day pulling up the floorboards to get something to cover the checks.

Anything, I thought, to get those hemorrhages stopped. So that was the one clause I put in the contract. Evidently, over and above the condition of the jaw, there is a cancerous condition of the lungs—and it is beyond treatment. But if at least we could stop these gruesome hemorrhages. So, when Pool said he could do just that, I found a sufficient dismal comfort in his assurance.

Now—an hour ago—I have talked with him by phone. And, with much embarrassed coughing, he retracts. The hemorrhages cannot be stopped.

He did, however, suggest about three X-ray treatments a week. But he said that, if she stayed at Doctors Hospital, it would only be for these—hence, since the day-to-day costs would be so great, we may as well take my mother home, and try to find some mode of treatment nearer home.

Do you have any notions at all, Bill? As to how I might proceed, to the best advantage of all concerned? As things line up now, I am to drive into NYC on Sunday morning and bring my mother back home, to an address in Weehauken, where my parents have lived since they came to this area in 1915.

Looking over the letter, I note one possible ambiguity. The hemorrhages are not of the lungs, but of the jaw. I presume the treatments would be to lower their frequency. (I realize now that I did not ask Pool what they were to do, explicitly.)

So, if you have any notions whatever as to how we might inquire into arrangements for these treatments, and possibly into some hospitalization generally (for the old man is not competent to deal with the calamities, and I really do not see how, with our sparse resources here, we could do an adequate job). . . . I'd be grateful, slavishly, for a word from you. If you wanted to phone, you could call us here, reversing the charges, Netcong 709–J.

Pool, by the way, said that he'd be glad to discuss the case with anyone who wanted to know of his experiences with it.

Oof! Meanwhile, best luck.

Sincerely,
K.B.

[B]   [Andover]
November 17, 1951

Dear Bill,

Herewith the "arguments" for chapters in T.B.L. (Turds a Beddy Love.)[198]

Imagistically, there's a lot of internal relations I did not consciously contrive at the time. Note, for instance, the close of Part One (on p. 60). It is completely "prophetic" of the story's later development, though I had no such schematism consciously in mind. The rustle of water, heard behind the mist, attains its fulfillment in the final words of the book. The barking dog is the yapping of the hero (notably in passages like pp. 140–145—a dismal variant of that gent I call "Kennel Bark"). The "twitter of unrelated bird-notes" is in the very _form_ of the last chapter. (Birds also as "augury." Nay more, as nursery word for turd, which lurks also in Towards of the title. For such a bird, see form of Brancusi's "Golden Bird.") The meeting with Alter Ego, etc., is aspect of the regressive, masturbation theme. (See also same theme in the story-within-a-story, with the "dummy policeman" as symbol for the sense of guilt.) For corrosion theme, cf. the many aspects of rodents; also p. 157, on "slow acids of the mind." And on p. 209, even God (always a term for ultimate motivation) is classed as a rodent. Middle of 210: I'd now interpret the "eye" as also ambiguously "I." (An internal aspect of the person, dissociatively tracking the lonely ego. Also, of course, as a God, or principle of moral judgment. After I finished the book, by the way, the obsession of that eye pursued me terribly. And I damned near went to the priests for help. But there were reasons whereby I could not have solved my personal tangle by this route. So I kept hanging on, until finally I worked out other ways, ways that required such sitting-on-the-lid as resulted in the years of hypertension.)

Could also trace a course of progressive dissociation through the book. (What I call, for analyzing such plots generally, the "separating-out.") Simplest instance: passage where he is talking in public telephone booth, speaking in a dismal voice while smiling in order to mislead a stranger who is standing outside looking through the glass. Or at end of p. 102.

Enough—thought I could go on. One thing certain: There is something much more drastic than the merely "intellectualistic" going on in that book. And eventually, I dare hope, I'll be able to teach people how to read it. And I'll swear to God, Bill, I have never for a moment doubted this fact: Once people know how to read that book, they will know that it is one of the fundamental works of fiction in our literature, generally in the line of Hawthorne. And it is made for spouting, "as a gargoyle would speak which, in times of storm, spouted forth words," an expression on p. 9 that already involves us in the storm-piss-diction nexus, and all the ultimate relationships between style and eating, sucking, spewing, farting, belching, and other bodily processes of intake and outgo. (I originally wrote, by lapsus typewriteri, "relationsips.") O, vive Rabelais, who knew that you really do eat beefy diction; and further knew, as our toilet-idealists don't, that there are the same by-products from the assimilation of words as scrupulous theologians worried about, with regard to the Eucharist.

Shinny, shinny, shinny.

Meanwhile, Bill, let me here again say on the page, as I have said by phone: I am grateful to you, beyond words, for your good offices as regards the problems with relation to my mother.[199]

Sincerely,
K.B.

Am still, among the many interruptions, working back through your books again. I've got in deep enough to want to do a really thorough job. Tentatively, have decided on this procedure: Spin from <u>Al Que Quiere</u>. Try to formulate and illustrate every essential motivational strand in that book. Then treat the others in terms of it (noting modifications, transformations, additions, etc. in the later volumes). According to my interpretation, by the way, the element you are trying to specify in the prose theorizing of <u>Spring and All</u> is what I would call the "socio-anagogic" motive ("natural" things as seen through the perspective supplied by man's <u>social</u> pageantry).

I already have enough notes to do a dozen articles. But this thing is out to be as "definitive" as I can make it. Hence, its completion is still some weeks off. But, Deo Volente, it's going to be, and it's going to be by somebody who is ready to recognize the spirit and honesty of every step along your way. And by somebody, you baystard, who will have read you more closely than you ever read yourself. (Did <u>you</u> ever index the steps in your poems?)

[B]   [Andover]
January 22, 1952

Dear Bill,

> Prithee, I pray, do let you give me leave
> To speak in iambs pentametrically,
> Avowing you have robbed me of my rights
> In saying not how much it is I owe
> By way of bills to Honest Doctor Bill.
> (including not only the wear and tear, but also the phone calls.)
> Spick. Quos ego—

Otherwise, how are you?

Sincerely,
K.B.

Sorry I couldna get there, to hear your bleat.[200] But was keeping myself turned towards a song-and-dance I was shedyuled to give on the 17th.

[P]   [Rutherford]
Jan 23, 1952

Dear Ken,

      Your iambs are wasted on me

      redundant, excessive but still

      since you labor the point I shall see

      if Floss will not send you a bill.

I damned near DIED reading my 10 pages to the wolves.[201] I could hear them growling before I had got half way down the first page. I was nervous enough as it was, I had not taken a cocktail thinking I'd keep my tongue free, I didn't eat what was on my plate, but as the pressure mounted my old heart began to torment itself until it was a painful lump in my chest. I had to grit my teeth and grind out the words from a parched throat.

They wanted to kill me. That Irishman, Hackett, former editor of the <u>New Republic</u> I think was the only one who defended me at least vocally.[202] It was a stand off otherwise, half the guys went away scowling, the other grinning. I felt better as soon as I had finished the reading.

                                  Ho hum,

                                  Bill

[B]   [Andover]
January 25, 1952

Dear Bill,

Herewith the herewith. And many thanks for the bestirrings.

But what would you say about a guy who, after witnessing so many ultimate moments, testifies that he damn near killed himself trying to kill off blank verse?

Haint there many langwiches? And haint that one of them?

Thank God somebody else goes nuts once in a while, so that <u>I</u> can get a chance to sit back and feel normal. Up here in my study, I get damned sick of throwing myself down with a dull thud. How I'd have enjoyed sitting there watching the young man avow that all verse should be generically Rutherford, specifically W.C.W.

Remember the savant who, writing in English, tried to decide (without prejudice) whether it's more natural for the adjective to follow the noun, as in French, or to precede it, as in English. One guess as to what he concluded.

(Am in a jam for the time being. So have had to delay my lucubrations on you. But I'll get there, bejeez, I oath. And before long.)

Sincerely,
K.B.

Just happened to note title of a poem in recent <u>Hopkins Review</u>. "Posterity as Breath." Assuming that the title is accurate, here's what I would expect, in advance: "Posterity" would have furtive connotations of "posterior." "Breath" would thus be such kind of pneuma, or spirit, as is in humbler, non-cryptological parlance, called "farts." But heck, I enclose the poem herewith. Maintaining that the stranded dead whale is a toyd, whether the lady knows it or not. . . . Yours, as ever, for poetic treasure.

Come to think of it, the next poem seems to have its fingers in such substance, too. Or am I just a King Midas, with a Midas touch that can turn everything to such problematical gold?

[P]   [Rutherford]
May 25, 1952

Dear Ken,

I took the bull by the cock, without your permission, and signed your name to my nomination of Kenneth Beaudoin for the Gold Medal to be given by the Institute in poetry in 1953.[203] I'd like to see the guy get it which he hasn't the vaguest chance of doing so long as there are such pushers as blah blah blah blah is in the field.

Maybe I shouldn't a done this. If you object, say so and I'll withdraw your name.

Hope to see you during this open season.

Best,
Bill

[B]   [Andover]
[June 4, 1952]

Dear Bill,

Thanks for relevant documents.[204] Am pondering same, and letting my judgment mellow.

More soon.

Meanwhile, wd. say: I grant that the items are by a good workman.

But am still wondering, as regards the Official Trumpets. (Where's the scope? Or where's the succinct statuary? Learn me, dawlink.)

KB

[P]   [Rutherford]
June 11, 1952

Dear Ken,

When I'm able I'll come up and see you—before July 4. 'S a promise.

Meanwhile don't worry about the guy.[205] I'll withdraw the nomination. I don't even know if he was eligible but he didn't have the vaguest chance of getting it anyway. I was merely caught short and rather liked his informal approach. He's better than you may think, but I'll acknowledge you have to see more of his work.

A better guy, if I had thought of him or even known of him, is Louis Grudin whose "GUST ON SPRING STREET" is one of the really powerful poems in the modern language. (From THE OUTER LAND Dial Press.)[206] Why don't YOU nominate HIM? I'll be your backer.

Anyhow, forget Beaudoin.

Yrs,
Bill

[B]   [Andover]
June 12, 1952

Dear Bill,

Two words, in haste, to say: Am all in a flutter, slapping things together for my six-week stint at Indiana U., beginning in about a week.[207]

As for that golden medallity: There are three people who ought to get it in a row (I don't care about the order). They are Marianne Moore, Wallace Stevens, and you. (Or have some of you three been honorably bumped off already?) I understand that Marianne Moore has suggested Stevens. What I'd like to do is to suggest this club-offer. If you know of any way of my officially doing so, let me know. In the meantime, until that Necessary Business is out of the way, I don't think I'll plug for anybody else. (Years ago, I decided that I'd like to do a kind of "triptych" on you three. So far, I've only contrived somewhat of one-third, on M.M.[208] But, bejeez, I do avow: I'm taking all your books with me this summer, plus all the notes I have already husbanded or wived or whatever—and I'm going to try my damnedest both to get the article lined up and to try it out on the dog by peddling it in the classroom.)

If you ever read Chamisso's <u>Peter Schlemihl</u>, and have any brand new things to say about it, do rush them hither.[209] I am giving a public lecture on it (a subject of my own choosing) on June 25th, at Bloomington. (In case you haven't read it, it's about a gent who became separated from his shadow. I say as much in hopes that maybe you haven't read it, but might like to extemporize on Shadows, which is or are the morbid subject of my smiling talk.)

In case you can trek hither before I decamp (and here's hoping you can):

As things are now, we're expecting the McKeons (from U. of Chicago) for midday meal on Monday, June 16th (that makes a lot of ems).[210] So, if you and Floss could turn up then, all to the good. (We're having toikey.) Perhaps, should add that at this writing there are no local ailments. In the evening, we go to see the younger son enact a very thought-provoking major role in "Wild-Cat Willie Gets Girl-Trouble," a graduation play which has enticed me, as a Specialist in Sin–Ballix, because I am informed that at a strategic point Michael Wildcat Willie when shaving nearly cuts off his nose.

If you'd negotiate, may I repeat: Netcong 2–0709–J

In haste, to meet the mails.

Sincerely,

K.B.

[B]   [Andover]
November 11, 1952

Dear Bill,

Good luck, you old stinker.[211]

I love you just like nothing at all, and that's the greatest of all.

Could I persuade you to look on the other side, and read one of my prose poems?

Every honor you get gives me profound delight and makes me ashamed all over again, that I haven't got that article done yet. But I'll get it done. And the other side will make it apparent why I must, God willens.[212]

A toi,
K.B.

[P]   [Rutherford]
Nov 1/52

Dear Kenneth—Yes, do come to see us. Tuesday or Monday. Bill gets tired very easily, so I'll just say he wants to see people but not for long visits.[213] Looking forward then to next week.

Sincerely,
Floss

[P]   [Rutherford]
Nov 18/52

Dear Kenneth,

When I wrote the first card, Bill didn't think he was up to having you come to lunch. Now he says please come, or come late in the afternoon and stay for supper. I think lunch would be better, but I'm doing as he asks. He can't write himself, but he is going to in time. Again, until next week.

Floss

[P]   [Rutherford]
6/8/53

Dear Ken,

It was nice of Libbie to invite us for a day in the country. We have it in mind as soon as it shall be possible.

Meanwhile here is this—whatever it may mean. It comes, as I receive it, from E.P.[214]

What did you think of Elizabeth Bowen's address at the Institute affair— I saw you leaning back with your eyes closed as if listening.[215] I was very much moved but the audience seemed not paying much attention. So it goes.

Best,

Bill

[P]   [Rutherford]
[June 1953]

It may mean something that signatories are almost all from small "state" universities.[216]

ALARMED by the neglect of the Greek and Latin classics, millenary source of light and guide in judgment of ideas and forms in the occident; by lack of curiosity concerning what is current in contemporary foreign languages both in the west and in the orient; by growing carelessness in the use of language both private and public, and insensitiveness to the values of the literary arts which serve to maintain language in a healthy condition for civilized use; by the torpor of a pseudo-scholarship which does not mean any activity of the mind but mere retrospect.

WE URGE, TOWARD A REORIENTATION, that instead of hunting out the provenance of every bit of rubble used in the construction of literary works, the student of literature ask, and answer on the basis of evidence supplied by the works themselves, these three questions:

1. To what degree of awareness has the given author attained?

2. What was his aim and purpose in writing at all?

3. What part of his discoveries is of use now, or is likely to be of use tomorrow, in maintaining the life of the mind here or elsewhere?

Clark Emery (University of Miami)
Ashley Brown (Washington and Lee University)
Hugh Kenner (University of California)
Rudd Fleming (University of Maryland)
L. R. Lind (University of Kansas)
Amiya Chakravarty (University of Kansas)
H. M. McLuhan (University of Toronto)

W. F. Stead (Trinity College)

Margaret Bates (Catholic University of America)

Robert Stallman (University of Connecticut)

As our means of disseminating this statement are limited, we ask those who receive it to give it what publicity they can, especially by reprinting it in full, and to express their agreement or dissent in as lively a manner as possible. We request that any communications be addressed to: W. James, P.O. box 6964, Washington 20, D.C.

[B]   [Andover]
June 9, 1953

Dear Bill,

How.

Sure, you must come out, as soon as you feel like it. Can make the decision at the last minute, if you phone us (Netcong 2–0709–J). Or we can arrange it beforehand, whereat you might fare better banquet-wise.

We're expecting Dick Lewis and his wife up from Princeton soon (around the fifteenth).[217] It would be nice if you came then. But we don't yet know exactly when it will be. (Incidentally, there are few trains to Cranberry Lake now, a little less few to Netcong, but plenty to Dover.[218] So when you think of coming, look at all three spots along the line, take the nearest one if it fits your schedule, but if you have chosen one further down the line, we'll be glad to meet it. And in any case, we'll certainly use the whole range for your trip back. Difference between Cranberry Lake and Netcong is completely negligible, and difference between Netcong and Dover is so nearly so that we somewhat incline to think of that as the norm.)

I'm glad that I seemed to be listening to Elizabeth Bowen's address. For I was, most earnestly and respectfully, doing just that. But her slow pace, heroically undertaken to take account of her impediment and outwit it, got me so nervous that I simply couldn't follow the sentences. I tried again and again; and every bit I heard sounded good and solid; but I just couldn't stand the strain— so I kept getting lost, not after a few sentences just, but after a few words. So I still don't know what she said. But I do know that what she said wasn't the usual piffle that is at those doings usually pooped forth. I knew I was in the presence of something I should respect; I got that from the sequences I did contrive to follow. But honest to God, Bill, that pace, which was slower than Roosevelt and Churchill put together, got me so godam nervous that I could have followed her better had she been talking too fast in French or German. Perhaps if I hadn't been medicated besides—but with that dimension added, too . . . well . . .

But that brings us to our next subject. Thanks indeed for the Statement, urging toward a Reorientation. The three questions are not bad. But breathes there the question putter with soul so dead who never to himself hath said: "I can put three better ones"?

My three would be:

1. What equals what in a given work? (That is, what is "good," what "bad," what desirable, what undesirable, what heroic, what villainous, what cowardly, etc. I mean. I mean, not what judgments do we have about the work in these regards, but what judgments does the work itself seem to have about such matters?)

2. What is the work a cure for? (All works are "medicine." Otherwise, why bother to write them? But I won't try to explain that to you, for I realize that it's out of your field.)

3. What are the stages of the work's unfolding? (For by its process, the work "processes" us, if I may borrow from the most indecent modern cant.)

Am writing an article for which, at this point in my first draft, your item seems so fit that I think I'll snatch at it. I'll quote theirs, pay it my respects, then add the inevitable. However, as per the vid. sup.

Meanwhile, Bill, the pond is plenteous, the land is lush, and I for the moment am mellow, with pen in one hand and drink in the other. And, having turned off the radio, what more could I ask for, besides fame, and ten million dollars, and a bit less heart-consciousness?

May we somehow, Dopo, always forever flourish. Meanwhile, the best from here to you and Floss—and spick.

Sincerely,

K.B.

Yes, I thought Bowen was <u>very</u> good—chopping out bit by bit sentences that really flowed as she had written them. Your coming doesn't have to have any link with the <u>Lewis's</u> visit. Only any time we know in advance of anyone's coming whom you might like to see, we'll let you know. But hope you'll just come up on your own very soon.

Love,

Libbie

[P]   [Rutherford]
Oct 12/53

Dear Libbie,

If this coming Sunday is o.k. with you, we can drive up to Cranberry Lake with our Mr. Bill. Then if you could meet us at the store or the clubhouse, that would be wonderful. Possibly it would be best to phone you when we get there, as young Bill is often later in getting away than he plans, being an M.D. like his dad.[219]

So, if the weather is good and you are in a receiving spell, we'll see you Sunday. It will be a pleasure. I know you will find Bill greatly improved and barring the unforeseen.[220] I have hopes of even more return to normal.

Our best to you all.

Florence

[P]   [Rutherford]
11/4/53

Dear Ken,

The enclosed letter from Norman Pearson explains itself.[221] If you will risk your record and go to the trouble of forwarding it to him I am sure that it would be properly handled and promptly returned to you. I would be extremely grateful to you for the service.

Perhaps you would like to write direct to Pearson yourself. If so do so as it would be better than carrying on the necessary arrangements through a third person. But if you dislike the whole idea I'll tell Norman about it.

The expense of it will be my responsibility though I shall have to ask you to make the necessary initial outlay. We had a swell time at your place though as usual the very moderate amount of liquor I imbibed seems to have gone to my tongue. I apologize.

Best to Libbie and the boys.

Bill

31 October 1953

Dear Bill,

I may or may not know my own strength (which isn't much), but I obviously don't know Yale's (which can sometimes be surprising). At least I ought to have made full inquiries before writing Floss about my query of a copy of

Burke's recording of your poems. For I find that the Library is going in whole hog for recordings, in connection with what the university likes to call audio-visual education, and is assembling a vast series of collections of many sorts. They are eager to have this recording, or others like it; and if Burke could send me the wire recording, I will have it back to him promptly with a disk for him, and one for you too if you would like it. Yale's own copy they will take off on another wire, since they prefer the fidelity of wire transcripts, as well as finding them easier to store and make available to the students. They will play off Burke's once, and take the recordings off their own wire so as to save wear on his. You write him, or I'll write him, if you send me his address.

As to the Quevedo, we'll wait until my introduction is off the press, which should be in a few weeks.[222] Then we can see. I'll send you one, though you won't need to read it.

Have just been in Boston to a meeting of the New England College English Association, before which you spoke in Hartford, and heard your name on all sides. Samuel Morse French was very excited about the fine essay you sent him on Wallace S., and someone named Milton Hindus told me proudly that you had either written, or promised to write, something on Whitman for him.[223] They had a Whitman session on the program, which I chaired, or rather rocked.

Thirlwall sent me an immaculate precis of the <u>Paterson</u> material, which answers my immediate purposes nicely.[224] French told me that a part of the 5th part was either out, or just to appear, and thought it one of your <u>very</u> best. That's being alive in the finest sense! Let the juices keep on running!?

Yrs,

Norman

[P]   [Andover]
November 5, 1953

Dear Bill,

How.

Delighted to hear from you. Was afraid that I had tired you, with my ways that tire me. But, blee me, I recall no lingual laxations. (Have we ever thus indulged, really, since the easy early days? The days ohne souci, or sans Sorge. Oh, were there ever such . . .)

But as regards The Record, tell 'em I am Imperious. If Pearson will arrange for me to bring it into NYC, at some Official Place, I'll be glad to participate.

(Only requirement being that they must agree to excise <u>my</u> horrendously nasalized interpositions. Can I be wholly as bad as <u>that</u>?)

Under these conditions, there'll be no charge—though I guess somebody ought to buy me a drink. But I won't mail it, or otherwise ship it—and my experience with these machines leads me to think that they should record from my machine, which I would bring with me. (Incidentally, my machine is not wire, but tape. A Brush.)

This is the first time in my life I've ever had a chance to be a prima donna. And it's wonderful. Jeez, what you poets get away with! As regards you, I'm all for it. But when I think of politics like Tate . . . oof![225]

Meanwhile, am preparing for a lecture on Bentham, whose attempts to drive the Imaginative element out of language were much more imaginative than most poets' attempts to keep it in.[226]

Best greetings to you, and Floss, and the family.

Sincerely,

As regards a discussion we were having: "Midnight" wouldn't be an ideal example of an accent on a short syllable, since the two consonants, "dn" would make a long quantity, so far as Latin scansion is concerned. To be a perfect example, it would have to be "mi'night," if there were such. Opening <u>Paterson</u>, I note: "To make a start, / out of particulars."[227] "Particulars" would be a perfect example of an accent on a short syllable. Heck—not perfect example. To be perfect, the "u" of "particular" should be short, since long "u" has a "y" sound that slows up the "c" by adding to it. Though the "o" of "of" is short, the syllable would be counted long in Latin scansion because of the f-p. So I guess "out of" would be, in English, something midway between a trochee and a spondee (as regards the kind of tests I had in mind). "-ulars" would be midway between an iamb and a spondee. By mere accent, the first line would be merely two iambs. But by quantitative tests the sounds would be much subtler. For instance, the long "o" of "to" would place "to make" midway between iamb and spondee. Lots of chances here, yes?

[P]   [Rutherford]
May 11, 1954

Dear Ken & Libbie,

Here it is spring again—an inch of snow on the ground and two blankets on the bed. Hail to thee blithe spirit! even though it may not be the skylark!

We'll have to be seeing you one of these days. By the way, have you read Ezra Pound's translation from the Greek of Sophocles, "The Women of Trachis" (in Hudson Review) very interesting.[228]

The Columbia Broadcasting Co., it may not be the right name, has been after me to make a recording of a reading of my poetry. It came to me that I might ask you if I could not induce them to take their apparatus up to your farm and do it there using the reading that you have already made—and which I shall never be able to do for anyone again.[229] I haven't yet got their consent to do so but they may call up any day now. I want to be ready for them.

Apart from that how are you both? Recently we journeyed to the national capitol (Not to see the prize ape recently active there) for a short stay of just three days. I had been given a commission to write an article on an exhibition of American Primitives.[230] Very impressive. Those old boys (and gals) had a lot to put down in paint about the world about them. I was thrilled with them and only hope I did them credit. The article is to be printed in one of those swanky art magazines costing a dollar or two, see if I can get it to you.

There have been other activities on the writing front which I'll report on time. Poetry has accepted the Coda of a long, 30 p., three-part poem which will not be published till next year, etc., etc.[231] It's slow work but after all it's only to keep busy that I write at all so I have no kick—the panic occasionally comes over me that at any moment I may find myself with no more projects to occupy my seething brain and then—as in the past, all my life—I turn and look behind me to try and see how far the hounds are behind me.

It's heartening to realize that I still have two or three (or more) friends I can turn to when I want to spill over. Is your older boy at college yet. I occasionally think of him and his younger brother wishing them luck. My older boy's wife expects a baby any day now—he said it is not fair to bring up an only child: most men do not look for such an excuse for their rutting. Same to you.

Best luck,
Bill

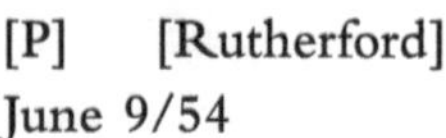

[P]   [Rutherford]
June 9/54

Dear Libbie,

Can't remember if Kenneth is here or there just now, so will you be kind enough to call it to his attention? (The enclosed letter.) I suppose M. Hindus wants to know for sure if K.B. is going to add his bit.[232]

Still hoping to get up to see you all some day. We'll make it eventually!

Floss

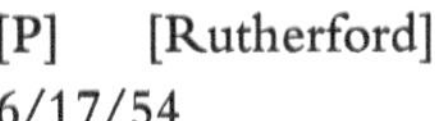

[P]   [Rutherford]
6/17/54

Dear Ken,

How did you make out with the Librarian of Rutgers? Did he arrange to have the record of my reading re-recorded? Has there been any hitch to the proceedings? Lemme know the details.

And what about the man from Brandeis? Are you going to write the note for him on Whitman? Drop him a note so that I may be able to face him.

? ? ? ?

Wishing you the same.

Your pal with a question mark about his neck,

(better than a dead albatross)

w.c.w.

No! I'll be damned if I do

Bill

[B]   [Andover]
July 19, 1954

Dear Bill,

How.

Is this, the herewith, a sin? Trying to decide whether I could make precise my feeling that Whitman's <u>first lines</u> are always different in rhythm from the typical <u>developments</u> in his verse, I copied out a batch of first lines.[233]

And when I looked at them "en masse," I saw that, with but a bit of rear-ranging, they could be made into a medley.

(Am in a Whitman swirl at the moment. Have done the first draft of an essay on the <u>Vistas</u>, am now trying in general to sum up the <u>Leaves</u>, and then for a wind-up I'd like to analyze the "Lilacs." But I still am not sure whether I can meet the deadline, though sometimes I am. Do you know if anyone has

made anything of the fact that the trinity of images in the Lincoln poem—
lilacs, star, and singing bird—are scent, sight, and sound respectively? References to scent are rare in Whitman, though there are indications that his leaves
of grass may have had strong olfactory connotations for him personally. Some
passages clearly show a strong identification of scent with woman, too, though
he also liked the sniff of his own armpits, he says. Your star-lines that Stevens
quotes, by the way, are much better than the ones he writes on them, though
his are quite good, too.)[234]

Yours for ensemble-Individuality,

Sincerely,

K.B.

Everything is in a fantastic jam hereabouts at the moment. Granny had a stroke
recently, and is still in bad shape, though slowly recovering somewhat. Carpenters have ripped a chunk of our house apart, for patching and an addition. And
I am uncomfortably trying to pick my way through a jumble of notes, while
leaving enough mail unanswered to complete my wretchedness at public relations. Oof!

Though savants have denied that the bird Whitman heard singing really
was a thrush, we should certainly take him at his word when he says that it
was a hermit.

Don't bother to return the Whitmaniana.

First O Songs for a prelude
by W. Omnific Whitman
As I ponder'd in silence,
Starting from fish-shaped Paumanok where I was born;
As I lay with my head in your lap, Camerado,
Thou who hast slept all night upon the storm;
Vigil strange I kept on the field one night,
This moment yearning and thoughtful sitting alone.

Over the carnage rose prophetic a voice
From pent-up aching rivers.
A march in the ranks hard-prest, and the road unknown,
Spirit whose work is done—spirit of dreadful hours!

(Now list to my morning's romanza, I tell the signs of the Answerer.
An old man bending I come upon new faces.)

Lo, the unbounded sea!
Flood-tide below me! I see you face to face!
In cabin'd ships at sea,
Out of the cradle endlessly rocking,
Over the Western sea hither from Niphon come
As I ebb'd with the ocean of life,
Facing west from California's shore,
Rise, O days, from your fathomless deeps, till you loftier, fiercer
sweep.
Give me the splendid silent sun with all his beams full-dazzling.
O to make the most jubilant song!
A song for occupations!
(Ah, little recks the laborer.)
A song of the rolling earth, and of words according
I hear America singing, the varied carols I hear.
These I singing in spring collect for lovers,
Trickle drops! my blue veins leaving!
America always! Always our old foliage!

Come, said the Muse;
Come, my tan-faced children.

I sing the body electric,
Weapon shapely, naked, wan,
Scented herbage of my breast,
Myself and mine gymnastic ever,
Full of life now, compact, visible,
I celebrate myself and sing myself;
Me imperturbe, standing at ease in Nature.

On journeys through the States we start,
Among the men and women, the multitude,
In paths untrodden,
The prairie grass dividing, its special odor breathing—
Not heaving from my ribb'd breast only,
Afoot and light-hearted I take to the open road.

You who celebrate bygones,
Are you the new person drawn toward me?

Whoever you are, I fear you are walking the walks of dreams.
Behold this swarthy face, these gray eyes;
Passing stranger! you do not know how longingly I look upon you.

To get betimes in Boston town I rose this morning early,
When lilacs last in the door-yard bloom'd
On the beach at night
By blue Ontario's shore.

Respondez! Respondez!
Here, take this gift—
Come, I will make the continent indissoluble.
O take my hand, Walt Whitman!
As Adam early in the morning
To the garden anew ascending.

[P]   [Rutherford]
July 24, 1954

Dear Ken,

Here in the country by the sea—your letter was forwarded to me (on rereading this, it sounds like the beginning of a Millay sonnet, I must be losing my manhood even more rapidly than I suspect). I write to urge you not to fall by the way but to complete the essay on Whitman before the deadline shall arrive.[235] I count on you to do this. You wouldn't let an old pal down. I would love to read what you have to say and would count it a privilege to appear in the same book with you.

No, I never saw mention of the trilogy being associated with the 3 senses.[236] Good for you. It is interesting.

That's all I have to say. I hope the reconstruction is going well. Find time to finish the article is the ardent wish of your co-defendant,

Bill
William Carlos Williams

[B]   [Andover]
[May 4, 1955]

Dear Bill,

Many thanks indeed for your generous note. And thanks to Floss, too. And best luck to you on your trip.[237] (Me, I'm now getting ready for a one-night stand at Cornell this Friday.) When you get back, we hope that we can arrange for another visit from you and the Thirlwalls. Here's looking forward to then.

Sincerely,

K.B.

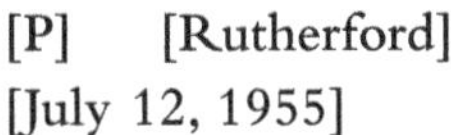

[P] [Rutherford]
June 29, 1955

Dear Ken,

This ain't the letter I promised you. That's coming when I find the time to think for a time first.

This is merely to bear a request for a young woman that wants a recommendation from you for a Guggenheim fellowship. Blame it on me, she never even thought of you as a possible sponsor. If you receive the request, after you have seen her work, act on it as you think best.

The name is Denise Goodman.[238] I think she has the makings.

We had a good time last week or so ago that Sunday—it might have been in the time of Aristotle since it is part of the infinite past. We have been talking of your proposed trip to California after your younger son goes to college next year. Good luck to you and Libbie at that time. Be sure to stop off at Santa Fe on your way! You ain't seen nothin yet.

See you again as soon as we are able.

Best,

Bill

[P] [Rutherford]
[July 12, 1955]

Dear Ken,

You had every reason, from what I have since discovered in your book of poems,[239] to refuse to accept my casual opinion of them given in such an off-hand manner when I was at the farm. I have been reading them again as I told you I would and have been much moved, I have just started to reread them beginning at the back of the book with the "Rhapsody under the Autumn Moon" which I find now to be seriously good as anything I have ever read. If I ask you to change the insignificant inversion in the 6th line[240] you'll know how to take the poem being so superbly well conceived and executed. Beautiful work. I was full of admiration for what you had done and made available for me and for anyone who can read and enjoy such a poem.

Now that I have begun I'll go back slowly as I am able and what I discover I'll tell you about as I am able. I like the controlled freedom of the line you have used in the poem of which I am speaking. Very good.

Best,

Bill

[B]   [Andover]
July 18, 1955

Dear Bill,

Heckaroo, that's a bonus! Many thanks for the kind words. But you violated the rules. The rules were: You were simply to tell me what you considered to be the "soft spots" and why. I wasn't fishing for some more kind words. I was fishing for some statements about your own aversions.

Point is:

The one claim I make for the book is that it has brought the most unusual diversity of responses, with some persons even loathing what others have said that they prefer. So, in keeping with my Criticaster's Guile, I have begun trying to use it as a Personnel Director might, to size up the characters of my subjects. Now I've probably spoiled the magic, but that's what I had in mind. In briefee weefy, I had hoped to get some formulas about yourself by yourself, while you were supposedly busy formulating me. Then you go and spoil things by thinking that you had hurt my feelings, and reporting on things that you like.

Jeez, strange as it may seem, I ain't averse to your suddenly liking something I wrote, and saying so. As a matter of fact, God bless you, even if you did violate the rules.

May you rot in hell, however, for giving my name to the lady poet. I agree with you that she is good. (Above all, I liked her description of the kids getting out of school and busting loose. But it's a very subversive idea—and since she published it, I trust that she already has a dossier in the F.B.I. files.) My bellyache is that, when I get to writing up one of those things for Moe,[241] I spend more godamn time on it than needed to write a chapter, and then, to cap it off, my batting average there has been pretty rotten, for years. In any case, now that the damage has been done, count me in. And my song in her behalf will be as sonorous as my cracked voice permits.

Wd. say: it was good to see you and your party, and to see you fresh from the benignity of being sunned upon by audiences. Best greetings, and to Floss. And I think you still owe me that report on soft spots.

Sincerely, personnelly

[P]   [Rutherford]
[July 19, 1955]

Dear Ken,

It'll be a hard job to tell you <u>exactly</u> what I mean.[242] That is why I haven't written you in detail before this and that is, I understand, <u>exactly</u> why you want to hear from me. It has to do with advances in the art of writing down a poem, as I conceive it, over what has been done in the past—even the very recent past. The way you think about a poem, the way you conceive of it in relation to the thought it contains, betrays you.

After all you cannot look in my writing for anything but the most advanced feeling for the art that I am capable of and you cannot look to my appreciation of your own work being my intimate and most understanding friend from any other standpoint.

To take a flier, I am completely through with the concept and the practice of blank verse. The counting of the five regular syllables makes me grind my teeth. So that in your later, longer poems when you adopt the form I can hardly read what you have written without a feeling of defeat.[243] I don't care what you're saying, it means nothing to me. That is why I praised in the poem I spoke of in last letter the loose treatment of the lines as being so refreshing.[244]

And the whole effect of, taking such a form as blank verse, and using it to contain a poem as one would contain evaporated milk in a can, is wrong. A poem is a construction and not what the poet has to say. That is a tough nut to crack but I believe and trust that you can crack it.

In other words, all my objections to your poems when they exist have to do with technique as if that can be spoken of separately from the body of the work itself—which is impossible. I'll send you a copy of one of my latest poems, in fact, the last—written 5 months ago and to be contained in my last book. If it means anything to you or not, keep it for as far as I know it may well be my last poem.

Cheerio! and pip pip!—I am going to devote myself to some prose from this time on as I am able. Best to Libbie.

Yours till hell freezes,

Bill

TRIBUTE TO THE PAINTERS
  Satyrs dance!
     all the deformities take wing
       centaurs
 leading to the rout of the vocables
    in the writings
of Gertrude
    Stein—but
      you cannot be
an artist
    by mere ineptitude.

The dream
    is in pursuit!
The neat figures of
    Paul Klee
      fill the canvass
but that
    is not the work
      of a child.

The cure began, perhaps,
    with the abstractions
      of Arabic art
Dürer
    with his Melancholy
      was ware of it—
the shattered masonry. Leonardo
    saw it
      the obsession
and ridiculed it
    in La Gioconda.
     Bosch's
congeries of tortured souls and devils
    who prey upon them
      fish

swallowing
    their own entrails
Freud
    Picasso
        Juan Gris
The letter from a friend
    saying:
        For the last
three nights
    I have slept like a baby
        without
liquor or dope of any sort!
    we know
        that a stasis
from a chrysalis
    has stretched its wings—
        like a bull
or the Minotaur
    or Beethoven
        in the scherzo
of his 9th Symphony
    stomped
        his heavy feet

I saw love
    mounted naked on a horse
        on a swan
the back of a fish
    the blood-thirsty conger eel
        and laughed
recalling the New
    in the pit
        among his fellows
when the indifferent chap
    with the machine gun
        was spraying the heap.
He
    had not yet been hit
        but smiled
comforting his companions.

Dreams possess me
>and the dance
>>of my thoughts
involving animals
>the blameless beasts
and there came to me
>just now
>>the knowledge of
the tyranny of the image
>and how

>men
in their designs
>have learned
>>to shatter it
whatever it may be
>that the trouble
>>in their minds
shall be quieted
>and put to bed
again.
>>>>>W.C.Williams

[P]   [Andover]
September 5, 1955

Dear Bill,

Confession. You had carefully clamped the pages of your poem in the wrong order. And it had me puzzled until this blunt truth dawned on me.

Now, getting them straight, I see that it is a very lovely poem, and very moving. (psst: though Marianne Moore warns against using "very.") Thanks much indeed for letting me see it, and letting me keep the copy.

I think I understand your resistance to corseted verse. The kind of straight-forwardness, or "naturalness," you aim at is to be got only by the methods you have so well developed. So far as your own work is concerned, you prove your point irrefutably.

My only faint answer is that there are other kinds of effects to be got. In my "Liber Momentorum,"[245] for instance, 94btm–95tp, the three lines at the top of p. 95 are substantially blank verse, concealed somewhat by the fact that the first three syllables are printed as a line by themselves. It seems to me that this particular kind of formalism is proper, as an offshoot from the preceding paragraph of prose. And something similar takes place, in the shift from free verse to rhymed, corseted verse on my "Invective and Prayer" item, on pp. 32–33.

Similarly, it seems to me that even today one may have a sonnet mood, and at such times let him write a sonnet. Or he may have a jog-trot contemplative mood—and then let him do post-Wordsworthian blank verse.

I am aware that I speak merely as a dilettante, hence sans authority. But frankly, if I could write the sort of thing I most urgently want to write, it would be a piece of highly fluctuant prose (ranging from narrative and fantasy to the most abstruse abstract reasoning) interspersed with versifying interludes that sometimes got the kind of effect you get so well and sometimes got wholly formalistic effects (as with Baudelaire's mighty "La Geante" sonnet, or a Goethean ding-dong lyric, for instance the formalistic yet dreamlike musicality of Mignon's song, "Kennst du das Land"). If I could get you to agree that such a form is allowable, then next I'd plead for individual corseted forms as fragments of such a totality.

Here's betting you'd like a lot the last chapter of Edward Sapir's book on Language (Harcourt, Brace).[246] I copy out this neatly summarizing bit: "Latin and Greek verse depends on the principle of contrasting weights; English verse, on the principle of contrasting stresses; French verse, on the principles of number and echo; Chinese verse, on the principles of number, echo, and contrasting pitches. Each of these rhythmic systems proceeds from the unconscious dynamic habit of the language, falling from the lips of the folk." He defines thought as "nothing but language denuded of its outward garb." And language is "the collective art of expression."

It was good to see you all the other day, and I hope you're none the worse for wear to do with the trip. Also, the visit came just right for me, as I had finished with all my odds and ends of work, and was ready to turn in the direction of preparations for the teaching bout (which begins on the twelfth). I cleared the slate by the simple but drastic decision to forget about my book until the long vacation this winter. Meanwhile here I sit, drinkless at cocktail hour, but mildly Serpasilious, though not unmindful that the smell of ripening grapes rises to rebuke my a-Dionysiac lethargy.

Best greetings to you and Floss—and let's plan for another visit.

Sincerely,

Your reference to dreamlike thoughts of animals interested me a lot. Why not try to pin them all down? (Or perhaps you are doing just that.) I once started to tell Harold Rosenberg about a dog.[247] He interrupted me by saying "Oh, I know what you're going to say. You're going to say that dogs have the characters of their owners." I was going to tell him about a very mean dog I once had.

[P] [Rutherford]
Sept. 7, 1955

Dear Ken,

Thanks for the tip out of Marianne's cookbook, it is a good one that I'll profit by.[248] I'll never use "very" again without scrutinizing the context carefully. It's amazing how careless or asleep we can be about those things. By the way, I never hear from the Moore any more I wonder what, if anything, has happened. She used to send me her books whenever published and I always did the same for her. Has she outstripped me in the number of her publications; therefore? I refuse to change my ways unless convinced that my contributions, and someone convinces me of it, are no longer welcome. We should see each other oftener.

Keep the poem.[249] I meant it for you when I sent it.

Of course you are right, there are many ways to write a poem. All I meant to say is that I do not like blank verse as a recourse when I face the modern poem. There is so much that should come first. Undoubtedly I am prejudiced in favor of a more experimental approach. There is so little time, why repeat the forms of the past?

I am so harassed with or by the serious guys with their intellectual troubles that they think anything they say in whatever form they <u>think</u> they are adopting so long as they are permitted to speak at all, that they forget that the form of the poem is the poem . . . that I have become sensitive, hypersensitive, to a very common situation. (That "very" again).

I'd rather not write at all than use an—a spent form in making or attempting to make my constructions. Can that be why M.M. is through with me? since she cannot agree with my experiments? It is along the line of our discussion.

But I'm too impatient. I detest doctrinaire formula worship which it is not when a friend is using a convenient verse for to speak his mind. The fault is mine, but you so pleased me in your epigrammatic verses and the one longer piece[250] of which we have already spoken that I became impatient when I thought you slow to win the rest of my approval. After all you are my friend, I wanted you to succeed in everything, even to teach me in my own art.

It was a good afternoon, I wish it could be repeated. I wish for impossible things: that we could communicate in ways that would surpass ordinary communication. That is where I feel my inadequacy: I'm not up to it any more—if I was ever up to it, but these engineers and physicists that ignore the profundities and simplicities of the human intellect give me a swift pain in the ass.

Bog, go bury your bone,

Bill

Tell Libbie, I'm working day and night—with necessary layoffs for recuperation—on that "long short story" I outlined for her and hope to have it finished in a month—at least a first draught of it.[251] I warn her that I am feeding on her warmth. Where else shall we find comfort but out of a woman? Many women! Ha!

W.

[B]   [Andover]
Sept. 8, 1955

Dear Floss and Bill,

I think this is going to work out fine. Have you any objections to my proceeding along the lines in my letter to Hannah?[252] Do you have any people who would definitely want a copy of the record—you mentioned some fellow up at Yale, I believe, who might be interested?

It was good to have you here last week. We shall see you again when we all go up to Thirlwall's some time later in the fall—but if you can get a ride with your young ones any time do come up again sooner.

Love,

Lib.

Sept. 8, 1955

Dear Hannah,

Many thanks for all the information about the records, and all your trouble in getting it, and in such good detail so that we know just what is involved. I think we should go ahead with the Audio-Video people. I will play the recording carefully again, and get an idea about the exact time it takes, maybe getting Butch[253] to do a little cutting in between pieces to make it fit.

The whole business of an organization to sell the records won't come up at this time at all, as the only reason we want the acetate made is to get the perishable tape recording onto a matrix, to avoid rerecording and the terrific loss in fidelity when this is done.

The financing of the $54.25 can, I think, be easily accomplished by having people who want copies of the record divide up the total cost. If we had say 15 records run off, two to go to the Library of Congress, and then collect $5. a piece for the others from people who want a copy (I can think of four or five among our close friends who would be eager to do this)—the cost would be covered, and the acetate could go to Bill for his use in the future, whenever he wants it.

Would the Institute be willing to pay ten bucks for its two records, or would it insist upon the wholesale price?

I'll clear with Bill, and make a careful time check on the recording, and write you again in a couple of days.

As I said before, this recording is really good; much better I think than any of the other readings by the modern poets—it brings out the character of the reader marvelously, and adds a lot to the understanding of the poems too. We wouldn't be so anxious about getting it on permanent records, if it weren't so good.

Some day when all has calmed down here, I'll write you a <u>personal</u> letter and bring you up to date on family activities.

Love,

Lib

⤳

[B]   [Andover]
Oct. 6, 1955

Dear Bill,

I have disappointing news about the recording. Rickie Leacock took the tape into some of his experts in this field with the idea of filtering out machine noise and polishing up the sound for recording, and they say that the original recording is made so light that when it is blown up sufficiently for recording on regular records, the noise of the machine makes too much inter-ference—and that because the recording was made so light, it can't be blown up successfully.[254] But they can make duplicate tapes, just like the one we have, without any loss in fidelity, and I am asking them to make one for you. This you will have for use if anyone does decide a record can be made of it. This is all the more disappointing because these fellows in the movie and recording business thought the reading was very very interesting.

Before I got this report from Rickie, I had found out from a good recording company, that the making of the stamp and records from it would have been around or over a hundred dollars, because of its length, etc.

So we are just about back where we were in the beginning, which burns me up. Except we shall have a couple of good tapes to preserve the reading just as it is. I'm passing on this info to Hannah Josephson, asking her if a tape could serve her purposes.

The commercial reproducing company says that the usual way of reproducing now, is on tapes not records. But of course this won't serve people who have record players, and not recorders. So again *#%$_&%*) ("_$&%'_-(with your four-letter word vocabulary, you shouldn't have any trouble filling in for me.)

We received your beautiful little new book[255] and it is very fine indeed both inside and out. KB has already read it and will write you soon.

We hope to see you before too long. Love to you and Floss.

Lib

He was <u>very</u> pleased with long poem, which I have not yet read.[256]

[B]   [Andover]
November 7, 1955

Dear Bill,

Yes, you were right. I see it now. The kind of thing you were after in this new book (and the kind of thing you got beautifully) makes iambic pentameter seem almost ludicrously malapropos.

The first time I read the "Asphodel" poem,[257] it seemed so completely <u>dissolving</u> that I actually began to feel faint. All the little nodules of fight had been melted, turned into a succession of breathings-out (each tercet being in effect one such moment). The most disarming kind of utterance one could imagine. Ironically, however, your "titular" moment is iambic tetrameter:

> Of asphodel, that greeny flower,
> I come, my sweet, to sing to you!

What shall we make of that?

I have delayed writing you, not just because I have been busy (I have been being fantastically busy with the schoolwork), but also because of embarrassment. This is not the sort of book that one can merely be "complimentary" about. It is a profoundly moving book. And everything I started to say seemed inadequate, so inadequate that I couldn't bring myself to say it. Indeed, I'd like to avoid the issue still longer—but I'd better say something, just to avoid misunderstandings.

The coda of the "Asphodel" poem sums up racingly. Its swift introduction of all the essential elements (each one dwelt on just long enough) is marked by a mixture of fervor and skill that has the quality of perfect fulfillment. Here, I felt, the sheer Logic of Language was speaking, using you—one might say— as its medium, and under the sign of a brave naturalism (poet merging with scientist).

Of the shorter poems, I most preferred "The Sparrow."[258] Its accuracy, its comicality, the poet's democratic identification with a mutt among birds: that all makes one feel good. In the first poem, were you in effect saying that, as the negress was of a marigold tinge, so marigolds are negroid? (I mean: as regards the sheerly visual dimension of the poem, not its possible figuring of a dark realm beyond the "objects.")[259]

Incidentally, might I ask whether, in the closing lines of "Asphodel," you in any way thought, however fleetingly, of your earlier lines on the saxifrage? I refer to the associations that are by you connected with "and begun again to penetrate / into all crevices." (Jeez, all of a sudden I realize, too, that the refrain you quote from Spenser's "Prothalamion" is iambic pentameter—and fits quite neatly as parenthesis to your remarks on "the pomp and ceremony/ of marriage." It is another kind of "summarizing" line, like your "titular" statement.)[260]

This is just "on account," Bill. More later. And I am all the more determined that I must pull all my notes together and try to finish up that essay I've been planning for, on your verse. I owe it to myself to get that done. Meanwhile, I at least have the satisfaction of plugging for you with my students. One of my "counselees" took a spontaneous shine to you—and we are discussing your verse in our conference periods. The class itself I have been able to "alert" only secondarily this term (via Marianne Moore's pages on you in Predilections),[261] since we are now stressing other aspects of the subject. But I hope it will be different next term, when we stress Poetics.

Meanwhile, whenever the thought of our adventures abroad makes me uneasy, I am heartened all over again by the thought of your verse (and of your prose, too, for that matter). I tell myself with patriotic fervor: There must be something sound in a country that could produce a guy like that.

But to my chores (and they are manifold). More anon. And best greetings, and to Floss.

Sincerely,

K.B.

Also, I'll send some, more formal, lines to McDowell.[262]

[B]   November 7, 1955

Dear Bill,

Here's the note I wrote to McDowell.[263] Heck, it's got a lotta woodenhood. But I figure that some of the spots, taken out here and there, might be serviceable.

Incidentally, here's a paragraph in a letter by someone I don't even know, written to someone else I barely know. Most of what this writer says has to do with technicalities of printing, typesetting machines, and the like. I never read anything so circumstantial. He evidently lives happily in a world of minute technological particulars. And the genius of his attitude shows through here, too:

Just the other day I was looking at some pictures you took at my mother's home in Everett. You and I are trying to balance a croquet ball on the head of a mallet. Helen and Jean and my mother are bent over looking for four-leaf clovers. She was only a little girl at that time. It doesn't seem possible that so many years have passed.

(The "she," as made clear by the previous paragraph, is Jean.)

How time does fly,

K.B.

Mr. David McDowell, Editor
Random House, Inc.
457 Madison Avenue
New York 22, N.Y.

Dear Mr. McDowell,

Thank you greatly indeed for sending me a copy of William Carlos Williams's new book, <u>Journey to Love</u>.

Since receiving it, I have read it several times, both for itself and in connection with a study of Bill Williams's poetry on which I have been taking notes for some years.

I can well understand why he lays so much store by the long "Asphodel" poem. The trouble is: I found it so profoundly moving, everything I would say about it seems inadequate.

To begin with: Its rhythm has dissolved all the little nodules of fight, becoming like a perfect succession of breathings-out. And its coda sums up racingly. The swift introduction of all the essential elements (each one dwelt on just long enough) is marked by a mixture of fervor and skill that has the quality of complete fulfillment. Here, I felt, the sheer Logic of Language was speaking, using the poet as its medium, and under the sign of a brave naturalism (poet merging with scientist). The whole is a retrospect that has the quality of a call towards the future.

Of the shorter poems, I most preferred "The Sparrow." Its accuracy, its comicality, the poet's democratic identification with a mutt among birds: that all makes one feel good.

This is summational poetry, yet done face to face, wholly without official posturing. And out of simple things, it builds the visionary.

Here are some ad interim notions that occur to me now. If any of them can be of use, you're welcome to them. But it is a fact, alas! that all these remarks seem woefully wooden, when I turn back to the verse itself.

Sincerely,
Kenneth Burke

[B]   [Rutherford]
Nov. 17, '55

Dear Ken & Libbie,

You, Libbie, have nothing to feel self conscious about in appearing in your swimming suit among company. The photos were quite interesting. All I remember of the incident was the soreness of my tail from sitting slightly askew on the hard ground for an hour or more. The snap-shots didn't show THAT.

Thanks, Ken for the notice on my book of poems, I never have met up with a publication that has happened with as little fanfare as that one. Aside from a simple notice in the <u>Times</u> two lines, on the publication date it was as if a mere garbage scow had been launched. Private letters from friends is all I have to show for it and not too many from them. So your enthusiastic letter was welcome. Something you might enjoy hearing about is the (relative) popularity of "The Sparrow" among my male friends: in addition to your liking the poem, Win Scott of Santa Fe also likes and spoke of it.[264]

We've just been out to Buffalo on the Phoebe Snow, quite a come down for Floss after her two month's plane ride of last summer all over the west coast.[265] The cars are unconscionably slow after air travel though even Floss was inclined to hesitate after she had read of that latest wreck outside of Denver. When she heard that it was brought on by sabotage she was relieved, no reason why she may not travel by air in the future.

I'm plugging away at the compositions I outlined for Libbie when I saw you last. There were three of them—including the play which may never be written though when I was in Buffalo I saw the nurse who is to be one of the protagonists and questioned her about one of the minor female characters who is nevertheless important to me.[266] What I am actually working on now is the first of the short stories. It's going slowly ahead, all too slowly. The second story I haven't even touched.

The weather at least continues ideal, the bareness of these fall days with their clear days is to my taste perfect. Take care of yourselves.

Bill

[B]   [Andover]
November 19, 1955

Dear Bill,

Godammit, Bill. Here, after having been so long in acknowledging your book, here, after that apparently unpardonable delay, here I am writing you, and hoping for a soon answer even. If you think I should simply go f-q myself, I'll humbly accept your judgment, and act on it to the best of my abilities. But I dare fondly hope otherwise.

Point is:

I have a student who is studying poetry with me. Did I say "studying poetry"? No, rather, she is studying one poet; namely, yourself.

She likes your poetry so much, it is a delight to work with her. And though her major is chemistry (which marks her as a rarity at Bennington), she is showing an unusual perception in her analysis of your verse. She is a very genuine student, and her way of liking you is a tribute both to you and to herself.

Well, anyhow, after going over your poem, "The Birth of Venus," we were left with two questions.[267] First, in the last line of the first stanza, we weren't quite sure how to interpret "without cost." Second, in the first and third stanzas, you have a relation between small waves and pebbles; in the last line of the first stanza, there is a corresponding relation between "long swell" and rock. And we wondered what you had in mind, as regards these two sets. It's understandable why, if pebbles went with wavelets, rocks would go with swells; but just what might be the relation between pebbles-wavelets and rock-swell? (Incidentally, they seem like an imagistic analogue of the relation between particular and general.)

If you felt like giving us a helping hand on those points, we'd be grateful and entranced. So I'm sending you this note, just on the chance that you might feel inclined and have the time.

(Incidentally again, the relation is not just between long swell and rock, but long swell and rocks's teeth. But we particularly noticed rock because the place of "rocks" in the opening poem of the volume (<u>Collected Later Poems</u>) made it one of the words for us to watch especially.)

Here's hoping you'll feel moved to spick. Anyhow, best greetings. (The more I think of your "Sparrow" poem, the more felicitous it seems to me.)[268]

Sincerely, and to Floss,

K.B.

⌒

[P]   [Rutherford]

Christmas card for 1955—

To you all—we did enjoy our visit with you and wish it were easier to do it oftener—

Bill and Floss

⌒

[P]   [Rutherford]
Sept. 26/56

Dear Ken,

We thank you and Libbie for a good time last Saturday, it was a superb day as to weather. I must have Druid blood in my veins nothing makes me happier than a walk alone in the woods such a walk not of very serious proportions but as enjoyed beyond the cleared place back of your house and garden. I came out across the road from what you still call the barn and ran into your daughter, I didn't realize she was there. Jack didn't know she is a professor at C.C.N.Y. and is going to look her up.[269]

As to that operation, see DeBell at once and get it done. Don't forget to mention that you want a local.

Well I guess that's all I have to say for the moment, we had a good time and enjoyed a delicious meal, I'm not much on the drinks nowadays if I ever was but they also went the way of their kind with the same effect that Socrates and his friends enjoyed before us but we didn't loosen up the way we have done in the past. Maybe it was your feeling of loss in the absence of your two boys away at school that caused it. Who can tell? After I have reached 80 there may come other times if not long before that.

I have always heard that old age is garrulous, <u>tien!</u> Have a successful operation. Best to Libbie.

Bill

[B]   [Andover]
[1956]

Dear Floss and Bill,

Yes, do please scold us. We have it coming to us. But the guy was a "prominent" New York surgeon with forty years of experience, and he had treated KB for tension and knew and understood the problems involved—so we thought. Some day I must have a long talk with Bill and find out just what the "relatives of the patient" can do when everyone in the hospital who comes in to see the patient says he needs attention badly "but we can't do anything for him until the doctor sees him," and this goes on for twelve hours (third day after the operation with only one visit from the Dr. early the 2nd day before the swelling set in), and when I call the Dr. I get his wife who says don't worry, you know he is a difficult patient and a very tense person and I say—that's just why I AM worried—and finally the Dr. has KB's phone cut off at the hospital so he can't bother him (Are Drs. supposed not to be bothered?)—and at just what point can a relative of the patient get in another doctor—as far as I can make out, <u>never</u>. Well, anyhow he finally saw KB and realized that the guy would just die if he didn't do something, and he talked the whole thing over with him (KB was scared, and so was I), gave him relief from both ends of the alimentary canal (another question for Bill, just how long can a person lie bloated with no action either way, without developing gangrene or something?

Three days? four days?) and proceeded to pull him out of it. The telephone was connected, the Dr.'s wife told me to just call them any time I had anything on my mind (I said: "I don't like to bother you.") But for several weeks KB had painful trouble with elimination and we were worried. He seems perfectly all right now. But I shall be very scared to ever let him in a hospital again unless I have someone like Bill to advise me. He can go into shock and never pull out of it, if he feels he has an unsympathetic doctor. The reason this surgeon was "unsympathetic" was that he had forgotten to come to the operation (he admits he is forgetful) and he knew that KB knew that he had forgotten to come. Bad situation from the start.

Enough of wailing.

It is so good to have Floss's note saying that all is well with you. We too feel pretty good, waiting for the boys to come home for the holidays—the phone will ring any time now—and after then we go to Florida. The only thing that can keep the Florida trip from being a success is if they charge just much too much for everything—we are prepared for the worst—but they may go beyond what we think is the worst!

Wish we had had another visit with you this fall. I'm afraid we WERE a little sad at that time, not able to make it the truly happy day it should have been, for we do so much enjoy those days when you come. We shall work out a new way of life, given a little time. You are lucky to have your boys not too far away, even with their problems it is better not to have that feeling that they are in another part of the world. I am wondering how these problems have worked out. Next winter we go to California, Palo Alto—some Ford foundation behavioral group—good deal financially as KB can do his own writing, but such a long long way from Harvard University! It is surely the kids that kick the parents out of the nest.

Take care of yourselves. And do write. Mail will be forwarded whenever we have an address (KB says to everyone our address in the south will be General Delivery, Segregationville) (I wouldn't be surprised if there were such a place). And if we find a heavenly place, we shall surely let you know about it if there were the least chance of your joining us.

Your generosity ("I had planned to ask you to stay with us") makes that goddam hospital experience just a little worse in my memory—we have put DeBell on a pedestal around here since this fiasco.

I am sending you a 35–cent book worth a million. Do please read it.

Best of love, from KB and me.

Libbie

[P] [Andover]
October 15, 1956

Dear Bill,

How. 'Twas good to see you, though I grant, however reluctantly, that it was not one of our happier occasions.

Meanwhile, my silence has been due to the fact that I committed a grievous Dummheit.

I went to a local guy for a diagnosis of my hernia. He diagnosed it as bilateral, inguinal hernia—and in the same breath said that he could do the operation for two hundred dollars plus hospital expenses, and could arrange for me to go to the hospital the very next day.

On the grounds that it was a minor operation, and could be over with so soon, while DeBell was so much farther off, thereby involving more difficulties about visits from Shorty, etc., I bought the proposition.

So far as I can make out, from things we know and things I heard while lying three-fourths anesthetized in the operating room, the operation, which was originally scheduled for 10:30, was moved ahead to somewhere around 8 or 8:30. And this caused a slip-up whereby, as I lay doped to the gills and all but ultimately out, on the operating table, everybody began asking where the hell the surgeon might be. And he was home having breakfast, nearly three-quarters of an hour away. Various things involved in this delay gradually worked me up into a fury, so that apparently I was squirting adrenalin during the operation. Anyhow, we know that I was in the operating room for two hours, for an operation that should have required much less time—so I had quite a batch of dope to get out of me afterwards.

All that, let us say, is hidden behind the fog of my anesthesia and the mystique of "medical ethics" (which is supposedly designed for the protection of the patients, but so far as I can see functions splendidly for the protection of the doctors). Anything to do with all that part of the job was behind a wall of total silence. For me to so much as mention any of my experiences in the operating room was to say an unforgivably dirty word. One intern, at one point, growled that "writers talk too much,"—which of course is the truth, but still. . . .

Anyhow, point is: Whatever went wrong there is hidden in conjecture, and that's that. But the next step is brutally clear: That for some reason best known to himself, the dirty bastard purely and simply denied me adequate sedation—

so I lay there day after day, night after night, in stony steely vigil, following the hospital noises, in an anguish of unremitting wakefulness. I was not his patient, I was his prisoner—and the experience was something little short of terror.

Home now, I find my insomnia (which was a problem before) increased to between two and three times its former grandeur. And, two weeks after the operation, my urine scalds me.

How much damage has been done to me, I do not know. But my mind is like a steel trap, and I have not yet found the trick of relaxing it. True, now that I am out of the hospital my clown has prescribed sufficient sedation (after disappearing for a week on a grouse-hunting trip in Maine)—but even at that, I have had to take twice the amt. prescribed. (I was to take $1\frac{1}{2}$ gr. of Nembutal at bedtime; but when, after taking such a dose at 11 o'clock, I found myself still busily buzzing at 1:30, I decided that more was needed—and with the dose doubled I got five hours' sleep, and might have got more had it not been for the scalding effect.)

I hate, I hate, I hate.

Oh jeez, fellow, could I but have had a humane guy like you to attend me. Jeez, what a beating I took from this clown, this bedside-manner shirtfront. Oof!

Meanwhile, best greetings to thee and Floss. And the weather here now is fantastically beauteous—if only I weren't somehow mulling over some ineffable fury, somewhere in my depths.

Sincerely,

[P]   [Rutherford]
Oct. 17/56

Dear Ken,

It's over anyhow, though you did have more discomfort than should have been necessary but the comfort that Libbie meant to you was worth it. I must say that your surgeon could have been more on the job in the follow up than he seems to have been. The urethritis sometimes can be annoying but should be easy to take care of. Let me know if it doesn't soon disappear. It sounds from here as if you had recently passed through an Inferno! You didn't tell me that you had had the damned thing on BOTH sides.

They say that for a loving husband every baby his wife has he suffers as if it was his own. I wonder how Libbie feels after this experience, as if she had

had twins perhaps? I know it's not a joking matter but at least you're home again. You don't have even a baby to show for it.

The country must be superb this year, even here in the suburbs it would be hard to beat it. This is one time I miss the car—but I really don't even then for I would be able then to pay you a visit.[270] Maybe it will be instead to be in Florida.

Cheerio (as much as you can manage it)

Sincerely,

Bill

[P]   [Andover]
December 24, 1956

Dear Bill,

Merry Christological (post-Christological) greetings, and hopes for a happy annual rebirth. Meanwhile, I continue to envy you your opportunities to be thus in different scenes. It's what I need, to help me add the necessary angles to my speculations on scene-act and agent-act ratios.[271] But I must go on sublimating, by reading metaphysicians and theologians and such, with their brands of scenic over-allness (what John Wild, a philosophy guy at Havvud, would call their "overarching" terminologies).[272] And you should have picked up much lore for subtilizing thoughts on the "hierarchal psychosis." ... Can't remember whether I previously sent you the glad tidings, that I have reduced my racket to a somewhat free-verse definition of man, thus:

> Man is
> the symbol-using animal
> inventor of the negative
> separated from his natural condition by instruments
> of his own making
> and goaded by the spirit of hierarchy.

This fall, a batch of medical expenses swiftly made us poorer by One Grand— so I consider myself permanently maimed. However, we have decided that the only known cure for such an ailment is to act just a little bit as though one had several oil wells. So, after the young gents return to Harvard following the holidays, we're going to drive south in our elegant 1950 Pontiac, and look for an inexpensive hole we can crawl into, until it's time for us to return as a

Welcoming Committee for the boys during their winter vacation. I can already hear myself wailing, each time I pay a bill. However, the anguish is eased somewhat by the fact that I have been offered a one-year fellowship with one of the Ford Fund projects (at Stanford, bejeez), my tenure to begin next fall. This opportunity comes at a most beauteous moment, from the standpoint of my own "project" on the Motivorum bizz. So I got my scheduled return to Bennington postponed for a year, and dare think that I can get one book, and maybe two, cleared away before I return to teaching. (My dream is to have the whole thing done, and to spend a year trying to find out just how simple I could make my notions, from the pedagogical angle.) At present, am in the thick of speculation on Catharsis. It's a gruesomely easy subject to gas about, so I'm having one devil of a job trying to condense it into solidities, while at the same time permitting it its range. Very vexing. The only cheering thought on the subject is that so many Greek tragedies were lost, so one can become an authority almost by confining himself to the two-volume Random House edition of the Greek plays (plus some Loeb editions for tracking down "key terms" in the ones which are to be given special attention). My greatest contribution to date is to have figured out (by theorizing doubtless to be scored as unsound) that the missing pages of Aristotle's on the subject would be different, depending on their place in his <u>Poetics</u> (namely: whether they came before or after the crucial definition in Chapter 6 of the treatise as we now have it). But I must stop now, as Shorty is leaving for town. And if this doesn't go off now, it'll linger here for at least two more days. . . . Best luck.

Sincerely,

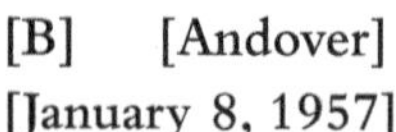

[B]   [Andover]
[January 8, 1957]

Dear Bill—We have heard tell that you picked up Five Grandeurs, though we haven't yet heard from what source.[273] Meanwhile, am sending this quickie to record our rejoicing (as if that were necessary!). Maybe we'll be seeing you in Florida (you can wave to us on the other side of the R.R. tracks). I'll tell you where we are when I know where we are. (We're scheduled to leave about Wednesday, D.V.) Incidentally, I have been happily hit, too (by a wholesome portion of the Ford Fund bounty, but it doesn't EVENTUATE for some months).[274] Today we cleaned the car—and, surprise! under the mud there was still a gleaming garb, so we'll start out proudly. . . . Best to you both.

Sincerely,

K.B.

[P]   [Rutherford]
July 2, 1957

Dear Libbie:

We had a good quiet time, I enjoyed it including the drinks and the dinner, which was delicious. The thundershower and the scamper with you under the towel to shelter left me breathless but I enjoyed it. Floss has plans for a visit in August which she will write you about.

Enclosed you will find the poem. Hope you can find something to enjoy about it. And when you find the time please show it to Ken's daughter Frances who applauded, with an affirmative nod and a grin, when I confessed that I am a feminist.

Take care of yourself. And Ken.

Affectionately,

Bill

THE BIRTH
A 40 odd year old Para 10
    Navarra
        or Navatta she didn't know
uncomplaining
    in the little room
        where we had been working all night long
dozing off
    by 10 or 15 minute intervals
        her great pendulous belly
marked
    by contraction rings
        under the skin
No progress.
It was restfully quiet
    approaching dawn on Guinea Hill
        in those days.
Wha's a ma', Doc?
    It do'n wanna come.
That finally roused me.
I got me a strong sheet
    wrapped it
        tight
around her belly.

When the pains seized her again
            the direction
was changed
            not
                  against her own backbone
but downward
            toward the exit.
                  It began to move—stupid
not to have thought of that earlier.
Finally
            without a cry out of her
                  more than a low animal moaning
the head emerged
            up to the neck.
It took its own time
            rotating.
I thought of a good joke
            about an infant
                  at that moment of its career
and smiled to myself quietly
            behind my mask.
                  I am a feminist.
After a while
            I was able
                  to extract the shoulders
one at a time
            a tight fit.
                  Madonna!
13 ½ pounds!
            Not a man among us
                  can have equaled
that.
            W.C.W.

[P]   [Andover]
August 19, 1957

Dear Bill,

    The typewriter is still throbbing with a heartfelt note I wrote to Jack
about the Wm. Wms. Letters.[275]

Shopping around among same, I see your selectivities emerging nicely. You knew what you were after—and I'm sure that's one big reason why you got so many good things done.

The next time you're out, you must inscribe p. 105 to me.[276]

Incidentally, as I told Jack, I am taking all your books with me on my trip west, in the hopes that, sometime between now and spring, I can put my many notes on you into shape as an article.

The thing that comes through quite convincingly in the letters is your vigor (which is, I suppose, a subdivision of your directness). The thing I didn't understand about your "Contact" line (when we used to haggle about it decades ago) was its subterranean relationship to your profession as a medico. I can only say in my defense that you yourself often talked about 'place' in a way designed to obscure this relationship.

I gave several reasons to Jack why your letters to me made me gloomy. But I think I forgot the main one; namely: that I'm trying to do a stretch sans alky, and the serpasil that helps hold me down seems to act not just as a "tranquilizer," but also as a flattener-outer.

Incidentally, we much enjoyed that poem you sent to Shorty, though it seemed to have lost some of the sharp lines it had when you were describing to her the incident around which it was written. Why not go back and look over some of your earlier drafts, before you started cutting? Though Revision by Omission is Rule No. 1, I guess it haint <u>always</u> right.

In a little over two weeks, we start our long drive west, not being due back here until late June.

Best luck, and to Floss.

Sincerely,

If this is a niggardly letter, I can only say in my defense: I have just read advance copies of a Knopf reprint of <u>Phil. of Litry Frm</u>.[277] A very nice job indeed—yet I haven't yet been able to work up a letter thanking the editors for their valiant work. I'm so "tranquil" I'm <u>sullen</u>.

[B]   [Andover]
November 23, 1957

Dear Bill,

Holla! While people are waiting on five phones, I take time out to dictate this hurried note. For I discover that my usually Better Half was a bit unbetter, in telling you of "sensarionism" where the text had said "sensationism."[278] So I write in haste, admonishing, lest you tree the wrong bark.

At moment, am all in a tizzy-wizzy while, encased in serpasiliousness, I get ready to Defend my Honor at the Center[279] next Tewes Day. Shall speak on my proprietary medicine, Dramatism. (Usually, to defend it, I have to show that it doesn't imply a disrespect for Lyricism. On the contrary! But this time, I am sure, no one will attack from that quarter. This time I guess I'll have to prove that it's as far from Lyricism as the human mind can get outside the laboratory.)

Meanwhile, yes, 'twas good to see the Wmses—a goodly bit of lil ole N. Jersey. Yes. Sorry we were so <u>non compotes</u> as regards finding a place whereat to eat. But jeez, we obviously meant well—all over the place.

Holla! Yes! Be sinyuh both, afore long.

Sincerely,

K.B.

[P]   [Andover]
October 18, 1958

Dear Bill,

Hello, bejeez!

I wonder if you have any ideas anent the enclosed. For instance, what should I throw out? (Not all of it, I hope.)

In particular, I wonder about the "Concluding Apostrophe," which was not in the original at all, but derives from my teaching a pretty student here about the all-importance of pood-pulling in Faulkner.[280] (Long live the Beauty Clinic, as regards the Thinking of the Body.)

I was mighty sorry that we had to miss the celebrating of your seventy-fifth revolution about the sun. But I was in the thick of things here. (In fact, that's about the only way one can be here, as regards the relation to things.)

Meanwhile, wd. say:

It's been a long time.

Fond greetings to you and Floss from both of us, yes.

Sincerely,

[P]   [Rutherford]
Oct. 24, 1958

Dear Ken,

Your animadversions on the subject of disgruntlement received, laid out as I am by a further stroke if not flat on my back at least thinking to be as I am able.[281] It should happen to a dog! poor pup.

Me, I'm more of the anapestic strain than the iambic so although I sympathize with you I can't wax too enthusiastic about the poem. What the hell, I'm in no mood for philosophic poetry or at present for poetry at all, God forgive me.

Sorry to be in such a mood. Let's hope I recover. Best love to Libbie. I did see poems sent to me, a small booklet, in a letter by Louis Zukofsky that I do thoroughly approve of.[282] Do you know him well enough to ask him to send you a copy of it, the only way you will ever see it.

I only wish we could meet again as we used to. Maybe across the table over a beef stew we could come to grips over this poem of yours for which I thank you.[283] Keep a stiff upper lip.

Affectionately yours,

Bill

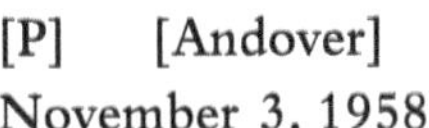

[P]   [Andover]
November 3, 1958

Dear Bill,

Helndamnaysh! Take it ease.[284]

Seventy-five revolutions around the sun—you ole revolutionary! And many more to go, each time putting a black curse upon my attempts to get you to agree to my attempts at violation of your Rule No. 1, "no ideas but in things" (that is, no ideas but in images).

Meanwhile, the only thing that is keeping me from suicide is the fact that all this paper work is just about killing me—so I must fight like a fiend to keep alive.

We have a date for next summer. (School here ending near the end of June.) In the interim, take it ease. And don't answer fan-mail from guys like me,—just go non-responsive, just as though you hadn't been not only a poet (for whom phones never ring) but a doctor (for whom phones never stop ringing).

No, that didn't quite turn out right. Phones ring for Rutherfordian poets, too. It's only <u>in principle</u> that they don't ring. (For critics, phones positively un-ring.)

Meanwhile, I keep wondering: What kind of pests are anapests? And if the damned word believes in itself, why is the accent on the first syllable?

Good luck, ole dope. And all our love to you and Floss.

Sincerely,

[P]   [Rutherford]
Nov 25/58

Dear Libbie,

We were happy to have your letter and to get news from you all. Bill is coming along <u>slowly</u> this time.[285] The depression following the cerebral episodes are the worst feature of the thing. It was a real tragedy to Bill to have to miss the Johns' Hopkins festival and the reading he was to have given in Wash. D.C. the following Monday—We had not seen the clipping you sent. Bill's comment was—I'll bet Robert Frost and Winters were the two mentioned in the paper!—Maybe it was just as well that Bill didn't get there, for between Frost and Winters, Bill would have been an outcast, and how![286]

How nice that you will be in Boston for awhile—it's a fine city—it has dignity—I always feel <u>good</u> when I'm there, by which I mean self respecting. People are polite—considerate—and most helpful about everything. And there is much to see and beautiful towns in every direction of historic interest. I know you'll love it. I've missed not seeing you—this summer—family matters can create havoc—can't they? We had many years of it with both our mothers (not alcoholic but senility)—one 102 years old and one 84—both crippled with broken hips—and handicapped by deafness. It's something! The mental lapses are the hardest features to cope with. At first I was shocked—when my mother slipped—she had been so keen—alert—independent but gradually I accepted and didn't react. The same for Bill's mother. Let's hope Kenneth's dad can be deprived of the liquor—which I have come to believe is the very devil to all who over do it. You'll have to assure K.B. that there is nothing for <u>him</u> to fear for the future. He and Bill are fortunate to be creative men—and age doesn't cut them off from what they have been doing—as it does to men like Ken's father. <u>They</u> are lost souls—and it's a blot on our set up.

I didn't intend delivering a lecture. Excuse it. We had tentative plans for a trip either to the West Indies or S. America this winter, but we have been advised by Bill's physician not to attempt it this year. So we will be at the above address where the door is always open—but you never come!

Our very best to you all—

Affectionately,

Floss

[P]
c/o Edward Richman,
Dudley Road,
Bedford, Mass.,
December 28, 1958.

Dear Bill,

Greetings, old toughie.

My institutional battle is over until March. So, in the meantime, all I need do is fight with myself, the which I do in more ways than you could shake a stick at.

The world is run by platitude, with less and less of latitude, and more and more ingratitude, to be—and less and less beatitude, and more and more white ratitude; and there you have my attitude, for free. (But lest we educators suffer guilt, we educate our students to the hilt.)

Where was we? I was saying you're good, and you were saying I stinnick. Manifestly, I was losing.

Anyhow, for the time bean, here I am with the Concord river flowing through my back yard. (Within a stone's throw, literally.) The owner of a big house (as rambling as one's guts) has gone south—and our job is but to keep the place reasonably and decently occupied. We're doing it as reasonably and decently as we can, except that he seems to have poisoned the rats just before he left—and many an untoward breath has thus necessarily been in and exhaled. Anyhow, it's nice to walk on the water (that's how we take our constitutionals each aft). My troubled dreams—are they because I was so exhausted from my term's work at Bennington, plus the still more exacting relaxation afterwards? or because I smell the poisoned rats in my sleep? (I sometimes dream of trying to step among a whole wilderness of thick, ripe, honey-colored turds) or because this winding house is a perfect setting for a murder mystery? (the first night, I awoke in terror, hearing a knock down there somewhere in the dark, and would I dare go down to answer? I shiver anew, even as I write of it) or because of the books I have been reading? (such as Jonathan Edwards and his urgent sense of sin) or because of my entangled speculations? (showing how, if you peer long enough into the same word, you can dimly make out there either free will or determinism).

There's still so much to be scraped up. Why don't they make quick with the bombs? And save us the trouble.

If only I could persuade myself that heaven is a place where one can swill bourbon without a hangover, then I could figure out some reason for things. Otherwise, I'm greatly bepuzzed. (Anyhow, only the other day I was peddling you on the morning star that dissolves into dawn—what a quick beauty! And the first thing tomorrow, I review you on "The Use of Force."[287] I'm getting ready for next term, too.)

Meanwhile, good luck, Dopo. And more anon.

Sin erely,

[P]   [Rutherford]
Jan. 1, 1959

Dear Ken & Libbie,

This is a personal letter to you Ken but since I'm thinking of you both together far off in the literary sticks of Harvard and adjacent New England places about Concord (never realized the significance of the word before this) I included Libbie in my general address.

That was a beautiful letter you sent me, all the old nonchalance and verve came to life again. I needed just such a letter in my present state, it did me good, rescued me from myself and allowed me to breathe again—deeply.[288] When a man has such understanding friends he can never be licked. Come on let's go again!

Your note on the house you're living in gives me too the creeps, I betcha Libbie never woke up when the tap on the door interrupted your dreams. Who was it? A special delivery? Or just nothin' but your own over-wrought imagination, poor sons of bitches that we are all caught in the same trap. I don't blame you for paling up with your Benedictine friar in Sussex and trying to make a go of it. Our Carolinians are Baptists so I have recently read.

I'm about ready to launch that new book on my mother's notes. I deceived her into allowing me to jot down under her specific interjection about 20 years ago. McD.[289] is to bring it out in June. Its name will be: YES, MRS. WILLIAMS, a personal record. It'll run to a little more than 200 pages with a 20 page introduction by yours truly and a note on Mother as translator from the Spanish.

The worst thing to do about my present life is that with this most recent stroke, although I can sleep fairly well I am eternally so depressed that I can't live with myself, and my slightest error in conducting my life is exaggerated until it becomes an obsession. Everything I do goes wrong and I never seem to learn by experience.

Are you going to stay up there until New Jersey opens up and the boys will be ready to return? The older boy seemed to be headed toward physics, what about his brother the Freshman—or is he already a sophomore?

Floss reads to me since I cannot read for myself—but I dread over-tiring her. We're going out tonight for supper at Bill's mother-in-law. My stupid mind keeps doing pinwheels without rest. It is fatiguing. When I can sleep (as I usually can) it is bearable. Last night Floss tells me I slept through the New Year's racket. God be praised.

That was a wonderful letter, old friend, try it on again when you have the time. And love to Libbie from both Floss and myself. Oh I have A PLAY SCHERDULD FOR PRUDUCTION any day now at a N.Y. Off Broadway theater, <u>MANY LOVES</u> which came out in New Directions about 20 years ago.[290] It will be advertised in the papers now that the strike is over. I don't dare think of it.

Bill

⁊

[P]   [Rutherford]
August 25/59

Dear Kenneth—Just a note to tell you that Bill is in N.Y. Hospital while he was operated on for cancer of the signoid (lower bowel). He is doing well and we think that barring the unforeseen he will be O.K. I don't know why Bill insisted that I write to you, but he did. So, am doing so. He hasn't wanted to tell anyone.

Hope you all are having a good summer—with plenty of water in the pond!

Best to Libbie and the boys too.

Floss

⁊

[P]   [Andover]

August 26, 1959

Dear Bill,

Helndamnaysh! Greetings from Burke the Bellyache to Toughie Two-Gun Bill. Tochangethefigure, I hear from Floss that America's Most Human Poet has been under going a slight revision. That ain't fair. Time after time, I have started to write you all about my symptoms, but always desisted because they kept changing (I at least <u>think</u> I invented the concept of the Migratory Symptom, though mine change like the position of the hands on a clock—each moment unique yet circulating so that they keep coming back to the same situations).[291]

Only a week or two ago, we got a card from Jack Thrillwell, escaping somewhere in Europe and I wondered about your next trip here, when he gets back.[292] Would that be feasible soon?

My year at Bennington (the first time I ever taught full time) nearly slew me. As a result, I came home seeing double and the mere thought of a pretty young college girl was enough to make me freeze at 98 in the sun/ "From now on," I susurrously exhaled, "call me Old Meanie. Down with Eros—long live Thanatos." Then, after clearing away a couple of overdue reviews, I got tangled in an essay ingeniously entitled "Body and Mind"—and a glance at the motionless cyclone of my room would be enough to tell you what a state the mindless body of that essay is in. I have been trying to decide just what is the relation between sheerly verbal action and sheerly physical motion. Just what is the difference, for instance, in the meaning of the words, "taste of an orange," if said or heard by someone who has tasted an orange and by someone who hasn't? It involves the Existentialist essence-existence bizz, but I hope without the Existentialist bulshide. . . . Trying to decide—though what the hell's the difference what I decide? Also, I had an offer to teach a term at Berkeley—but I decided that I really must take this whole year off and try to get these godam books and things out of the road. (We'll probably canter down to the Gulf side of Florida for the peak of the winter.)

Meanwhile, take it ease, me frenn. And we'll be looking for you hereabouts before long. The pond so far this year has been ample. You'd think water grew on trees. We've had water to burn. Come out and feed the mosquitoes by our idyllic shores.

Shorty joins me in sending fondest greetings.

Sincerely,

K.B.

Best to you and Love,

Lib.

⤳

[B]   [Tampa, Florida]
3/11/60

Dear Bill,

Naturally, I can't be sure that this will reach you. For you're a bit more than a stone's throw away. Two stone throws, in fact, which is certainly our nearest for any length of time.

God knows, as regards beginnings, "A" is certainly a species of same.[293] Then comes "Round of fiddles playing Bach." That, then, presumably, is what we are to be about? (As I said today, I think that, somewhere along the line, it should involve the distinction between dance rhythms and verbal rhythms, plus their possible overlaps. That's the only way his problem makes ultimate sense to me, so far as sheer words are concerned, except insofar as one suicidally hopes by words to transcend words, as we all somehow do while also not wanting to do anything of the sort—for how be the Bible-book animal, sans words?)

Might not that start be said to come to a head, (44btm) where, when on the sumjick of transferring "the design / Of the fugue" to poetry, our hero says:

At eventide

Venus come up

(the few bits thereafter puzzle me a bit, but seem reasonable).

See on complex and simple, p. 53. and note what all it grows out of, on that very same page.

62. "in terms of mathematical/function." Every time he aims at rediscovering the art of Lucretius, I naturally glow, though I also grant that it's a tough job.

91. Nice Spinoza-stuff, as also elsewhere in the text. Spinoza is the best Jew next to the guy who dictated the Bible—and besides, his text hasn't yet got garbled, as Big Shot's did.

99. "writing its signature different / each time so / you cannot get your money back." There our hero names his problem. It's the problem of all Eternal Rebeginnings (along with the fact that we live only by rerebeginning repeatedly).

P. 100–101. This I must copy out, to use:

> Most honorable Sir,
>   We perused your MS.
> with boundless delight. And
> we hurry to swear by our ancestors
> we have never read any other
> that equals its mastery.
> Were we to publish your work,
> we could never presume again on
> our public and name
> to print books of a standard
> not up to yours.
> For we cannot imagine
> that the next ten thousand years
> will offer its ectype.
> We must therefore refuse
> your work that shines as it were in the sky
> and beg you a thousand times
> to pardon our fault
> which impairs but our own offices.
>   Signed, Publishers.

109. "What is music which does not In any sense progress?" /

144tp. music as upper limit, speech as lower limit. I have already suggested how I would reduce this. /

152–3. "His name sounded / very familiar, / But I got used to it." As thus amended, splongdeed!

166 and thereabouts. Was much interested in his reduction to terms of teaching. Maybe it's not the very best reduction, but there are certainly many not nearly so good.

173. Good on senses.

203. "I grow sick hearing myself / Unable to stop." Yes, the cruelest cut of all. And that reminds me of his best assorted wisecrack, on p. 28:

Saying, It's a hard world anyway,

Not many of us will get out of it alive.

214–216. The story of the dog is beautifully told. And it grows neatly out of the stuffo on the guilty geezer who had read Das Kapital.

221tp. "I have to reread several times / to find out what I meant." He said it, I didn't.

I like in principle his every attempt to round out images with ideas. (There's no necessary reason for his thus qualifying your slogan, "No ideas but in things": but it allows for a freer step from lyric to drama, in case that is what one does happen to want.) And I was happy to see how things got to swinging towards the close. Or rather, I was for a while. Then it began to seem like logorrhoea, at which point I found myself wanting an astringent, at which point he threw in the kitchen sink. Eauque, if that's what he really wants. But does he?

Dubito, ergo sum.

In any case, I agree with you, he writes an honest line. (That's what you teach us, insofar as we are able to learn your lesson. And it's most interesting to see how, by remembering you when reading Pound, he brought in Charlie Marcus instead of the Douglasite bulshido, though necessarily sans certainty.)[294] But jeez, if you don't consider pp. 112–117 absolutely hideous, then prithee learn me!

Where, then, was we?

I was saying yestiddy that the guy is good insofar as (a) he can let it roll out nachurl and (b) he's entangled with the problem of beginnings (as every good Jew should be, if he begins with Genesis). I mean I was thus bleating earlier this very day, that now seems so long discarded.

How many years has it been, since we thus this aft yiped togidda?

And I was saying how I loathed Eliot in his later phases, not for his religion but for his advertising of it. (I'll wholly respect any man's religion if, like Valery, he keeps quiet about it. But, whatever virtues I concede to the <u>Quartets</u>, I despise (and I mean DESPISE) our hero's stylistic tricks for saying in effect: Please leave me alone to pray here all by myself all here alone just me and my God, I'll be there at such-and-such an hour, and if you want to look in and photograph me, you can, but please respect my privacy, and I promise you that, if you don't press the bulb, I'll do it for you, after my fashion, like Cinarra, and thereby I, rather than you, will get the revenues for my conversion which, I am sure you will agree, is most important to me, if not in the afterlife, at least in the late years of my life here and now.)

O.K., good guy. I admit, we couldn't get together enough to work these things out. I admit, I owe you a damned good article <u>on you</u>, whereas you <u>owe me nothing</u>. I admit, you are preeminently entitled to demand that I recognize how good you are, whereas you are not required to know one poopin thing about what I'm after, all my years out there on the commuting fringe. Peccavi, peccavi.[295]

Dawlink!

Sincerely thine,
K.B.

[B]   [Andover]
April 8, 1960

Dear Floss and Bill,

Back at the Old Stand, after plowing through a fantastic amount of rainwater all the way home. 'Tis good to have your friendly notes, and to be assured that we didn't give you a bum steer in persuading you to risk a month among the unrealities of Florida real estate.[296] (As the world retreats more and more into the realm of sheer Symbolism, I seek solace in the thought that, at least, one's ailments are real enough.)

We were most fortunate in having you there, to help make the bad weather be as though mellow.

Bill's "Song" is a Delight.[297] And it should inaugurate our proposed investigation under Auspicious Auspices. The last stanza puts a surprising lot together, suggests many possibilities.

At this stage, however, I think I should resolutely suppress all asseveration on my part, and should confine myself merely to some questions.

My job, at this stage, is to ask questions without, as far as convenient, indicating what I may have in mind. However, for later comparison, I should knock out some notes which I don't send at this time, but which I shall send later, after we have "explored" for a while.

The first questions, then, would be:

Would you give me a set of synonyms, kindred images, related anecdotes, metaphors, etc. for "ear" and another set for "eye"? I mean in general, not necessarily as related to this particular poem. For instance, but no, there I'd be horning in already!

The second question:

Would you give me some similar improvisings as regards the idea of merging division?

Third question:

Though I recognize that the word "lie" in the penultimate line has nothing to do with falsehood, suppose the last line of the poem got lost. Could you imagine a scholiast who, with only this garbled text to go by and unaware that there was a lost last line, sought to explain why ear and eye "lie"? Could you, arbitrarily, think up an argument for him?

Toot toot! Ding ding! We're on our way. And I betcha we can have some fun, in our old age.

Sincerely,
K.B.

[B]   [Andover]
4/13/60

Dear Floss and Bill,

Thanks so much for following us all the way—it must have been good for us for we came the whole way without even a minor accident or up-set though we drove constantly in a pouring rain. We thought of you, too, on your way home, and were a little worried because of the crowd at Sarasota. So glad all went smoothly.

We are very glad to be back home—all the bulbs are bursting out of the ground—and everything smells so good. KB says how wonderful to look out and see all that fine soil that things can grow in. The boys were here and we had a happy week with them.

Bill's poem is very very fine and lovely. So much said in few words, and gently.

How's the recalcitrant hand?[298] Keep at it. The way now is from the felt object back to the brain—not vice versa—and this is the way it was in the beginning, amen! And who am I to be reminding the wise Dr?

The moles are on their way out (thanks to Butch for tying the strings)—but they are taking their time, clinging on for dear life.

When we get back from Penn State—and spring is really here, then you must come up.[299] We'll find a way.

Till then, take care. And please more poems.

Love,
Lib.

Have you ever tried doing the same thing with both hands at the same time?

[B]   [Andover]
And/or,
4/16/60

Dear Bill,

How's our project going?[300] Meanwhile, jeez what a jam I'm of a sudden inny winny! Just back from Philadelphia, where I gave a talk under the mouthful of title, "The Philosophy and Psychology of Language," I now find myself squoze by a dozen chores before we leave next Tuesday for my nine-day stint (or Roving Commission, or whatever) at Penn State.

The head of the Poetry Class there has asked if I'd officiate at one meeting. And I'm wondering if you'd let me read 'em your charming "Shell Song."[301] (My idea is that I'd read it, along with items by some others, sans giving names of authors, then let them comment for a while, and then end by divulging names of authors.)

I hope that those questions I asked, by way of warming up, didn't seem too far afield, or such. And I hope that you and Floss are enjoying the Northern stirrings, so different from Florido. (Last week, for several days when I should have been working on my notes, I did some ecstacatic puttering around in the woods—and so far I haven't missed the derned old sea one particle.)

I'd be grateful if you'd send a quick Yes or No to me via the enclosed envelope. Here's hoping . . .

Sincerely,
K.B.

[B]   [Andover]
5/31/60

Dear Bill,

Jeez, how wrong you have been, in saying all those stinko things to darling Floss about me and my not-answering.

Your poem <u>went over beautifully</u>.[302] And I was so happy that it did. And I admit that I should have said so. But bejeez, Bill, I've been runragged.

So I dint get around to telling you about it. Ats all.

Of course I'm sorry you wouldn't play my game.[303] But why in the heck should you? (I refer to those questions in an earlier letter, questions that even I myself thought of as but ways of beginning to get ready to begin.)

You ole duffer, it's a beautiful poem. That's beyond question. But there are some twists and turns still to be considered. The main problem is: I had some notes I wanted to send you, and where the hell are they?

I'll run across them, when I'm looking for something else. And then I'll send them along.

But in the meantime . . . how about coming out here, whenever it suits your fancy? Call us up even, on the spur of the moment (just to make sure that we're here).

You grand old bloke, with your grandesse blokess, come on out, and let's mill and mellow around, and mull and mule and maggle to our hearts' content.

Ah, shinny! Maybe I just can't tell you how nice it was for us that you and Floss came to muss around with us there in Florido. Maybe I'm too stinko twisted. But you have imagination, so figure it out for yourself.

Look, you baystard. The only thing I hold against Jarrell is that <u>I</u> was saying, for years, in <u>my</u> classes, that you were our <u>most humane</u> poet.[304] God damn it, I did just that. Then that latecomer can pop up and file the claim.

. . .

6/3/60

Found, some days later, among my Unfinished Business. Hell, Bill, how can we go on, except by Unfinished Business? Meanwhile, you ole stinkeroo, good lucktyuh.

Sincerely,
K.B.

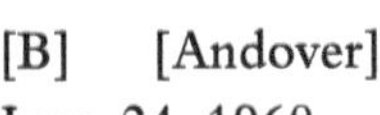

[B]   [Andover]
June 24, 1960

Dear Bill,

At last, I got clear of the jobs for a day or two. Also, I located my notes on your (enthusiastically acclaimed) "Song" anent shells and such.[305]

But I haint gonna transcribe my notes now (the notes that led me to ask you those tentative questions). Rather, I'm hoping that I can spring them on you some time this summer, maybe, and see where we go from there.

In the meantime, there's one consideration of mere business. The second stanza seems to suggest that "scallops" and "lion's paws" are in different bins, whereas "lion's paws" are a species of scallop. Thus, so far as the sheer "logic" of the alignment is concerned, "scallops" are to "lion's paws" as "shoes" are to "tennis shoes." But though I doubt whether that's what you consciously wanted, my theory of the poem's underlying alignments can go along with your usage. For there is a sense in which such a line-up in the second stanza implicitly contains the line-up in the third.

I see the development along these lines:

Stanza One. Writing a poem about shells, our hero astutely writes it about "one" shell. Next, instead of saying "This one shell is beautiful," he turns things around, and supposedly starts by talking not about shells but about "beauty." So, whereas things started a long way off, we are given as a starter, within the conditions of this symbol-system, "Beauty is a shell."

Next, she turns into a girl. She is _la_ beaute. But things move fast. So, before the stanza is over, "she" is under the "sway" of an "it." (I refer to the formula, "its way," in which I beg leave to hear "it sway.")

So, all told, as regards the first stanza, we have an opposing of feminine and neuter, in terms of a shell, which is equated with beauty.

As regards the second stanza: "Lion's paws" are certainly gents, though under the sign of subsidence ("retreating waves"). The neuter isn't as neutral as it might be. And, if "lion's paws" are gents, then at first glance "scallops" are ladies (except for the sheerly technical problem I have already mentioned in this regard).

Now, then, what happens in the third and final stanza? "Retreating waves" will become transformed into "undying accents." That is to say: the masculine and/or neutral principle will have its way, poesy-wise. In one sense, "retreating," in another sense it will be "undying." (Secondarily, that's the difference between "waves" and "accents," as regards total translation of these motives into terms of imagery.)

Next, all of a sudden, what of "ear" and "eye" turning up here in the third stanza? Well, first of all, it's probably ear-and-eye because eye-and-ear would be the cliché (including maybe medically on the side, eye-ear-and-nose).

We have gone from connotations of feminine and (neutrally) masculine to talk of ear and eye lying down together. We started with a lady shell which, whatever her sway, is presumably sheathlike, since shells mostly are.

But lions-and-scallops also suggest lions-and-lambs. And in their way, as regards the realm of the "undying," _they_ will lie down together, too. So, all told, both sexual and non-sexual ideas of lying down together are here enabled to lie down together.

But why "eye" and "ear" particularly? Might there also be included here a merging of the motives associated with painting and the motives associated with poetry? (And would the <u>personal</u> equation for the ego-eye of painting be such motives as are represented by painters like Hartley and Demuth?)[306] Or is the ear penetrated, and does the eye penetrate?

Now you know how much subtlety and complexity I see in that lovely, simple poem. And possibly you also know what I meant when I said that I wished you'd try, as an experiment, improvising on the word "lie" as if the "down" had been lost.

Meanwhile, I wanna say in my defense: I did not ask Mrs. Hermes to send you those books of mine. I go by a rule of this sort: If a critic doesn't know a poet, it's the critic's fault; and if the poet doesn't know the critic, it's the critic's fault. Needless to say, it's an ironic rule.

But thanks much indeed for sending us those copies of the Nashon.[307] Also, incidentally, on receiving a copy of their anthology recently, I was happy to see that we were both in there though here's hoping that you got more for your pages than I did for mine. (Psst: I got <u>nothing</u>.)

Holla!

Sincerely,
K.B.

[B]   [Andover]
June 25, 1960

Dear Bill,

Helndamnaysh! I don't think I got my point across at all, in my note of yesterday. So let's try again. At one stage in my godam novel, <u>TBL</u>, the guy says:[308]

> Even at this moment I realized that for any act, or any way of thinking, there is a tender word and a harsh word, equally applicable. Caution may be called vacillation, acquiescence may be called toadying, sturdiness may be called obstinacy. I knew there was deceit in my using the harsh words only—but unless we adopt a false position, we cannot get our truths stated.

Or, in my <u>Rhetoric</u>, when discussing Carlyle's doctrine (in <u>Sartor Resartus</u>) treating all appearances as "clothes":

This doctrine brings him to the ultimate mystery, the Symbol as Enigma, as both clarification and obfuscation, speech and silence, publicity and secrecy. For it simultaneously expresses and conceals the thing symbolized.

Then I quote, from Carlyle:

Of kin to the so incalculable influences of Concealment, and connected with still greater things, is the wondrous agency of <u>Symbols</u>. In a symbol there is concealment yet revelation: here, therefore, by Silence and by Speech acting together, comes a doubled significance.

(See in particular his two chapters on "The World in Clothes" and "Symbols.")

I take it that the psychology implied in the esthetic of Imagism fits perfectly with what Carlyle says of "Symbols." Hence it becomes a way of both saying and not-saying, a mode of "truth" that is also in a sense a "half-lie." And particularly because of the double meaning of "lie" in English, whenever a writer says something such as, "Behind such-and-such, there lies such-and-such a principle," I often try, for purely experimental purposes, reading the verb in the "wrong" sense (frequently with revealing results!). The same "spying," of course, goes for my own past uses of the word. (Recently on occasion I have consciously used the ambiguity.)

As regards your poem, I am naturally much interested in trying to see how many motivational strands might be implicit in the principle or ultimate unification stated in terms of eye and ear (including also the enigmatic merging of sexual antithesis in old age while, in my own case at least, there is an association of seeing with "penetrating" and of hearing with "being penetrated").[308]

The steps in the poem seem to strike a series of glancing blows, as each moment of stability is found to contain an element of instability that requires you to hurry on. And though the "lying" down together of eye and ear is a perfect "solution" for the poem as poem, obviously we're but <u>beginning</u>, once we ask what all might be implicit in that image.

"Division" and "Unification" each have their peculiar kinds of problems, with varying kinds of <u>ad hoc</u> "solutions." And I think that this lil "Song" of yours is a byoot for the way it stirs up those waters.

Strangely enough, I was particularly boisterous yesterday because I had just finished revising a dialogue, "Prologue in Heaven," the first draft of which I wrote in Englewood last winter.[309] It's a discussion between The Lord and

Satan, with The Lord telling Satan of his plans to create a symbol-using animal on Earth, and explaining how, though he would make the best possible of worlds, he can't make a symbol-using animal without allowing for the kind of orneriness that is intrinsic to symbol-using. Satan, who is a young hot-head admirer of The Lord, is indignant about human vices. He considers people "revolting." And though he doesn't mind all the stupid things they will say about him, he is indignant at what he takes to be self-importance with regard to The Lord. (I found it amusing thus to revise the character of Satan, and to "prophesy" how things were going to turn out, as the result of man's "symbolicity.")[310]

But, to the grind.

Sincerely,

K.B.

[B]   [Andover]
July 8, 1960

Dear Bill,

Herewith a quickie to depose (I'm trying to line up some talks I'm scheduled to give at Georgetown U., on 11th, 12th, 13th inst.):

(1) Your poem anent the "Ultimate Bear-Hug" is most impressive.[311] In the style of German <u>der</u> Tod rather than French <u>la</u> mort! More on that when we next confabulate.

(2) I expect to be back sometime on Thursday, the 14th. Any visit any time thereafter would be grand. (There's probably going to be a bright young anthropologist and famille here on Sat. and Sun. He's a slavish admirer of your work—and I'm sure he'd pee his pants with delight if you turned up while he is here. He did a poem on you, which I tried to get Mack Rosenthal to take for his W.C.W. number of <u>The Nation</u>—but no go.)

(3) Positively helndamnation NO, as regards publishing my "3 A.M. Impromptu on Zukofsky." 'Tis too untrimmed. And above all, when and if I air my reservations on Eliot, I want to do so in ways that don't give The Enemy so many opportunities to smack back. Besides, you're a better man to review the book anyhow. After all, you're a poet full time. And you're the guy who told me to learn how to write from Zukofsky. If, in the course of your review, you want to quote a bit of my letter, <u>specifically from parts to do solely with Zukofsky</u>, that's O.K. with me, though I'd like to get a chance to pass on

whatever excerpts you used. You could give credit to "a guy who has just fin-ished a dialogue between The Lord and Satan, but who insists that it is purely imaginary."

Best greetings, and to Floss—and we'll hope to be seeing you both soon.

Sincerely,

K.B.

[B]   [Andover]
Aug. 8, 1960

Dear Bill,

The play is a beaut—all of it: trusting husband, frustrated woman, the bum, the hot number, the cop—all—and the stage arrangements, if properly worked out, could be extremely effective—the busted house, the cellar hole—the room around it.[312]

And I am engrossed with <u>Yes, Mrs. Williams</u>—the slow building of a char-acter and a situation between mother and son.[313] Some beautiful passages. Will have more to say about Mrs. Williams when I finish the book.

Did you want me to return the play ms. after KB has read it? Or can we pass it on to others who might be interested?

We did not hear from the guy about the tape.[314]

Rereading your letter, you say you want the ms. returned soon. KB will read it tonight, and back it will come to you. I am so glad you let us see it.

Best love to you both,

Lib

I told the plot of the play to the Cowleys who have just been visiting with us and they were much amused and interested.[315]

Tues. Letter from Princeton guy received. Still hope you've located your tape of reading. Will tell him so.

[B]   [Andover]
Aug. 11, 1960

Dear Floss,

I am so glad you found the tape—it was made by professionals in a New York studio and is an improvement on the original (they were able to remove some of the hum).[316] However, as I wrote Mr. Francis, any technician making a record of the reading might want to return to the original and do his own job of screening out background noises. Until then, it is good to have this copy to lend around to interested people. We were delighted that it (ours) had kept in such good condition. Do let me know what Mr. Francis thinks of it—he should be very pleased with it. Bill does a <u>fine</u> job.

So glad Bill had a good time in Indiana.[317]

By the way, the original recording was made 6/21/51 (not 55) and I don't know the date of the professional copying of the tape. The '55 might have been our mistake since KB's handwriting is so bad on the original, the '51 could have been taken for '55.

In haste, but with lots of love,

Lib.

I am working on a bird drawing—it might turn out to be a crane instead of a pelican!

[B]   [Andover]
Oct. 24, 1960

Dear Floss and Bill,

Being confined to my bed for a couple of days last weekend with a sore throat (the boys were here and they took over the cooking). I read right straight through <u>The Build Up</u> and found it a fascinating book in many many ways.[318] How sorry I am I can't immediately ask you a lot of questions to fill out the story from where you leave off, but I believe Floss has told me some of it and I'm trying to remember and piece it all together. The flavor, the tone of the book is perfect and brings back the feeling of the whole era wherever you are, or were. To me, Bill was the instrument but the book is actually written by Floss through her eyes (except for some few passages)—it is Floss telling the story of her family and they are all wonderful characters.

I am so curious to know if the house of stone <u>was</u> built in Monroe (we drive right through there on the way from Andover to Bennington and I have always remarked what a beautiful spot it is—got lost up around the head of Greenwood Lake once and came down a mountain side right into Monroe) and if so, whether it is still there.[319] And what happened to "Joe"—I remember Floss' saying she had taken care of her mother for years in her own home. What a woman she must have been, tho' one is really endeared to the father.

And is your artistic nephew the son of "Ives"? The drive behind Gurlie was very characteristic of that period, in Asheville as well as Rutherford, and my parents, from another country, also involved in it though with a somewhat different emphasis, and it was always drilled into us that we had to "prove" ourselves intellectually and there was always the background of the struggle to "belong" and to belong well—in some way. I can't be sure, but I do believe it's somewhat different now with the same age group. The drive, or the reasons for any drive, seem to be elsewhere—I'm not exactly sure where.

Well, Michael goes off to the Army on Nov. 15th for two years. He may spend them at a desk job in Fort Dix (sorting mail or filing papers—after basic training) or be sent abroad. He'd like to go to Germany, but is afraid he might be sent to Korea. Butch is well and happy with his star gazing via intricate machines, telescopes and cameras and new chemicals.

Was reading somewhere yesterday that whale oil is an extremely important ingredient in certain car-lubrication compounds, in the making of <u>plastics</u>, and of cosmetics—i.e. our wonderful machines must have a little of it to run the way they should. Also they now have extremely efficient ways of <u>harvesting</u> it—though there was no word mentioned of plans to assure its continued production.

Please write news of both of you, and of the sons and grandchildren too. Hope their problems are getting solved and that the kids, too, are growing up OK. And that Bill is working. We hear of his poetry going to be read at a poetry center in NY soon and of something honorary at Nat'l Arts Foundation (?) in Feb. (?).[320]

Best love to you both,

Lib

And <u>many thanks</u> for sending the book. And <u>autographed</u>, too.[321] KB says he is writing when the midterm papers and grades are done.

[B]	[Bennington]
[December 17, 1960]

Bill, you generous old rummy. I've been trying for some days to write you a letter. But the graciousness of yours, plus the mad seventeen-things-at-once situation we're now in as the term explodes (I'm now frantically reading papers and writing reports), must perforce "necessitate" (to use a favorite word of the students) my delaying until the rush is o'er (December 21st). Meanwhile, this is just a quickie to say thanks, jeez thanks. Also, as I'll explain later, your poem has a spot, which I can quote to great advantage in connection with an essay I have to write soon (for a textbook edition of <u>Timon of Athens</u>).[322] Meanwhile, best love to The Bill and the Floss, or whatever that book was called.

K.B.

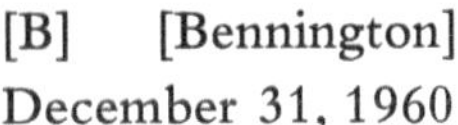

[B]   [Bennington]
December 31, 1960

Dear Bill,

Now it can be told, you mellow generous old baystard, you. The family has gone shopping, and I snuk a coupla slugs of Old Grand Dad (jeez, I can't even spell it!), and the year grinds to a close.

Our countryman, Barnum, admonished that one should never give a sucker a break. So, my first impulse was to ship you a bbl. of my latest versifyings.

But for all the crudity of my befuzzlement, I'm just somehow decent enough not to do ennithing of the sort. (Since you said that you liked the middle ones best, I even bethought me of a shrewdness wherein, to get the blessing, I'd tell how I had come across a whole new batch of middle ones, whereupon I'd parade some of my later sputterings.)

Bill, you're such a mellow generous old baystard, you're so riddled with humanity, you're poetry is so charmingly different from what I despise more and more in that shrewd God-seller, Eliot, I'll just tell you a story about local doings:

We have arrangements here whereby we have (if I may use a subversive word) <u>Contact</u> with a few students, technically known as "Counselees." One of my such, a remarkable girl who has been on all kinds of forced marches (even unto Tashkent, in the course of her odysseys), of a sudden showed me a poem she had done. I was astonied, on several scores. But most of all I was astonied on these two scores: (1) Although an exchange student from Poland, she was much tougher than I would ever be about distrust of "propaganda"; and (2) she wanted to write poetry a la Wallace Stevens.

I says, says I: "So that's what you'd do? And a good move it is. But could there be a better move?" And without waiting for her to ask me what such a move might be, I went on, to say (I mean: I goes on to say): "Look. Stevens is an excellent poet. But he's a mixture of poetry and insurance. How about a guy who is a mixture of poetry and medicine?"

There was your contact, you baystard. And you did such a beautiful job of it, the A.M.A. would have thrown you out, except that the fish bones were never that accurate. (Ironically enough, this student's surname is Fischbein, through no fault of hers.) Or fish legs.

Well, at this point, the rest of the family turned up, and broke the continuity. They turn out to have been the equivalent of that visitor from Porlock who turned up at Coleridge's and broke the continuity exactly when he was writing down his dream of Kubla Khan. But this was no dream. For critics are insomniacs.

Bill, the story is purely and simply this: I owe you an article, an article about you. And if Bigshot but grants me the time, I'm going to do it. And if He grants me the time, He'll also grant me the eloquence. And so, I'll write that eloquent article about you that I have long been taking notes on and getting up steam for.

Poetry and medicine! I watched you finger that dog's paw down in Floridoh, looking for sand burrs, with your weaker hand yet—and I saw how quickly the dog knew that here was guy who knew his business.[323] (In my philanthropic worries a bit sooner, I nearly got bitten.)

Yet, I'll bet it never even crossed your mind what an act that was. Probably you were just having Contact, in this case with a stray mutt on the beach.

That's what you demanded of us all, in our work. And it's what you got, in yours. And you were proved right right right. (Well, not as right as all that; for now and then I wish you were a bit more to the left, e.g., with regard to Cuba.)

Dear Bill, I respect you so much, and I am so grateful to you for your typically spontaneous letter, I will not ask you to repeat one word of it in public. Let the others batten and fatten on your kind assurances.

You're a mellow one, you baystard. And it is my boast that I know how mellow you are, in line after line (along with your cantankerousness, of course!).

And now, ending the old year and/or starting the new year right, I would say, for the both of us, who love you both: Do flourish; and do let's have lots of good moments yet, come next year.

Sincerely,

K.B.

[B]   [Andover]
August 22, 1961

Dear Bill,

Ja, die Welt ist dumm.

Aber nein, du hast mir kein Buch gesandt.[324]

Back from Chicawguh, I have by now got 25 pages of my godam <u>Poetics</u> definitively revised.[325] (Or more or less definitively.)

The Latin word for "man" (<u>vir</u>) means a male of arms-bearing age. From it we get the word "virtue." The Greek word for "Mars" (Ares) comes from the same root as the Greek word for "virtue" (arete).

Our word "Beauty" goes back to the Latin word for "war" (belloum), and beyond that to an earlier form, duellum. Both are tied up with the Latin word for "good" (bonus, earlier duonus).

Am I wrong, or is it true, that English has no word to rhyme with "music"? (Not quite: I made up a reference to "the Falls at Hoosick," but the poor Indians helped out with that one.)

Anyhow, we got good rhymes for "sit and think."

Holla!

Sincerely,

K.B.

[B]   [Englewood, Florida]
[December 1961]

Dear Floss and Bill,

We didn't get out any Christmas cards this year because we were involved with packing and moving down here just before the holidays. We have a fine house (inside plumbing! and central heat) and will be here until April 1. Then we shall return to Andover for a long spring, which I am looking forward to.

KB is finishing the <u>Symbolic</u> ms. and I am typing it.[326] He has just enough speaking engagements here and there to break the monotony of straight revision, which is fine.

I, too, enjoyed the very fine poems of Bill's and also the article of Lowell's, and was going to write you about them, but KB's letter went out meanwhile and he is speaking for both of us.[327] We are so anxious to know how things are going for you, and hope Floss will find time to drop us a card.

Best love, and all the good wishes in the world for the New Year,

Lib

I don't know whether other people's calamities make you feel any better or not—but KB is on a strict diet, no liquor, etc. to bring down his blood pressure, and I am having my front teeth pulled this weekend! However, the b/p is now down to 155 or thereabouts, and I am looking forward to sporting my store teeth next week!

Greetings to the Jrs. Are any of them living with you now? How are the grandchildren? Also say hello to Madelein when you see her.

[B]   [Kingston, NJ]
January 14, 1962

Dear Bill,

Have just read the article by Robert Lowell on you in the current <u>Hudson Rev.</u>

It gives me a chance to say why I haven't written the article on you that I have long wanted to write.

I have not written it because I'd love to have done a long piece having exactly the quality of those warm and brilliant and thoroughly just pages by Lowell.

Mea culpa, mea maxima culpa. Forgive, Bill—but at least let me hereby formally subscribe to the quality of the perceptions and sentiments so persuasively set down by Lowell.

Meanwhile, I'm in the midst of revising a chapter on hermeneutic burdens having to do with the subtle interrelationships btw. Sphinx and sphincter. (I'm already two weeks past the self-imposed deadline for the book as a whole, and I'm not halfway through the revision.)

Best greetings, and to Floss. And if you have but a fraction of your poems' felicity, then surely you're all afloat with joy. (Why did my Ucs make me first write "job"?)

We're here, quite comfortably fixed, until the end of March. No problems except my worst enemy, meself. Wish we could see you.

Sincerely,

K.B.

I append a few lines from a recent poem, perhaps not intrinsically worth considering, but of diaristic relevance:

Meanwhile me,
A vile old man,
Inclined to an old man's greed,
Seeing the seamy side,
Powerlessly exclaiming

<u>Bring on your bombs, your bugs, and the trick chemicals</u>
<u>Get this damned business done</u>

<u>But in the interim</u>
<u>Curse me for a not-yet-housebroken cur</u>
<u>And rub my nose in filthy lucre</u>.[328]

[B]   [Andover]
July 12, 1962

Dear Bill,

After working my dam fool head off, and then falling into a sloth that which none could be slothier, I am gradually pulling the self together. And I now seize my trusty Qwert Uiop (or, if you will, my Asdf Gh Jkl, or do I mean my Zxcv Bnm?—though I resolutely refuse to call it a "#$%_&'()*"). And I wanna thank you greatly for the hand-attested copy of your <u>Pictures From Brueghel</u>.[329]

Jeez, many things there are nice and fresh! He writes the poem "Because it's there to be written."[330] That's quick and jaunty. Levitaysh is all. I always had some erudite ideas about that famous red wheelbarrow—and I find them confirmed on p. 57.[331]

As for the Brueghel ones: Though I admit that I prefer finger painting to word-painting, I must say you do wonders with that form. And I got much interested in trying to make exactly how the ending of your lines, as printed on the page, differs from the sheerly logical breaks, with some transitions fitting indeterminately on one or the other side of a slope between two sentences. The shifts are very subtle. In one of my early stories (which you never loved!) I tried one thus: "Ampersand placing the germs into the blood through the sucking of lice not affable skulls whom the madam lay with the man so aloof from us as he stood on stilts that passing dogs stopped to befoul them." But after that effort, I collapsed. In your case I have in mind, for instance, the closing lines on p. 9:

under a tree

whose shade
carelessly
he does not share the
resting
center of
their workaday world

"He does not share" goes first of all with "shade," then shades off indetermi-nately into "the resting center."[332] The more closely you watch such, the more it maketh to be dizzy.

I have pedantically marked out quite a number of the poems, in the attempt to see whether, by inspecting the lot, I could spot some corresponding formula (which is <u>my</u> kind of un—and to heck with you!). But I'm still left trailing, and not likely to catch up.

What you were able to do, while picking your way through all the butch-ery and botchery that the freedom-loving (or do I mean money-loving?) inhuman race visited upon the areas this side The Meadows, what you found a way of doing was to keep on saying that there were all sorts of things to write zippy zappy lines about—<u>and without lying</u>, Bejeez, lines without lying! Lines under the sign of Levitaysh—and the sharpness of the lines themselves proves that the levitaysh is really there, if one is but a Billiam Charlie Billiams while one is looking.

All your lines go well. Then all of a sudden there's a line that is so essentially you, I hear you and see you right <u>hic et nunc</u>. You materialize in your sparkling bad-boy best. The shrewd scholastics tell us that, if we do have to go to Heaven, which looks like one hell of a bore to me, we'll be there at the height of all our powers. Just like so many of those lines of yours. And if you now and then feel bum, just bear in mind the fact that the human body can't go on living up to the requirements imposed upon it by brisk verse such as yours.

You baystard, you stinkeroo, you're good! You just are. And don't ever try to deny it. For you have committed yourself, again and again. Us critics and the John Birch Societies have got the dope on you. You could go down a filthy city street, and find there a poem as lovely as a babbling brook in June. And again and again you proved your point: The poem "was there to be written." And that's subversive.

But, though it was undeniably there as has been scientifically and/or poet-ically proved by the writing of it, it couldn't have existed except through the agency of Billiam Charlie Billiams.

Eauque, dear Dopo. And thank you very much indeed for sending us that book, with that precious wobbly signature.[333] You baystard, you stinkeroo. We prize that, because we know what to prize.

And with all our love to Floss,

Sincerely,

K.B.

Dear Fellow North-Jerseyite: Is it poss. that you and Floss may be out this way this summer sometime, in that local cranberry bog writ large? If so, that would be wonderf. And d'yuh know? Come next wint, we're planning to go south again to Floridoah. You should give the area another chawnst. Think it o'er!

K.B.

Route 1—Box 327 AA
Englewood, Florida
March 5, 1963

Dear Floss,

Over the radio we have heard the news about Bill, and we want to write you.

The guy seems to me so perennial, I found myself saying to Shorty, "I must write a letter to Bill this morning."

Even though that month you and he were here was so vexing (for what else can a place like this be in bad weather!)—and I felt guilty for having lured you here by false premises—there is that place up the road where you stayed. It has always seemed like a bond, and now it will seem more so. And above all I remember the whip-poor-will, calling from sumewhere across the bay, on that early morning we came regretfully for the drive to the airport, and your return north.

I hope I can someday finish not too inadequately in Bill's honor the article for which I have long been taking notes, and which I have not finished so far because I could not get what seemed to me the exact mixture of admiration and analysis I thought was needed. (I remember writing him in both delight and envy when I read the article on him by Lowell.)

We know you will be swamped with letters, so please do not feel that you should acknowledge this. But do keep us in mind and keep in mind the thought that we'd love to see you.

This spring we plan to be at Penn State. Then, as things look now, we'll be at Andover all summer. And maybe we could meet some time then.

Bill's work is eternally fresh. And he is written into the very constitution of our country. Who better combined skill and the spontaneity of personality? I think of him as still among us. I always shall.

Sincerely, with love,

K.B.

Notes

1921–1929

1. Most of Williams's letters originate from 9 Ridge Road, Rutherford, New Jersey, where he lived and practiced medicine most of his life.

2. Paul Mariani, *William Carlos Williams: A New World Naked* (New York: Norton & Co., 1981), 174. Robert McAlmon (1896–1956) "first broached the subject to Williams of starting a new little magazine with him now that *Others* was finished." Williams and McAlmon were coeditors of *Contact* 1–4.

3. Jack Selzer, *Kenneth Burke in Greenwich Village: Conversing with the Moderns, 1915–1931* (Madison: University of Wisconsin Press, 1996), 190. The story to which Williams refers may be either "My Dear Mrs. Wurtelbach" or "The White Oxen."

4. Gilbert Vivian Seldes (1893–1970) was the managing editor of *Dial* from 1920 to 1923.

5. Kenneth Burke, "Heaven's First Law," review of *Sour Grapes*, by William Carlos Williams, *Dial* 72 (February 1922): 197–200.

6. Burke used two of Williams's poems in his essay: "January" and "The Great Figure."

7. This is a reference to Burke, "Puritans Defended," review of *The Influence of Puritanism* by John Stephen Flynn, *Literary Review* (1 February 1921): 2.

8. Burke may have sent these, in part, because he was currently working on de Gourmont. See his "Approaches to Rémy de Gourmont," *Dial* 70 (February 1921): 125–38.

9. This may be a reference to Eugène Scribe (1791–1861).

10. Jules Laforgue (1860–87), one of the first French poets to compose in free verse and also one of the early influences on T. S. Eliot.

11. Burke, "The Armour of Jules Laforgue," *Contact* 3 (1921): 9–10; reprinted in *Contact* 1–4 (New York: Kraus, 1967): 9.

12. The long story that Burke mentions is most likely "The White Oxen," completed while he was staying in Asheville in the summer of 1920 (Selzer, *Kenneth Burke*, 88). Burke's characterizing the piece as "too much Huysmans and Little Review" refers to the fact that the *Little Review*, published in the mid to late twenties (edited by Margaret Anderson) often published experimental pieces and espoused liberal politics that frequently ran afoul of the censors. Joris-Karl Huysman (1848–1907) was a French novelist and critic who was part of the fin-de-siecle European authors known as the "decadents," whose works dwelt on morbid and ghoulish aspects of human experience.

13. Edvard Grieg (1843–1907) was a Norwegian composer, a romantic nationalist known chiefly for his impressionistic pieces for piano.

14. Jules Romains (1885–1972) was a French playwright most recognized for his comedies and social satires. The Malcolm Cowley poem to which Burke refers is "Day Coach," *Secession* (spring 1922): 1–3.

15. Selzer, *Kenneth Burke*, 86. This may be a reference to any of five stories that Burke composed while staying with his wife's family, the Batterhams, in Asheville, North Carolina: "The Olympians," "Portrait of an Arrived Critic," "The Soul of Tajn Kafha," "The Excursion," and "Mrs. Maecenas."

16. 134 West 15th St., New York, was the second of Burke's addresses in 1921; his first was 989 Boulevard, Weehauken, New Jersey; the third was 50 Charles St., New York.

17. See Robert McAlmon's "Essentials," *Little Review* 7 (1920): 69–71; "What has Djuna Barnes, or [Max] Bodenheim, or Malcolm Cowley, or Witter Bynner, Ben Hecht, Mark Turbyfill, and a few others to leave? Omit their names from their work,—all that any of them has even done, compiled in a book,—and who would recognize it? They produce neither conscious, accidental, nor perverse art" (69).

18. Selzer, *Kenneth Burke*, 190. This is a reference to Burke's "Dadaisme is France's Latest Literary Fad," published in *New York Tribune*.

19. McSorley's is an ale-house at 15 East 7th Street in the East Village; founded in 1854 and still in business, the bar used to be for men only—women were first admitted in 1971.

20. 13 February 1921, Robert McAlmon married Annie Winifred Ellerman (Bryher). The couple departed for Europe the next day.

21. Matthew Josephson (1899–1978), editor of *Broom* and associated with *Secession*. After interviewing Williams for the *Newark Ledger*, he instigated the first meeting between Burke and Williams, which occurred (in the company of himself and Robert McAlmon), 2 January 1921.

22. Robert McAlmon, "Apotheosis to Extinction [Credo]," *Contact* 1 (December 1920): 1.

23. Selzer, *Kenneth Burke,* 88. From April 15 until the end of September 1921, Burke and his wife Lily lived near the town of Monson, Maine.

24. Selzer, *Kenneth Burke*, 188. Lily Mary Batterham (1893–1969), from Asheville, North Carolina. Burke met her in Greenwich Village and they were married on 19 May 1919. She was the first of two sisters to whom Burke would be married. By Lily, he had three daughters: Jeanne Elspeth Chapin (b. 1920), Eleanor Duva "Happy" Leacock (1922–69), Frances Batterham Burke (b. 1926).

25. This may be a reference to Burke's work on his essay "Approaches to Rémy de Gourmont" as well as to a recent publication of de Gourmont's essays: "Lettres d'un satyr," *Mercure de France* (1919).

26. Stuart Davis (1892–1964), one of the most famous painters New Jersey ever produced, is also noteworthy for having been the artist of the descriptive frontispiece for the original *Kora in Hell* which may be seen in the Williams edition of the *Briarcliff Quarterly* (October 1946), 193. See also Williams's description of his first encounter with the artist in *I Wanted to Write a Poem: The Autobiography of the Works of a Poet*, ed. Edith Heal (Boston: Beacon, 1958), 29.

27. This is a reference to Oscar Williams whose name must have occasionally become confused with William Carlos Williams since they were both publishing about the same time and involved with little magazines as well. See also Babette Deutsch, review of *The Golden Darkness* by Oscar Williams, *Dial* (January 1922), 105.

28. Burke, "Approaches to Rémy de Gourmont," 70. The reference to "Eddie" in the following line appears to be Williams's returning Burke's play on names in his March 22, 1921, letter. Edmund Burke (1729–97) British statesman and philosopher.

29. Selzer, *Kenneth Burke*, 189. Scofield Thayer (1890–1982), editor, and James Watson, president, gained a controlling share of *Dial* in 1920. Thayer was the editor from 1919 to 1925. Noteworthy is the fact that the first issue of the refurbished magazine featured a story by Burke for which he was paid $100 (See Hans Bak, *Malcolm Cowley: The Formative Years* [Athens: University of Georgia Press, 1993], 153). Burke's "My Dear Mrs. Wurtelbach" was rejected by *Dial* in March (See Selzer, *Kenneth Burke*, 190).

30. Floyd Dell (1887–1969), prolific author, literary critic, and coeditor of *The Masses*. Edmund Burke (1729–97), British statesman and philosopher. Williams seems to be returning Burke's play on names in his March 22, 1921, letter

31. Burke, "My Dear Mrs. Wurtelbach," in *The Complete White Oxen* (Berkeley: University of California Press, 1968), 143; the passage to which Williams refers is from Burke's scatological conclusion of the story: "If there is one pure joy left with us, it is to pass a tight jobby."

32. At the bottom of this letter Williams drew a cartoon of a bearded man with a naked woman inscribed within the outline of his beard.

33. Selzer, *Kenneth Burke*, 191. The Burkes spent April through September in Monson, Maine, accompanied by Josephson and the artist Carl Sprinchorn.

34. John Gould Fletcher (1886–1950), "Review of *Kora in Hell*," *Freeman* 3 (May 18, 1921): 238.

35. Williams published Burke's "Ver Renatus Orbis Est" in *Contact* 4 (1921): 9.

36. *Contact* 4 was published in the autumn of 1921.

37. Robert McAlmon's London edition of *Contact* never saw publication.

38. Selzer, *Kenneth Burke*, 97. Burke's story "My Dear Mrs. Wurtelbach" was rejected by Williams in early 1921, but later placed in *Broom* in January 1923.

39. Williams, here, is joycing the name of the lead character in Burke's "My Dear Mrs. Wurtelbach."

40. Paul Scarron (1610–60), French comic playwright and poet who is most memorable for his parody of epic poetry.

41. This is probably his reference to *Contact* 4's manuscript.

42. Mariani, *A New World Naked*, 183. Florence ("Floss" or "Flossie") Herman Williams (1890–1976), Williams's wife. "Floss's neck problems had also been the direct result of Williams's fast driving, when he'd hit a railroad crossing at a fast clip and sent Floss's head smashing against the tin roof of their Ford, crushing one of her neck vertebrae."

43. Robert McAlmon, *McAlmon and the Lost Generation: A Self-Portrait* (Lincoln: University of Nebraska Press, 1962), 374. Wallace Gould (d. 1944), poet from Maine. "A great

mountain of a man. . . . He was a superb cook and for a time supported himself by baking three kinds of pound cake which he sold by mail. In Farmville, Virginia, he lived with Miss Mary Jackson . . . whom he eventually married."

44. Williams, *Kora in Hell: Improvisations* (Boston: Four Seas, 1920).

45. Selzer, *Kenneth Burke*, 191. The manuscript may be Burke's "The White Oxen."

46. Baroness Elsa Von Freytag-Loringhoven, "Thee I call 'Hamlet of Wedding-Ring': Criticism of William Carlos Williams' 'Kora in Hell' and why—," *Little Review* 7 (1921): 48–60. Baroness Von Freytag-Loringhoven (ca. 1870–1927) was an eccentric artist in the Dadaist tradition. For part 2, see *Little Review* 8 (1921): 108–11. For an account of their peculiar relationship, see also Mariani, *A New World Naked*, 160–64.

47. Selzer, *Kennneth Burke*, 190. The stories are very likely Burke's "The White Oxen" and "My Dear Mrs. Wurtelbach."

48. Mariani, *A New World Naked*, 202. In August, the Williamses often vacationed at the Haslunds' family farm (Florence's mother's side) in Wilmington, Vermont.

49. This is probably his reference to *Contact* 4's manuscript.

50. Selzer, *Kenneth Burke*, 191. This may be a reference to one of the following stories: "The Book of Yul," "A Progression" ("An Odyssey"), "In Quest of Olympus," "The Death of Tragedy." These were compositions that Burke had worked on while staying in Monson, Maine, with Matthew Josephson and Carl Sprinchorn.

51. The reference is to one of the following of Burke's publications: "Heroism and Books," review of *Romain Roland: The Man and His Work* by Stefan Zweig, *Dial* (January 1922): 92–93; "The Correspondence of Flaubert," *Dial* (February 1922): 147–55; "Heaven's First Law," 197–200; or to his "Portrait of an Arrived Critic," *Dial* (April 1922).

52. Williams, *Sour Grapes: A Book of Poems* (Boston: Four Seas, 1921).

53. Burke, "David Wassermann," *Little Review* 8 (autumn 1921): 24–37.

54. Jean Cocteau (1889–1963) and Paul Morand (1888–1976) were some of the French authors to whom Williams referred.

55. This may be a reference to Williams's having sent Burke's "The White Oxen" to Robert McAlmon for his consideration in the European edition of *Contact*.

56. Williams, *The Autobiography of William Carlos Williams* (New York: New Directions, 1967), 135. Alfred Kreymborg (1883–1966) founded *Others* in 1915 and coedited the first two issues of *Broom* with Harold Loeb (1921). Williams remembered Kreymborg as the central figure in the Grantwood group: "Several writers were involved, but the focus of my own enthusiasm was the house occupied by Alfred and Gertrude Kreymborg to which, on every possible occasion, I went madly in my flivver to help with the magazine which had saved my life as a writer."

57. In November 1921, Burke was completing the essay on Walter Pater that he first placed in the magazine *1924* and later included in his collection *Counter-Statement* as "Three Adepts of 'Pure' Literature." Williams's reference to Arnold may derive from the fact that the essay, in its original form, contained a short segment on Arnold.

58. Paul Rosenfeld (1890–1946), music critic on *Dial* (1920–27).

59. Edgar Williams (b. 1884), Williams's brother, was graduated from the Massachusetts Institute of Technology with honors in architecture, and won the Prix de Rome, an award which allowed him to study three years at the Academy there.

60. This may be a reference to either *Spring and All* (Paris: Contact, 1923) or to *The Great American Novel* (Paris: Three Mountains, 1923).

61. The advanced copy of *Dial* to which Williams refers contained Burke's review of Williams's *Sour Grapes*. Burke, "Heaven's First Law." *Dial* 72 (February 1922): 197–200. It is noteworthy to point out that the title of Burke's review derives from the conclusion of Williams's Christmas Eve letter of 1921.

62. Williams, *Autobiography*, 165. Wallace Gould stayed with the Williams in Rutherford for the winter of 1922.

63. In 1922, the Burkes bought their seventy-acre farm in Andover for $1500 and began to settle in during the spring of that year.

64. Shi, *Matthew Josephson,* 60. This is a reference to Matthew Josephson and Gorham Munson's *Secession.* "Late in 1921, Josephson decided along with Gorham Munson to publish a new magazine. Low printing costs in postwar Europe made it relatively easy for anyone with enough time and energy to publish a review."

65. Guterrez is a figure associated with the Christopher Columbus segment of Williams's *In The American Grain.*

66. Malcolm Cowley, "Day Coach," *Secession* 1 (spring 1922): 1–3.

67. e. e. cummings, "on the Madam's best april the," *Secession* 2 (July 1922): 1; cummings, "and I imagine," *Secession* 2 (July 1922): 2; cummings, "life hurl my," *Secession* 2 (July 1922): 3; cummings, "working man with hand so hairy-sturdy," *Secession* 2 (July 1922): 4; Cowley, "A Solemn Music," *Secession* 2 (July 1922): 2; Cowley, "Two Swans," *Secession* 2 (July 1922): 3; Burke, "Book of Yul," *Secession* 2 (July 1922): 7–17; Josephson, "The Oblate," *Secession* 2 (July 1922): 21–29.

68. Giuseppi Leopardi (1798–1837). Williams used Leopardi's work as one of the background sources for his Columbus segment of *In The American Grain.*

69. Cranberry Lake is situated four miles from Burke's house in Andover, New Jersey.

70. Paul Herman Williams, "Bobby," Williams's second and last child, born 13 September 1916.

71. Gorham Munson (1896–1969): founder with Matthew Josephson of *Secession* (1922–24).

72. Selzer, *Kenneth Burke*, 191. Burke, who also served as coeditor for some issues, was helping Munson secure manuscripts for *Secession.* They published Williams's "The Hothouse Plant" in the third issue (See Mariani, *A New World Naked*, 202).

73. Burke worked as the acting manager of *Dial* in 1922 and 1923 (Selzer, *Kenneth Burke,* 54).

74. This reference might be to any of five translations Burke undertook during this period; Hans Purrmann, "From the Workshop of Matisse," *Dial* 70 (April 1921): 428–42; Hugo von Hofmannsthal, "Lucidor: Characters for an Unwritten Comedy," *Dial* 73

(August 1922): 121–32; Richard Specht, "Arthur Schnitzler," *Dial* (September 1922): 241–45; Thomas Mann, "Tristan," *Dial* (December 1922): 593–610.

75. Blaise Cendrars (1887–1961): French novelist and poet who edited *Anthologie nègre*, Paris, Éditions de la Sirène, 1921.

76. Williams, *Autobiography*, 55. Charlie Demuth (1883–1936), the painter of flowers and "The Great Figure" to whom Williams dedicated *Spring and All* (1921). "The Hothouse Plant" is the poem referred to here. In 1902, while at medical school, Williams met Demuth at Mrs. Chain's boarding house on Locust St. "I have had several but not many intimate friendships with men during my life, patterned, I suppose, on my youthful experience with my brother. There have been Ezra Pound, Charles Demuth, Bob McAlmon and a few others."

77. Mariani, *A New World Naked*, 208; Williams, *Autobiography*, 179. In order to prepare for the composition of *In The American Grain*, Williams took a year off his medical practice and rented a house in New York from September to January; he and his wife traveled in Europe during the second half of the year.

78. Yvor Winters, "Carlos Williams' New Book," review of *Sour Grapes*, by William Carlos Williams. *Poetry* (20 July 1922): 216–20. "Despite all Dr. Williams' passion to the contrary, he is greatly influenced by his contemporaries and predecessors—by which I do not mean to condemn him, but simply to indicate that he, like any good writer, is inextricably caught in Mr. Eliot's 'tradition'" (220).

79. While in Paris, Robert McAlmon privately published his own collection of short stories, *A Hasty Bunch* (Dijon: Contact Editions, 1922). The story that upset Williams so was "What Is Left Undone," *Little Review* 9, no. 3 (spring 1923): 32–43. The tale is hardly a veiled reference to Williams's frustration (Dr. Holden's in the story) with his inability to get time enough to write so beset was he with the doctoring of "dagos."

80. McAlmon, *McAlmon*, 4. Ernest Hemingway (1899–1961): "Bringing out Hemingway's first book was his [McAlmon's] most memorable publishing achievement."

81. This may be a reference to Burke's review of Williams's *Sour Grapes*. Burke takes his title from the closing lines of Williams's 1921 Christmas Eve letter.

82. Eleanor ("Happy") Duva Burke, born 2 July 1922.

83. McAlmon, *McAlmon*, 379. Lola Ridge (1871–1941): Arriving from Ireland in 1907, Ridge, who was also the American editor and agent for *Broom*, "wrote poems on the beauty and brutality of New York life, and her consistent theme was the martyrdom of the downtrodden." Williams fondly recalled his visits to her informal salon: "On Fridays, which was my day off, I'd stop over sometimes for a party during the evening. The group often met on the second floor of a small Fourteenth Street apartment, most often at Lola Ridge's, that Vestal of the Arts, a devout believer in the humanity of letters; narrow quarters where anyone might on occasion show up" (See Williams, *Autobiography*, 163).

84. William Carlos Williams, "The Attempt," *Secession* 3 (August 1922): 5; Williams, "The Hothouse Plant," *Secession* 4 (January 1923): 21.

85. Waldo Frank, "Hope," *Secession* 3 (August 1922): 1–4. This was an excerpt from Waldo Frank's novel, *City Block* (New York: Boni and Liveright, 1922).

86. Gorham Munson's review of cummings' *Tulips and Chimneys* actually occurred in the next issue: Gorham Munson, "Syrinx," *Secession* 5 (July 1923): 2–11; Williams, "The Hothouse Plant," 21. Wallace Stevens "Last Looks at the Lilacs," *Secession* 4 (January 1923): 19; Hart Crane, "Poster [Voyages I]," *Secession* 4 (January 1923): 20; Kenneth Burke, "In Quest of Olympus," *Secession* 4 (January 1923): 5–18.

87. Burke's meaning here has to do with the divergent views represented by these two groups: Irving Babbitt (1865–1933) and his close associate Paul Elmer More (1864–1937), both of whom taught at Harvard among other places, were leaders of the so-called New Humanists opposed to the decline in standards, both moral and cultural, that were current in the twenties and the thirties and thus promoted a return to traditional values; whereas, Carl Van Doren (1885–1950), atheist and Pulitzer prize winning author, critic, and teacher at Columbia, Burton Rascoe (1892–1957), associate editor of McCalls and later the literary editor for the *New York Tribune* (1923) as well as associations with many other leading newspapers and periodicals throughout the thirties, and John V. A. Weaver (1893–1938) literary editor of the *Brooklyn Daily Eagle* (1920–24) as well as novelist, screenwriter, and poet in the idiom of the street, were members of a loose confederacy of progressives and aesthetic rebels who, touting their various "isms," had targeted outmoded forms of expression that they identified with the genteel tradition.

88. This is probably a reference to the recent July publication of *Secession*.

89. Mariani, *A New World Naked*, 210. Burke acted as coeditor of the third number of Munson and Gorham's *Secession*. For some reason Williams had conceived a momentary dislike for Josephson, and it was Munson's mention of Josephson in his letter to Williams that put Williams off. Nevertheless, in 1925 he would be quick to support Josephson's counterattack on Mencken and Boyd in *Aesthete 25* (See Shi, *Matthew Josephson*, 101–2).

90. e. e. cummings, "Four Poems," *Secession* (July 1922): 1–4.

91. The offices of *Dial* were located at 152 West 13th St., New York City.

92. Mariani, *A New World Naked*, 206. This was to be the last of the first edition of *Contact* magazines.

93. Mariani, *A New World Naked*, 205. In February 1923, Ezra Pound informed Williams that William Bird of Three Mountains Press had sent Williams's *Great American Novel* to press. Williams had known Pound from his earliest days at medical school at the University of Pennsylvania.

94. Evelyn Scott (1893–1963), who had had an affair with Williams that lasted for over a year (1922–23), turned out novels, as the record shows, at a fairly steady pace: *Narrow House* (1921), *Escapade* (1923), *Migrations* (1927), *Ideals* (1927), *Wave* (1929), *Blue Rum* (under the pseudonym of Ernest Souza) (1930), *Calendar of Sin* (1931), *Breathe Upon These Slain* (1934), *Bread and a Sword* (1937), *Shadow of the Hawk* (1941). An explanation for Williams's use of "marionettes" derives from the fact that Kreymborg had brought out an edition of his plays: *Puppet Plays* (New York: Harcourt, Brace, 1923). Williams once played a role opposite Mina Loy in Alfred Kreymborg's Dadaist play *Lima Beans*, where the actors' actions were to appear wooden-like, as if manipulated by a marionette. Noteworthy, too,

is the fact that Williams had had a rupture with Kreymborg in 1918 caused by Kreymborg's selecting Edna St. Vincent Millay's *Da Capo* instead of a Williams's play to be performed by the Provincetown Players. Even though Williams would dedicate *Sour Grapes* to Kreymborg in 1921, they never recaptured their former closeness (155).

95. Williams, *Autobiography*, 180–83. Before their trip to Europe in 1924, Bill and Flossie drove down to Farmville, Virginia, to visit Wallace Gould in late September 1923.

96. Williams and his wife traveled in Europe from January through June 1924.

97. Mariani, *A New World Naked*, 229. On Tuesday, 25 March, Williams and his wife "took the train south down to Frascati for the day and noted that the train and the marketplace were jammed with people. He remembered hyacinths and violets and anemones blooming and belling everywhere."

98. Caracalla, Marcus Aurelius Antoninus, Roman emperor from 211–17, is most remembered for the Baths of Caracalla. This reference to the man who Gibbon termed "the common enemy of mankind" coupled with the mention of the public baths he had built as a sort of penance, may be an indirect means of apologizing for an unflattering remark Williams had made about Burke.

99. There is no record that the *Manuscript Editions* were ever published.

100. This may be a reference to Burke's January 1924 publication of *Broom* 6 in which he had published his short story "Prince Llan: An Ethical Masque in Seven Parts, Including a Prologue and Coda," (12–22).

101. Selzer, *Kenneth Burke*, 195. In the summer of 1924, Burke had contracted with *Dial* to translate the introduction of Spengler's *Decline of the West* for $120.

102. Mariani, *A New World Naked*, 231. Andreas Gaspar and Lajos Kassak were "coeditors of *MA* ('Today'), an avant-garde magazine published in Vienna."

103. Burke, "A Progression," *Secession* 7 (winter 1924): 21–30.

104. Mariani, *A New World Naked*, 231. This is a reference to Andreas Gaspar and Lajos Kassak, coeditors of *MA* ('Today'). While in Vienna, Gaspar had handed Williams the latest edition of *Secession*.

105. Gorham Munson, "The American Murkury," *Secession* 7 (winter 1924): 32. In response to an attack on *Aesthete; Model 1924*, Munson's salvo was directed both against the audience of *The American Mercury* and its primary author, H. L. Mencken.

106. Williams here is referring both to the text and ideas of Waldo Frank's *Our America* (New York: Boni and Liveright, 1919), "a book whose very title opposed it to the values of the genteel representatives of 'their America.' *Our America* was a nationalistic call to arms for a new generation of writers and artists . . . who, Frank hoped, could together counter the problems tabulated by Brooks and who might continue the anti-puritan, anti-genteel sentiments Frank observed in Huck Finn, Abraham Lincoln, and H. D. Thoreau" (See Selzer, *Kenneth Burke*, 33).

Nevertheless, Frank's congratulatory introduction to "My dear Jacques Copeau and Gaston Gallimard" [the former, once director of the magazine *Nouvelle Révue Française* and head of its associated *Théâtre du Vieux Colombier* (then playing in New York for the last two years); the later, director of the Publishing House of the *Nouvelle Révue Française*] as being the inspiration for the project, may be the source of Williams's defensiveness here ("They are trying to get hold of 'Our America'"), notwithstanding Frank's explanation of his anxiety of French influence and high culture: "If I looked up continuously from my page into the distant eye of Andre Gide, the chances were I should tear my page to bits" *Our America* (New York: Boni and Liveright, 1919), x.

107. Burke, *The White Oxen* (New York: A. and C. Boni, 1924).

108. Edwin Seavers had announced from Woodstock, New York, the founding of *1924* (Bak, *Malcolm Cowley,* 321).

109. Yvor Winters (1900–68), "The Testament of a Stone," *Secession* 8 (1924): 1–20.

110. Scofield Thayer had asked Burke to serve as his private secretary on his European trip. Burke refused (Selzer, *Kenneth Burke,* 197).

111. Emanuel Carnevali (1898–1942). Williams characterized him as one of the "prominent one-book men about New York" (Williams, *Autobiography,* 266). Contact Editions published his *A Hurried Man* in 1925.

112. Madeline and Andrew Spence were members of the Polytopics Club started by Williams in the early twenties. Young Bill Williams would marry their daughter, Daphne, in 1949. See Mariani, *A New World Naked,* 137–40, for a description of the club's activities. Cranberry Lake is about five miles from Burke's Andover home.

113. This letter and the letter dated 20 October are on *Dial* stationary.

114. Burton Rascoe (1892–1957) authored a column for the *Herald Tribune,* "The Bookman's Daybook" (Bak, *Malcolm Cowley,* 282); he may have been with Williams and Isabel Paterson during an interview she had with the poet in late July (Mariani, *A New World Naked,* 285).

115. This was written in Greek.

116. Burke is referring to Williams's comment in his 28 August 1925 letter.

117. *Dial's* office was at this address.

118. Burke here refers to his wife's sister Libbie Batterham, who would later become his second wife.

119. In part, the source of tension between Ernest Augustus Boyd (1887–1946) and the little magazine crowd may be found in the *American Mercury's* first issue, December 1923, where Boyd's "Aesthete: Model 1924" attacked the modern aesthetes (Bak, *Malcolm Cowley,* 294). Malcolm Cowley describes the event in full detail in his *Exile's Return,* 190–96. Also worth mentioning is the fact that Boyd authored a biography on Mencken: *H. L. Mencken* (New York: Robert McBride, 1925).

120. In November 1925, Scofield Thayer, motivated by a belief that Burke was intentionally undermining the publication, asked Burke to leave *Dial.* Marianne Moore and Sibley Watson prevented the dismissal (Selzer, *Kenneth Burke,* 133).

121. William Carlos Williams, *In The American Grain* (New York: Albert and Charles Boni, 1925.)

122. John F. Riordan (1903–88): as a young graduate of Yale Sheffield Scientific School in early twenties, Riordan, a successful mathematician and engineer, struck up a correspondence with Williams that continued for many years (Mariani, *A New World Naked,* 248).

123. This letter and the one dated 31 December are addressed to 40 Morton St., N.Y. Burke kept a room there from March to December and commuted to his Andover farm on weekends (Selzer, *Kenneth Burke*, 197).

124. The busiest part of the year for Williams's doctoring was the winter months.

125. Matthew Josephson, *Zola and His Time* (New York: Macaulay Co., 1928).

126. "Fight" was never published in *Dial*.

127. The tickets were for Madeleine Heyder's piano recital at Steinway Concert Hall, 109 W. 57th St., 15 April 1926.

128. Burke's review of *In The American Grain* was entitled "Subjective History," *Herald Tribune*, 14 March 1926, 7. Though Burke's appreciative review celebrates the vitality with which Williams brings to life the exploits of Columbus, Boone, DeSoto, and Eric the Red, midway through his essay Burke claims that the work: "tends toward a maximum of 'interpretation' and a minimum of research. . . . The purpose is poetry, not history. Williams seeks bravuras rather than facts" (7).

129. "The Five Dollar Guy," *New Masses* 1 (May 1926): 19–29. This is the story over which Williams lost a $5,000 lawsuit owing to his failure to alter the facts of the story enough to disguise its actual source (Williams, *Autobiography*, 241–42; Mariani, *A New World Naked*, 253–54).

130. Albert and Charles Boni of New York were Williams's first commercial publishers.

131. "Mike" was a friendly slur for the Irish.

132. This is a reference to the informal Sunday salons hosted by the Burkes at their Andover farm.

133. In 1929, Richard Johns started the journal *Pagany*, named in honor of Williams's *Voyage to Pagany* (Mariani, *A New World Naked*, 291). Although Williams was hesitant to assume any "critical editorial status" (Williams to Johns, 12 July 1929), he was currently involved with another periodical—he did compose the manifesto for Johns, a service for which he was paid. *A Return to Pagany, 1929–1932*, eds. Stephen Halpert and Richard Johns (Boston: Beacon, 1969), 11.

134. Williams's joyced version of *The Hound & Horn* (1927–34), a title derived from Ezra Pound's poem "The White Stag." R. P. Blackmur was its editor at the time.

135. A reference to Wall Street's Black Thursday, 24 October 1929. Williams's son Bill related the account of his father's having papered his attic study with stock charts that recorded the declining market published in the daily newspapers. (William Eric Williams, personal interview, 16 November 1993.)

136. *The Hound and Horn* was founded in 1927 by Lincoln Kirstein (1907–96).

137. Kenneth Burke, "Seventh Declamation," *Hound and Horn* 3 (fall 1929): 71–77.

138. Andre Gide (1869–1951), *Les Faux-Monnayeurs* (Paris: Gallimard, 1925).

139. Kenneth Burke, "Thomas Mann and Andre Gide," *Bookman* 73 (July 1930): 228–31.

140. "Rain" was the title of the poem.

141. André Gide (1869–1951), *Si le Grain ne Meurt* (Paris: Gallimard, 1928); *Les Faux-Monnayeurs* (Paris: Gallimard, 1925).

1930–1943

1. This letter is addressed to Room 3006, 61 Broadway, New York, where Burke stayed while he worked for Colonel Arthur Woods, who had hired him to study connections between drug addiction and crime at the Bureau of Social Hygiene in New York; Burke ghostwrote Woods's book *Dangerous Drugs* (1931) (Selzer, *Kenneth Burke,* 134).

2. Victor Francis Calverton, a pen name for George Goetz (1901–40), was a revolutionary Marxist and owner/editor of *Modern Quarterly* during the twenties and thirties. Although the cause of Williams's comment remains unclear, we do know that Burke had recently reviewed one of Calverton's books. Burke, "On Re and Dis," review of *The Never Spirit: A Sociological Criticism of Literature,* by C. F. Calverton. *Dial* 79 (August 1925): 165–69.

3. Burke published his "Tenth Declamation" in *Pagany* 1, no. 4 (October–December 1930): 19–22.

4. Williams published his "American Poetry, 1920–1930" in *Symposium* (January 1931), 60–84.

5. Lily's sister, Libbie (1897–1969), would later become Burke's second wife (18 December 1933).

6. *Miscellany* (New York: Harcourt, Brace, 1930).

7. *The Last Imagist Anthology* (New York: Covici, Friede, 1930). Rebecca West published an article in the *The Bookman* (September 1929) that cast the works of Joyce in a bad light. Williams's answer, "A Point for American Criticism," first printed in *transition, 1929*, is reprinted in his *Selected Essays,* 80–90.

8. Although this may be a direct reference to Robert de Billy's 1930 edition of Proust's *Lettres et Conversations,* between 1925 and 1930 eight separate volumes of Proust's correspondences were published.

9. The journal *transition* (1927–38) was founded by Eugene Jolas (1894–1952) and Elliot Paul (1891–1958). *New Review* (1931–32) was founded by Samuel Putnam (1892–1950).

10. This may be a reference to a magazine that Burke was considering as a sort of successor to *Dial.* It never saw publication.

11. Louis Zukofsky, "The Cantos of Ezra Pound," *Criterion* (January 1931): 424–40.

12. William Carlos Williams, "Excerpts from a Critical Sketch: The **XXX** Cantos of Ezra Pound," *Symposium* (April 1931): 257–63.

13. Kenneth Burke, *Counter-Statement* (New York: Harcourt, Brace and Company, 1931).

14. Kenneth Burke, *Towards a Better Life: Being a Series of Epistles, or Declamations* (New York: Harcourt, Brace and Company, 1932).

15. This is a reference to Burke's work on *Secession* with Matthew Josephson.

16. Burke reviewed this work. Kenneth Burke, "In Quest of the Way," review of *A New Model of the Universe,* by P. D. Ouspensky, *New Republic* 68 (September 1931): 104–6.

17. This is most likely a reference to the hero of Burke's novel, *Towards a Better Life:* John Neal.

18. Williams's use of "view" here is doubtlessly a reference to *View* magazine in which he had placed several essays and reviews.

19. Kenneth Burke, *Towards a Better Life: Being a Series of Epistles, or Declamations* (New York: Harcourt, Brace, 1932).

20. Burke lived on Bleecker Street in late 1931 (Selzer, *Kenneth Burke,*13).

21. Katherine Anne Porter, "Bouquet for October," *Pagany* (January–March 1932): 21–22.

22. Kenneth Burke, *Counter-Statement* (New York: Harcourt, Brace, 1931).

23. In 1644, John Milton (1608–74) composed "Areopagitica," a pamphlet in response to Cromwell's establishment of a Board of Censorship.

24. Frederick Winslow Taylor (1856–1915): American industrial engineer who was called the father of scientific management. He devised management methods for shops, offices, and industrial plants. "Black Friday" is a reference to the recent economic collapse.

25. These lines are from a popular drinking song, "Little Brown Jug."

26. This a reference to Burke's publication of *Declamations.*

27. William Carlos Williams, *Collected Poems, 1921–1931*, introduced by Wallace Stevens (New York: Objectivist Press, 1934).

28. See Burke to Williams, 15 October 1931.

29. This closing, derived from T. S. Eliot's *The Waste Land*, was a deliberate jab at Williams's prejudice against the poet.

30. This is a reference to the publication party for Burke's *Declamations.*

31. In November 1932, Williams and Nathanael West (1903–40) brought out *Contact* 3.

32. Kenneth Burke, *Towards a Better Life: Being a Series of Epistles, or Declamations* (New York: Harcourt, Brace, 1932).

33. Williams was soliciting manuscripts for another edition of *Contact* (Mariani, *A New World Naked*, 321).

34. William Carlos Williams, *The Embodiment of Knowledge*, ed. Ron Loewinsohn. (New York: New Directions, 1974).

35. Though in the early twenties Winters was a "young disciple" of Williams and he (Williams) had admired some poems of Winters presented to him by Burke (Mariani, *A New World Naked*, 245), it is likely that Williams still held a grudge against Winters for his *Sour Grapes* review. Still, Williams did not allow this animosity to prejudice his selection of manuscripts for the last number of the revived *Contact*, where a work of Winters was included.

36. *Contact* 3, coedited with Nathanael West, came out in November 1933.

37. Williams sent his *Embodiment of Knowledge* to Burke as a potential publication for the MSS Editions. "Burke had spotted John Dewey's influence in the *Embodiment* as a weakness" (Mariani, *A New World Naked*, 336). It is noteworthy to point out that the MSS Editions never came to fruition.

38. John Dewey (1859–1952). As he often did, Williams carelessly lumped such figures as Dewey and Max Eastman (1883–1969) together in a general group of "academics" who presumed to dictate what poetry should be, feeling that "their arrogance effectively divided them from the people they insisted on treating as so many counters" (Mariani, *A New World Naked*, 483).

39. After Burke returned *The Embodiment of Knowledge*, Williams tried *The White Mule* on him—it was only partially completed. But Williams was unable to publish the latter until 1934 when *The Magazine* (Beverly Hills, California) published nine chapters over a one-year period (Hugh Witemeyer, ed. *William Carlos Williams and James Laughlin: Selected Letters* [New York: Norton & Co., 1989], 2).

40. This batch of poems would become *Collected Poems 1921–1931*.

41. Franklin Spier was heading up the *Manuscript Editions*. See Burke to Williams, 5 January 1933.

42. Williams, *Collected Poems 1921–1931*. Maxim Lieber was a New York literary agent and anthologist who briefly represented Williams. His stationary bore the heading "Authors' Representative" and his office was located at 55 West Forty-second Street in New York. With Barrett Harper Clark (1890–1953), Lieber edited three editions of *Great Short Stories of the World*.

43. Charles Reznikoff (1894–1976) was among the group of objectivists that were contributors to the Objectivist Press, the original publishers. *Testimony: The U.S., 1895–1915* (New York: Black Sparrow Press, 1978). Burke did write an introduction for the work.

44. This a reference to Carl Rakosi's founding of the Objectivist Press.

45. *The First President* was the name of Williams's operatic project (William Carlos Williams, *The First President,* in *The New Caravan,* ed. Alfred Kreymborg, Lewis Mumford, and Paul Rosenfeld (New York: W. W. Norton, 1936), 563–602.

46. Wallace Stevens wrote the introduction for Williams's *Collected Poems*.

47. *Blast*, a proletarian news magazine—not to be confused with Wyndham Lewis's London *Blast*—was founded by Fred and Betty Miller.

48. Fred Miller was an unemployed tool designer and writer (Witemeyer, *William Carlos Williams*, 2). "Though they were still struggling to keep *Blast* alive, they did not have enough money even for rent. So, on May 1 [1934], [Williams] drove to their apartment, took them and their daughter and their few belongings, and then drove them up to his unheated summer cottage at West Haven to give them a place to stay for the summer" (Mariani, *A New World Naked*, 355).

49. This is a reference to the celebration of Burke's *Permanence and Change* (New York: New Republic, 1935).

50. Burke was awarded a Guggenheim Fellowship on 7 May 1935.

51. *Southern Review* was founded in 1935 by Cleanth Brooks (1906–94), Robert Penn Warren (1905–89), Albert Erskine, and Charles Pipkin (1899–1941). Kenneth Burke published an article in the first number of the journal: "Recent Poetry," review of *No Thanks*, by e. e. cummings (July 1935): 164–77.

52. As the letters attest, for years Burke had intended to compose a comprehensive article on the works of Williams.

53. Williams's oldest son, Bill, was at Williams College, and his youngest son, Paul, had just entered the University of Pennsylvania.

54. Kenneth Burke, *Attitudes Toward History* (New York: New Republic, 1937).

55. Kenneth Burke, "Reading While You Run," *New Republic* 93 (November 1937): 36–37.

56. *New Republic.*

57. Alfred Emanuel Smith (1873–1944) was four-time Democratic governor of the State of New York as well as the Democratic nominee for president in 1928.

58. A reference to Burke's infant son Anthony.

59. William Eric Williams (b. 1914). Dr. Williams still lives and practices medicine at 9 Ridge Rd.

60. In April 1939, Williams would find occasion to use his studies during his address to the First Inter-America Writers' Conference in Puerto Rico (Mariani, *A New World Naked,* 446). His "Federico Garcia Lorca" is a related essay from this period and may be the work to which Williams is referring. (*Selected Essays of William Carlos Williams* [New York: Random House 1954], 219–30). This essay was also published in the *Kenyon Review* in 1939.

61. Burke, *The Philosophy of Literary Form.* Although Burke published many of the sections of *The Philosophy of Literary Form* as separate essays in the late thirties, this is probably a reference to "On Musicality in Verse," first published in *Poetry* (October 1940): 31–40.

62. Although Burke had reviewed *Sour Grapes* ("Heaven's First Law"), he never did complete another article on the poet until after Williams's death. See Burke to Williams, October 1935; 31 October 1945; 9 June 1948; 24 August 1950; 31 December 1960; 14 January 1962.

63. This is a reference to Burke's "Freud—and the Analysis of Poetry," *American Journal of Sociology* 45 (November 1939): 391–417 [also in *The Philosophy of Literary Form.* The passage to which he refers is on page 239 of the book].

64. Philip Horton, "Anthology of a Mind," review of *The Complete Collected Poems of William Carlos Williams: 1906–1938, New Republic,* 21 December 1938, 208.

"Unfortunately, the manner habitually associated with his name is the stripped style, the end product of his early imagism and later naturalism. In its extreme form this style is little more than experimental, the application of a theory; its poetic achievement is almost nil" (208).

Williams's response came in the same periodical, 11 January 1939 (291): "Boy! that's pretty cagey shootin'. I wish I could split 'em that fine. . . . There's a certain amount of justice in what he said, . . . but if he had paid the least attention to the book as a thesis on the conception of form which it attempts to realize—if failingly—he could not have fallen into the pontifical manner which mars his first paragraph. . . . To hell with him. If he hadn't had Stevens to teach him how to look crookedly he wouldn't have had anything at all to say. Tell him to go wipe his nose."

65. Burke is referring to the usual Sunday gathering of the New York crowd at his Andover home as well as to a lawsuit that Williams lost owing to his failure to alter the facts of a story enough to disguise its actual source (Williams, *Autobiography*, 241–42; Mariani, *A New World Naked*, 253–54).

66. Leonard Stanley Brown: teacher and anthologist. Burke was a visiting lecturer in Brown's summer courses in the late 1930s. Charles Edward Eaton (b. 1916): poet. In later years, Eaton gave Williams an account of Frost's warning his students (Eaton was one of them) away from Williams's works (Mariani, *A New World Naked*, 454).

67. Kenneth Burke, "On Musicality in Verse as Illustrated by Some Lines of Coleridge," *Poetry* 57 (October 1940): 31–40.

68. On 16 April 1941, Williams presented his talk, "The Basis of Poetic Form," in the theater at the University of Puerto Rico (Mariani, *A New World Naked*, 446).

69. Ernest Hemingway, *For Whom the Bell Tolls* (New York: Scribner's, 1940).

70. This is a reference to Williams's "A Fault of Learning," *Partisan Review* 10 (September 1943): 466–68.

71. Kenneth Burke, "The Five Master Terms, Their Place in a 'Dramatistic' Grammar of Motives," *View* (June 1943): 50–52.

72. Ken is referring to a rebuttal to Williams's article by Max Eastman and John Dewey of the *Partisan Review* (Mariani, *A New World Naked*, 484).

73. This resentment that Burke held for Sidney Hook and his crowd at the *Partisan Review* had been established for some years. See his response to Hook's review of *Attitudes Toward History*, "Is Mr. Hook a Socialist?" *Partisan Review* 4 (January 1938): 40–44.

74. See Williams to Burke, 12 July 1943.

75. Max Lerner (1902–92) was educated at Yale (Ph.D.), published thousands of articles in the *New York Post, PM,* and the *New Republic,* along with fifteen books, and Max Eastman (1883–1969), in the early decades of the century, was an editor of radical magazines: *The Masses* (1913–17) and *The Liberator* (1918–22). Where Lerner had realized the limits of radicalism and opted instead for a more centrist liberalism and gradual reform, Eastman, in the early years, held onto radical Marxist views even unto the irrelevance of literature in the modern age: he was opposed to modernist poets, New Humanists, as well as critics and the professoriat, affirming that Marx, Pavlov, and Freud had rendered them useless (Kazin, *On Native Grounds,* 404).

76. The Grant anecdote appears in Williams's "A Fault of Learning."

77. In 1943, the same year she made *Jane Eyre,* Joan Fontaine (b. 1917) costarred with Charles Boyer in *The Constant Nymph.*

78. From 1943 to 1961, Burke taught at Bennington College.

79. Williams, "A Fault of Learning."

80. Delmore Schwartz (1913–66). The response to Williams's article was titled "The Politics of W. C. Williams," *Partisan Review* (October 1943).

81. William Carlos Williams, *The Wedge* (Cummington, Mass.: Cummington Press, 1944).

82. François Rabelais (1495?–1553). French physician and man of letters. This may be a reference to Rabelais' injunction, "Do as thou wilt," the only rule in his utopian Abbey of Thélème (*Gargantua and Pantagruel,* Book 1), which housed both nuns and monks.

1945–1963

1. Kenneth Burke, "Container and the Thing Contained," *Sewanee Review* 53 (1945): 56–78.

2. Burke, *A Grammar of Motives.*

3. Burke, *A Rhetoric of Motives.*

4. See Burke to Williams, 15 October 1945.

5. These references are to Karl Shapiro's *Essay on Rime* and his own talk, "Verse as Evidence of Thought," given at Briarcliff Junior College (Mariani, *A New World Naked,* 517).

6. Kenneth Burke, "The Temporizing Essence," *Kenyon Review* 7 (1975): 616–27. (From his final chapter of *A Grammar of Motives*). Burke also published two reviews in the same volume: "Careers without Careerism," a review of Eric Russell Bentley's *A Century of Hero-Worship,* and "The Work of Regeneration," a review of Margaret Young's *Angel in the Forest.*

7. Aulus Gellius, second century Latin author who lived both in Rome and Athens and authored for the edification of his children a collection of essays titled *Noctes Atticae.*

8. See Burke to Williams, 12 October 1945.

9. See Williams to Burke, 15 October 1945.

10. See Burke to Williams, 12 October 1945.

11. This is a reference to the medical procedure that Williams had set up for Burke's complaint of 12 October 1945.

12. The "Great Market": Prentice Hall. These are the proofs for his *A Grammar of Motives.*

13. See Williams to Burke, 23 October 1945.

14. *Quarterly Review of Literature* 2, no. 2 (1945). The piece contains several poems by Williams; an article by Williams, "The Fatal Blunder," which is a criticism of "place" in Eliot's "Ash Wednesday"; Kenneth Rexroth's review of Williams's *The Phoenix and the Tortoise* entitled "In Praise of Marriage."

15. Kenneth Burke, "Motives and Motifs in the Poetry of Marianne Moore." *Accent* 2 (spring 1942): 157–69; Also in appendix C of *A Grammar of Motives* (Berkeley: University of California Press, 1969). The passage to which he refers has to do with the distinction he draws between Marianne Moore's "imagism" from Williams's "objectivism" (486).

16. This may be a reference to Williams's letter published in the *Partisan Review,* "Notes Towards a Definition of Culture." Eliot's essay along with an article published in the 1942 *Partisan Review,* "the Music of Poetry," had Williams feeling that Eliot was appropriating ideas upon which he (Williams) had based his entire life's work, especially

on the relation of "place" to the formation of culture, or the contribution of rural life to a city's culture, without having given him any credit (Mariani, *A New World Naked*, 476, 489).

17. Burke, *A Rhetoric of Motives*.

18. See Burke to Williams, 31 October 1945.

19. Ibid.

20. Lourdes, in southwest France, was the site where Our Lady of Lourdes appeared to St. Bernadette in 1858, and since became a place where it was believed that miraculous cures were effected.

21. William Carlos Williams, *A Dream of Love* (New York: New Directions, 1948).

22. See Burke to Williams, 12 October 1945.

23. Ibid.

24. This is a reference to the Burkes' proposed plan to spend the winter in Florida.

25. On 30 September 1945, Vivienne Koch interviewed Williams for what would become a critical biography of the poet (Mariani, *A New World Naked*, 510); his feelings toward the interview were set down in Williams, "The Visit," *Later Poems*, 234. Williams, "At Kenneth Burke's Place," *Later Poems*, 256, is the sketch he dashed off (Witemeyer, *William Carlos Williams*, 122).

26. Thomas Childs Cochran (1902–99) published over ten books on American business. With William Miller, he wrote *The Age of Enterprise: A Social History of Industrial America* (New York: Macmillan, 1942). Among Matthew Josephson's publications is *The Robber Barons: The Great American Capitalists* (New York: Harcourt, Brace, 1934). Burke reviewed *The Age of Enterprise* in *Direction* 6 (spring 1943): 3–5.

27. See Burke to Williams, 12 October 1945.

28. Burke, *A Rhetoric of Motives*.

29. Burke, *A Grammar of Motives*.

30. The "trilogy" refers to Burke's *A Grammar of Motives*, *A Rhetoric of Motives*, and his proposed *Symbolic of Motives*, which was never written.

31. Will Durant, *The Story of Philosophy* (New York: Washington Square Press, 1933).

32. *Partisan Review*.

33. See Williams to Burke, 10 November 1945.

34. Burke's "Aristotle and Aquinas" may be found in *A Grammar of Motives* (Berkeley: University of California Press, 1969), 227–32.

35. This reference to literary form recalls the topic of their first discussions with one another in the early twenties. See Burke to Cowley, September 1920. Jay, *Selected Correspondence*, 77. "Matty" refers to Matthew Josephson.

36. This is a reference to a line in Williams's poem "The Visit": "I can see also / the dagger in the left hand when / the right hand strikes." *Later Poems* (234).

37. See Burke to Williams, 12 October 1945.

38. See Burke to Williams, 19 November 1945.

39. Williams, "Improvisations," *Kora in Hell*, 52–59.

40. See Burke to Williams, 19 November 1945.

41. Burke, *A Rhetoric of Motives.*

42. "Shorty" refers to Libbie Burke.

43. William Carlos Williams, "The Cod," *The Collected Earlier Poems* (New York: Objectivist Press, 1934), 333–34.

44. See Burke to Williams, 23 November 1945.

45. See Burke to Williams, 12 October 1945.

46. Williams, "Improvisations."

47. William Carlos Williams, *A Novelette and Other Prose (1921–1931)* (Toulon, France: To Press, 1931).

48. See Williams to Burke, 14 November 1945.

49. Williams, *A Novelette and Other Prose (1921–1931).*

50. See Williams to Burke, 18 November 1945.

51. See Burke to Williams, 19 November 1945.

52. This is a reference to the procedure Williams set up for Burke's complaint in Burke to Williams, 12 October 1945.

53. Burke, *A Grammar of Motives.*

54. This is a reference to "The Socractic Transcendence," *A Grammar of Motives*, 420–40.

55. On his 11 November 1945 visit to Burke's Andover home, Williams composed "At Kenneth Burke's Place," *Later Poems*, 256.

56. See Williams to Burke, 14 December 1945.

57. William Carlos Williams, *Paterson, Book One.* (1946; reprint, New York: New Directions, 1963).

58. Burke, *A Grammar of Motives.*

59. See Williams to Burke, 23 October 1945.

60. Williams may be referring here to his own article recently published in defense of Pound: "The Case for and against Ezra Pound," *PM* (25 November 1945): 16.

61. Burke, *A Grammar of Motives.*

62. Conrad Aiken (1889–1973). Although Williams's poems conclude Aiken's first anthology (*A Comprehensive Anthology of American Poetry, 1944*), the revised edition overlooked his work (*Modern Library Anthology of American Poetry, 1945*). Aiken was at Harvard with T. S. Eliot and introduced him to Ezra Pound.

63. William Carlos Williams, "Russia," *New Republic* (29 April 1946): 615.

64. William Carlos Williams, review of *The Granite Butterfly*, by Parker Tyler, *Accent* 6 (spring 1946): 203. Williams never missed a chance to get his jabs in: ". . . the best poem written by an American since *The Waste Land* . . . certainly by far the best long poem of our day. Perhaps I had better have said, the first long poem by an American that has managed to emerge since the sweet blight of *The Waste Land*" (203).

65. This is a reference to Burke's "Four Master Tropes" (appendix D) in *A Grammar of Motives*, 503–17.

66. See Williams to Burke, 20 April 1946.

67. Williams, "Russia," 615.

68. See Williams to Burke, 20 April 1946.

69. W. H. Auden (1907–73) taught at Bennington in 1946 and at the New School for Social Research from 1946 to 1947.

70. Laughlin's New Directions Press published *Paterson, Book Two* in 1948.

71. The Williamses stayed with the Abbotts in Buffalo. Charles Abbott (1900–61) was head of library at University of Buffalo and head of the Lockwood Library's Poetry Collection where Williams began to locate his manuscripts and notes in an attempt to keep them in one location (Witemeyer, *William Carlos Williams*, 100). Williams's account of his visits with the Abbotts clearly indicates a close relationship (Williams, *Autobiography*, 323–28). He also orchestrated the honorary degree Williams was to receive there in 1950 (Witemeyer, *William Carlos Williams*, 321).

72. This day Flossie and Williams were staying at the Viewcrest farmhouse just off the Mohawk Trail in Charlemont, Massachusetts (Mariani, *A New World Naked*, 530).

73. Arthur Schlesinger Jr., *The Age of Jackson* (Boston: Little, Brown, 1945).

74. In October 1946, the University of Buffalo awarded Williams an honorary LL.D.

75. *Briarcliff Quarterly* 3, no. 11 (October 1946). Kenneth Rexroth's "A Letter to William Carlos Williams" is included in this issue:
Dear Bill:

When I search the past for you,
Sometimes I think you are like
St. Francis, whose flesh went out
Like a happy cloud from him,
And merged with every lover—
(193)

76. Horace Gregory, *A History of American Poetry, 1900–40* (New York: Harcourt, Brace, 1946); Matthew Josephson, *Stendahl; or, The Pursuit of Happiness* (New York: Doubleday, 1946).

77. The New School for Social Research was chartered in 1919, founded by Thorstein Veblen, Charles Beard, John Dewey, and James Harvey Robinson. Burke started teaching there on a part-time basis in the early thirties (Jay, *Selected Correspondence*, 154).

78. Williams, *A Dream of Love*.

79. Burke, *A Grammar of Motives*.

80. Yvor Winters, *Edwin Arlington Robinson* (Norfolk, Conn.: New Directions, 1946).

81. James Laughlin started a correspondence with Williams in 1933; Laughlin's New Directions published *White Mule* in 1937. Their relationship, professional and personal, continued for the rest of Williams's life. Williams's objections to Winters' book have to do with his merely referring to the passage of the Robinson's poems being discussed without actually quoting from them. Thus, while discussing "Eros Turannos," instead of quoting from the poem, Winters places the following: "See 'Eros Turannos,' pages 32–33 of *Collected Poems of Robinson*" (32).

82. Reich, *Die Funktion des Orgasmus.*

83. See Williams to Burke, 22 December 1946.

84. Ibid.

85. Frederic Wertham, "Calling All Couriers," review of *The Mass Psychology of Fascism,* by Wilhelm Reich. *New Republic,* 2 December 1946, 734–37. A portion of the review is given over to Reich's *The Function of the Orgasm.*

86. See Burke to Williams, 19 November 1945.

87. See Williams to Burke, 22 December 1946.

88. See Burke to Williams, 8 January 1947.

89. See Williams to Burke, 22 December 1946.

90. See Williams to Burke, 9 January, 1947.

91. Theodore Roethke (1908–63), American poet.

92. Burke, *A Grammar of Motives,* 223–26.

93. See Williams to Burke, 31 January 1947.

94. See Williams to Burke, 22 December 1946.

95. Burke, *A Grammar of Motives.*

96. Burke, *A Rhetoric of Motives.*

97. See Williams to Burke, 31 January 1947 for the source of "Hands off."

98. James Donald Adams (1891–1968), *The Shape of Books to Come* (New York: Viking, 1944).

99. Gotthold Ephraim Lessing (1729–81) was an influential dramatist and critic of 18th century. Lessing stressed the Aristotelian unity of action in dramatic construction. Much of the phrasing that occurs in this passage closely resembles Burke's use of Lessing in his essay "Medium as 'Message,'" in *Language as Symbolic Action* (Berkeley: University of California Press, 1966), 413, 416.

100. William Hazlitt, "An Essay on the Principles of Human Action," *The Complete Works William Hazlitt,* 21 vols., ed. P. P. Howe (New York: AMS Press, 1967). Burke's ideas appear to have come from the passage where Hazlitt discusses the effects of a burn on the imagination of a child:

"In like manner I conceive that this idea of pain when combined by the imagination with other circumstances and transferred to the child's future being will still retain its original tendency to give pain, and that the recurrence of the same painful sensation is necessarily regarded with terror and aversion by the child, not from its being conceived of in connection with his own idea, but because it is conceived of as pain. It should also be remembered as the constant principle of all our reasonings, that the impression which the child has of himself as the subject of future pain is never anything more than an idea of imagination, and that he cannot possibly by a kind of anticipation feel that pain as a real sensation a single moment before it exists" (1:19).

At the bottom of his page, Hazlitt appended this note: "I wish the reader to be apprized, that I do not use the word *imagination* as contradistinguished from or opposed to reason, or the faculty by which we reflect upon and compare our ideas, but opposed to sensation, or memory. It has been shewn above that by the word *idea* is not meant a merely abstract idea" (1:19).

101. Three years after this letter, Burke published an article on Roethke: "The Vegetal Radicalism of T. Roethke," *Sewanee Review* 58 (1950): 68–108.

102. Richard P. Blackmur (1904–65), literary critic and lecturer at Princeton.

103. See Burke to Williams, 1 February 1947.

104. See Williams to Burke, 22 December 1946.

105. See Burke to Williams, 1 February 1947.

106. Stan Musial (b. 1920) played first base and the outfield for the St. Louis Cardinals, winning the National League's Most Valuable Player award three times.

107. See Williams to Burke, 22 December 1946.

108. Bonnie Golightly owned the Washington Square Bookstore in New York. The cause for the celebration was the Williams issue of the *Briarcliff Quarterly* (Witemeyer, *William Carlos Williams*, 132).

109. André Breton (1886–1966) French poet, critic, and surrealist advocate of subconscious expression who authored *Que est-ce que le surrealisme?* (1934).

110. Robert Bridges (1844–1930). Williams greatly appreciated Bridges's essay "Testament to Beauty," but he felt that Bridges had fallen short of achieving his aim (Mariani, *A New World Naked*, 547).

111. On 5 May 1945, Williams recorded forty-nine poems on acetate discs (Emily Mitchell Wallace, *A Bibliography of William Carlos Williams*, [Middletown, Conn.: Wesleyan University Press, 1968], 259). Lowell, as the consultant in poetry for the Library of Congress (1947–48), was having the recordings made for the Library (Mariani, *A New World Naked*, 550). Lowell attempted to pass the position down to Williams, but Williams's bad health prevented it (Witemeyer, *William Carlos Williams*, 151).

112. Harry Duncan and Paul Wightman Williams, whom Burke calls "the Cummington lassies" in his letter of 16 August 1949, ran the Cummington Press, located in Cummington, Massachusetts. They published two books by Williams: *The Wedge* and *The Clouds, Aigeltinger, Russia, &* (Cummington, Mass.: Wells College & Cummington Press, 1948).

113. Norman McLeod, married to Vivienne Koch, was the editorial and publication director of *Briarcliff Quarterly*. The name of Williams's article was "Literary Intelligence," (205–8).

114. Thurman Wesley Arnold (1891–1969) published several works on government and economics: *The Symbols of Government* (New Haven: Yale University Press, 1935), *The Folklore of Capitalism* (New Haven: Yale University Press, 1937), *The Bottlenecks of Business* (New York: Reynal and Hitchcock, 1940).

115. Williams was currently working on the second book of his epic. William Carlos Williams, *Paterson, Book Two.* (New York: New Directions, 1948).

116. See Williams to Burke, [1947].

117. John William Mackail, *Virgil and His Meaning to the World of Today* (Boston: Marshal Jones Co., 1922). Burke used the passage to which he refers in his "Poetics in Particular,

Language in General" chapter of *Language as Symbolic Action* (Berkeley: University of California Press, 1966), 36–37. Mackail's text sets down what he terms Virgil's "numerous, complex, and not easily reconcileable" motives. Such a poem must: 1. "be a national poem," 2. "vindicate interconnection of Rome with Italy," 3. "link up Rome and the new nation to the Greek civilization," 4. "emphasize the Roman state as distinct from Greece," 5. "bring well into the foreground of the picture the conflict between Rome and Carthage," 6. "celebrate the feats of the heroes," 7. "find expression for the romantic spirit, in its two principle fields of love and adventure," 8. "Possess direct vital human interest," 9. "connect its figures with larger and more August issues," 10. "exalt the new regime," 11. "draw the lineaments of an ideal rule," 12. "lift itself into a higher sphere, so as to touch the deepest springs of religion and philosophy" (74–76).

118. Burke, *A Rhetoric of Motives.*

119. Rémy de Gourmont, *Dissociations* (Paris: Éditions du Siècle, 1925).

120. Although Burke would find many occasions to discuss Coleridge, his comments here are closely akin to his passage about Coleridge's work in *The Philosophy of Literary Form* (New York: Vintage, 1957), 19–22.

121. Wallace Stevens, "The Figure of the Youth as Virile Poet," *Sewanee Review* 52 (1944): 493–529. Stevens's essay is the third part of a three-part symposium: "Entretiens De Pontigny: 1943."

122. Gustav Aschenbach was the hero of Thomas Mann's *Death in Venice*, which Burke had translated many years before (New York: Dial, 1924). Burke's allusion refers to the episode where Aschenbach, whose desires have finally overwhelmed his will and sense of propriety, uses cosmetics to appear younger for the fourteen-year-old boy, Tadzio, whom he's attempting to please.

123. Not literally true: Williams was thirteen years older than Burke.

124. Williams was at work on *Paterson, Book Two.*

125. See reference to Mackail in Burke to Williams, 14 February 1947.

126. Kenneth Burke, "Ideology and Myth," *Accent* 7 (summer 1947): 195–205.

127. This is a reference to the current president of the United States, Harry Truman. The *New York Times* headlines for Thursday 13 March 1947 read: "TRUMAN ACTS TO SAVE NATIONS FROM RED RULE; ASKS 400 MILLION TO AID GREECE AND TURKEY; CONGRESS FIGHT LIKELY BUT APPROVAL IS SEEN."

128. Thomas Good (1901–70) was a relatively minor British poet and critic. His most significant works are *Out of Circumstance* (London: The Fortune Press, 1954) and *Selected Poems of Thomas Good*, ed. Michael Hamburger (London: St. George's Press, 1974).

129. Julian Symons (1912–94), English author and literary critic.

130. Here Burke refers to his commuting between Andover and Bennington College.

131. Williams, his wife, and her sister Charlotte drove out to Salt Lake City, Utah, where he was paid $500 for his presence at a writers' conference hosted by the University of Utah, 7 July to 18 July 1947 (Witemeyer, *William Carlos Williams*, 141). Allen Tate was there as well; they all stayed in an empty sorority house on campus (Mariani, *A New World Naked*, 546).

132. Josephine Herbst (1892–1969). "Jo and he—husband John Herrmann—put down what cash they had on a small, seventeenth-century sandstone farmhouse nestling in a narrow valley near Erwinna, Pennsylvania, just over the Delaware from Frenchtown, N.J. An old covered bridge spanned the river at that point at one time, but such idyllic things can't last in our day. . . . They'd grow their own vegetables, live cheap, do their own work (o shades of Kenneth Burke), be, in short, the new peasant" (Williams, *Autobiography*, 270).

133. Williams may have been referring to Pope's 1725 "Preface to Shakespeare" where he states that: "One cannot therefore wonder, if Shakespear having at his first appearance no other aim in his writing than to procure a subsistence, directed his endeavours solely to hit the taste and humour that then prevailed" (462). *Poetry and Prose of Alexander Pope*, ed. Aubrey Williams (Boston: Houghton Mifflin, 1969).

134. Frederick Morgan. "William Carlos Williams: Imagery, Rhythm, Form," *Sewanee Review* 55, no. 4 (1947): 675–90. "A poet who deprives himself of meter as well as of the full resources of imagery finds his range of expression severely limited" (690).

135. Robert Lowell (1917–77). Lowell wrote an appreciative essay on *Patterson I*: "Thomas, Bishop, and Williams," *Sewanee Review* 55, no. 3 (July–September 1947): 493–503. This essay caused Williams to begin a correspondence and friendship with Lowell.

136. In August, Williams gave an address at the University of Washington in Seattle (Williams, *Autobiography*, 370).

137. Williams, "The Poem as Field of Action," *Selected Essays*, 280–91.

138. In February, while shoveling his car out of a snowdrift, Williams experienced pains in his chest that were subsequently diagnosed as "anterior thrombosis" (Mariani, *A New World Naked*, 556).

139. The National Institute of Arts and Letters awarded Williams and Allen Tate the Russell Loines Award for Poetry. The $1,000 prize was presented with an introduction by Marianne Moore (Mariani, *A New World Naked*, 469).

140. Williams, *The Clouds, Aigeltinger, Russia, &.*

141. William Carlos Williams, *Many Loves and Other Plays*, ed. J. C. Thirlwall (New York: New Directions, 1961). *The Cure*, included in this volume, is the play to which Williams refers.

142. This is a reference to the Burkes' annual winters in Florida.

143. In summer 1948, Williams's son, Dr. William Eric Williams, began to take over his father's practice at 9 Ridge Rd.

144. See Williams to Burke, 10 May 1948. William Carlos Williams, "The Poem as Field of Action," *Selected Essays* (New York: Random House, 1954), 280–91.

145. Arthur Fisher Bentley (1870–1957) was a social psychologist and author of *Relativity in Man and Society* (New York: Putnam and Sons, 1926). Francis Fergusson (1904–86) was on the faculties of The New School for Social Research, Bennington College, Princeton University, Indiana University, and Rutgers.

146. In the years following Williams's strokes, his son Dr. William Eric Williams often drove him to Andover to visit Burke. Personal interview, 18 November 1993.

147. Williams had taken both his essay "The Poem as Field of Action" *Selected Essays* (New York: Random House, 1954), 280–91, and his *Paterson, Book Two* (New York: New Directions, 1948) on his latest visit to Andover.

148. "Old Ipse Dixit": Aristotle.

149. Theodore Roethke, *The Lost Son and Other Poems,* (New York: Doubleday, 1948). Burke met Roethke at Bennington where they were both teaching. Williams stopped by to visit with them on his way home from a journey to Cummington (Mariani, *A New World Naked,* 493). Roethke solemnized his relationship to these two figures by dedicating to them his *Praise to the End* (Garden City, N.J.: Double Day, 1951). J. R. McLeod, *Theodore Roethke: A Biography* (Kent, Ohio: Kent State University Press, 1973), 7.

150. Kenneth Burke, *A Rhetoric of Motives* (New York: Prentice Hall, 1950).

151. Mark Schorer, Josephine Miles, and Gordon McKenzie, eds., *Criticism: The Foundations of Modern Literary Judgment* (New York: Harcourt, Brace, 1948).

152. This is a reference to Williams's July 1948 train journey to the Seattle Conference (Mariani, *A New World Naked,* 56–63).

153. William Carlos Williams, *Paterson, Book Three.* (New York: New Directions, 1949).

154. Ezra Pound was at St. Elizabeth mental institution as the prisoner/patient of the U.S. government.

155. *Vogue* (February 1949). The caption beneath this photograph taken by Joffe (incidentally, one of the best portraits of the author in his later years) could not have pleased Williams, especially the segment that described him as "one of the important, although comparatively unknown, contemporary American poets" (213).

156. William Carlos Williams, *A Dream of Love* (New York: New Directions, 1948). The performance group "We Present" was not a professional one according to Mariani, *A New World Naked,* 589.

157. After his latest stroke, Williams convalesced at Charles Abbott's place in Buffalo.

158. Francis Golffing and Barbara Gibbs were fairly prolific poets and authors in the forties and fifties, writing many books with such diverse subjects as the spiritual in art, women's movement. They copublished *Possibility: An Essay in Utopian Vision* (Francistown, N.H.: P. Lang, 1986). See note 112, 1945–1963, for "the Cummington Lassies."

159. See Williams to Burke, 8 July 1949.

160. Burke is attempting to parody Williams's poetics as well as to allude to his recent publication, *The Clouds, Aigeltinger, Russia, &.*

161. See Burke to Williams, 16 August 1949. This is Williams's response to Burke's parody of his style.

162. Malcolm Cowley was Burke's longest and oldest friend. At four and three respectively, they grew up in Pittsburgh where Cowley's father was the Burke family doctor. See Jay, *Selected Correspondence* and Selzer, *Kenneth Burke* for the fullest account of their relationship.

163. Williams's epic animosity toward Eliot and his works derived from many differences—aesthetic, political, philosophical, and spiritual. Here, Williams seems to be suggesting that Eliot's conversion to Anglicanism (1924), rather than offering a "cure," represented

a form of spiritual castration. Note, as well, his allusion to the archbishop Thomas Becket of Eliot's *Murder in the Cathedral.*

164. Kenneth Burke was a lecturer at Kenyon College in 1950. This letter is typed on English Department stationary from Kenyon College.

165. Williams's reception of the National Book Award's first Gold Medal for Poetry was announced in January, hence the stir of publicity referred to in the previous sentence. Ezra Pound was awarded the Bollingen Prize for poetry in 1950 for his *Pisan Cantos.* Though these kinds of contradictions have lost their ability to startle us, the controversy centered on the fact that the government-sponsored award was to be given to a man who was being held for treason by another branch of the government. (Mariani, *A New World Naked,* 576).

166. Richard P. Blackmur (1904–65): literary critic and lecturer at Princeton.

167. Williams's dislike for Blackmur may have stemmed from Blackmur's 1939 article on Williams that claimed that his poetry was "a remarkable, but sterile, sport." "John Wheelwright and Dr. Williams," *Partisan Review* (winter 1939): 114.

168. Williams and his wife were guests at Yaddo from 16 July to 2 August 1950. Guests in residence at the same time as Williams include Theodore Roethke, Cid Corman, Richard Eberhart, Gladys Fornell, Nicolas Calas, Eugenie Gershoy, Elaine Gottlieb, John D. Husband, Beryl Harold Levy, Pierre Marcelin, Philippe Thoby Marcelin, Jane Mayhall, Willson Osborne, Robel Paris, Simmons Persons, Hans Sahl, Charles Schucker, Harvey Shapiro, David Wagoner, Ben Weber, Jessamyn West, and Mitsu Yashima. Lesley Leduc, Yaddo Centennial Public Affairs Coordinator, letter to the editor, 4 July 2000.

169. Burke, "The Vegetal Radicalism of T. Roethke."

170. Edgar Allan Poe (1809–49) penned at least part of "The Raven" on the property that became Yaddo. Lesley Leduc, Yaddo Centennial Public Affairs Coordinator, letter to the editor, 23 October 2001.

171. Burke, *A Grammar of Motives.* In appendix C, Burke first copies down a passage from T. S. Eliot's introduction to Marianne Moore's *Selected Poems* (1935) that describes the strategy of imagism: "to introduce a peculiar concentration upon something visual, and to set in motion an expanding succession of concentric feelings" (489). Burke follows this passage with: "I think of William Carlos Williams. For though Williams differs much from Miss Moore in temperament and method, there is an important quality common to their modes of perception. It is what Williams has chosen to call by the trade name of 'objectivist'" (486).

172. Williams spent five weeks at the University of Washington, in Seattle, giving readings and lectures (Mariani, *A New World Naked,* 624). This letter is written on stationary from the Hotel Edmond Meany.

173. William Carlos Williams, *Make Light of It: Collected Stories* (New York: Random House, 1950); Williams, *Later Poems.*

174. In November 1951, T. S. Eliot gave four lectures on "The Aims of Education" at the University of Chicago. Peter Ackroyd, *T. S. Eliot: A Life* (New York: Simon and Schuster, 1984), 302.

175. William Carlos Williams, "Parade's End," *Sewanee Review* 59 (1951): 154–61.

176. R. P. Blackmur, "The Lion and the Honeycomb," *Hudson Review* 3 (winter 1951): 487–507.

177. See Williams to Burke, 20 January 1951.

178. This is a reference to the manuscript that would be printed in *American Scholar* 20, no. 1 (winter 1950–51): 86–104. The "American Scholar Forum" of that issue takes up a discussion of "The New Criticism." The next issue, *American Scholar* 20, no. 2 (spring 1951): 218–31, completed the discussion. The article purports to be a "stenographic record of a discussion held at the home of the Editor on Tuesday evening, August 22, 1950." Present were: Hiram Haydn (editor of *American Scholar*); Kenneth Burke, introduced as a teacher of theory and practice of literary criticism at Bennington College; Allen Tate, introduced as poet and critic, then teaching at New York University; Malcolm Cowley, introduced as one of the best known contemporary American literary critics; William Barrett, associate editor of *Partisan Review* and assistant professor of philosophy at NYU, and Gorham Davis. It is interesting to observe that Williams's support of Gorham Davis's views, though he calls his statements "unbalanced," may have been due to Gorham's attack on Eliot's "contention that a living literature depends upon a living tradition, and that a living tradition depends upon dogma, and that dogma in turn depends upon the definitions of the true church—and that we can have salvation socially, culturally, literally and personally only by acceptance of the church" (104).

179. This is a reference to Gorham Davis.

180. A. Hamilton Thompson (1873–1952).

181. Kenneth Burke, "The Vegetal Radicalism of T. Roethke."

182. Edgar Williams, Williams's brother, was an accomplished architect. His firm built the administration building for the 1939 World's Fair in Flushing, N.Y. (Mariani, *A New World Naked*, 398).

183. Louis Zukofsky (1904–78). Pound sent him to see Williams. They first met in a restaurant, 1 April 1928, where Zukofsky asked Williams to read one of his poems. David Oliphant and Thomas Zigal, eds., *William Carlos Williams and Others* (Austin: University of Texas Press, 1985), 116.

184. Here Burke is referring to Williams, *Autobiography*. In chapters 43 and 44 ("Of Medicine and Poetry" and "The City of the Hospital"), Williams discusses, among other things, the relationship between his writing and his doctoring.

185. Burke, *Language as Symbolic Action*. The passage to which Burke refers has to do with Williams's discourse on the objects of his poems, the people. "They were perfect, they seem to have been born perfect, to need nothing else. They were there, living before me, and I lived beside them, associated with them. . . . It isn't because they fascinated me by their evil doings that they were 'bad' boys or girls. Not at all. It was because they were there full of a perfection of the longest leap, the most unmitigated daring, the longest chances" (288).

Compare this with Burke's own lines in *Language as Symbolic Action*: "The poetic motive does indeed come to a head in the principle of perfection, as exemplified most obviously in the aim to produce a work in which the parts are in perfect relationship to one another. But the principle of perfection should not be viewed in too simple a sense. We should also use the expression ironically, as when we speak of perfect fools and perfect villains. . . . [This shows a] tendency to search out people who, for one reason or another, can be viewed as perfect villains, perfect enemies, and thus, if possible, can become perfect victims of retaliation" (38–39).

186. At the close of chapter 44, "The City of the Hospital," Williams discusses the private heroism, hardships, corruption, and slights that doctors and nurses often endured. Burke's quip about the F. Scott "Fitzgerald-peddlers" in the preceding sentence may be a reference to the recent publication of Arthur Mizener's *The Far Side of Paradise: A Biography of F. Scott Fitzgerald* (Boston: Houghton Mifflin, 1951).

187. Williams, *Autobiography*.

188. This is a reference to a passage in the *Autobiography* where Williams characterized the frank openness ("profligacy") of Nancy Cunard and Iris Tree's lesbian relationship as "asserting a veritable chastity of mind which no one could disturb" (221). In this passage, Burke believed he had found a perfect example of "hierarchic motives," that he had been attempting to explain to the poet.

189. The following is the passage he sent to Williams from the section of his *Rhetoric* titled "Pure Persuasion": "Go through the fantastic list of erotic aberrations in Krafft-Ebing's *Psychopathia Sexualis*. Examine his case histories of those many perverse sufferers with whom (as the translator and editor, Victor Robinson, put it) 'the ability to enjoy or perform the sexual act, in the normal manner, appeared to be the most difficult of the arts.' Look there for evidence of the hierarchic motive. And does it not show immediately, in that vast thesaurus of dominance and submission, with the many intermediate variants? Note the odd identifications whereby one seeks to get, roundabout and at a distance, what he would not take simply and directly. Note the recondite "nobility" in the cult of vile things. Consider how abandonment to forms of sexual expression that society deems degrading could be at once a rebellion and a self-accusation, a morbidly tense acceptance of the very judgments by which one refuses to be bound." *A Rhetoric of Motives*, 224.

190. Williams claimed on 164 of his *Autobiography* that "Kenneth Burke later took over Marianne's *Dial* job."

191. Gilbert Vivian Seldes (1893–1970) was the managing editor of *Dial* from 1920 to 1923.

192. Williams, *Autobiography*. Williams makes the first reference to Burke in comparison to the rustic life of John Herman and Josephine Herbst in their sandstone farmhouse near Erwinna, Pennsylvania (269); the second reference to "old Krumwiede" has to do with Williams's attempting to surprise bedbugs that were menacing the children in his hospital (97).

193. Williams, *Later Poems*, 45, 54. "The A, B, & C of It," and "Sometimes It Turns Dry and the Leaves Fall before They are Beautiful" are the titles to which Burke refers.

194. The passage to which Burke refers occurs in the first stanza:

> The old horse dies slow,
> By gradual degrees
> the fervor of his veins
> matches the leaves' (79)

195. Williams, "Eternity," *Later Poems*, 36.

196. Faust Science (or: knowledge, study of . . .)

> When man lies in his bed
> He thinks of very terrible things,
> Asks himself if great misfortune surrounds him
> While he rocks in the waves of eternity.
>
> When man stands on his feet
> He thinks of almost nothing.
> Smilingly he calls himself a scoundrel
> While he walks along the gallows' path happily.
>
> What concerns me now that I've become older,
> While sitting I remember how in the days of my youth
> With great lamentation and much discomfort
> I was Faust's Faust, my very own seductress.
> (Translated by Adam Steiner)

197. See Williams to Burke, 6 January 1951.

198. Kenneth Burke, *Towards a Better Life* (New York: Harcourt, Brace, 1932).

199. See Burke to Williams, 15 November 1951.

200. On 11 January 1952, Williams gave a talk at the University of Pennsylvania (Mariani, *A New World Naked*, 645).

201. The title of Williams's talk was "The American Spirit in Art," published in *Proceedings of the American Academy of Arts and Letters and the National Institute of Arts and Letters*, vol. 2 (1952), 51–59. Reprinted in *A Recognizable Image: William Carlos Williams on Art and Artists*, ed. Bram Dijkstra (New York: New Directions, 1978), 210–20. "Emerson had called for a national literature as long ago as 1837 in his address to the Harvard divinity students, and here was Williams at the end of 1951 again insisting that the National Institute heed what was truly distinctive in the American art experiment. [He was referring to the American expressionists.] Williams had hardly read through the opening lines of his speech, however, when the catcalls and boos began" (Mariani, *A New World Naked*, 643).

202. Francis Hackett (1883–1962) was an editor for the *New Republic* in the early twenties.

203. Kenneth Laurence Beaudoin (b. 1913).

204. See Williams to Burke, 25 May 1952.

205. Ibid.

206. Louis Grudin, *The Outerland* (New York: Dial, 1951). Although little is known of Williams's relationship with Grudin, it is perhaps telling that Grudin authored an attack on T. S. Eliot: *Mr. Eliot Among the Nightingales* (Paris: Drake, 1932).

207. In 1952 and 1958, Burke served as a lecturer at the University of Indiana. In 1958, he served as a Fellow in the School of Letters from 14 June to 26 July 1958. "The School of Letters (now defunct) had been brought to Indiana from Kenyon College by Indiana's president, Herman Wells." Kenneth R. Johnson, Chair of Department of English, Indiana University at Bloomington, letter to the editor, 16 November 2000.

208. Kenneth Burke, "Motives and Motifs in the Poetry of Marianne Moore." *Accent* 2 (spring 1942): 157–69.

209. Adelbert von Chamisso, *Peter Schlemihl* (Vienna: P. Stern, 1834).

210. Peter Richard McKeon. "One of Burke's tutors at the time [the early twenties] was Richard McKeon, then a young graduate student working on a dissertation on Spinoza. McKeon had befriended Burke on their ferry rides from New Jersey to Columbia a half dozen years before" (Selzer, *Kenneth Burke*, 41).

211. This blessing from Burke is a reference to Williams's most recent stroke, suffered in August.

212. On the reverse side of this letter, Burke sent the following note to Marcus "Marc" Cook Connelly (1890–1980), Pulitzer prize-winning dramatist (1930) and Yale professor (1947), who was also a member of the American Academy of Arts and Letters. Williams was awarded the Gold Medal posthumously in 1963.

November 11, 1952
Dear Marc Connelly,

Sorry I can't be there, to vote on the golden medal for poesy. But I have a notion—and I offer it for what it may be worth.

I think we should make a three-year decision. (I say this, realizing that my ignorance of the conditions may invalidate what I have to say.)

I think we should give the medal, in some succession or other, to three I consider a triptych: W. C. Williams, Marianne Moore, Wallace Stevens. I don't care what order, as long as it's all part of one parcel. But tentatively I'd suggest the order I have here used.

Maybe this suggestion musses up the rules. I don't know. But I devoutly believe every word of it.

Sincerely,

213. This is a reference to Williams's recovering from his latest stroke.

214. Ezra Pound. While confined at St. Elizabeth's asylum from 1945 to 1958, Pound sporadically fired off gnomic or scornful notes to Williams.

215. In May 1953, Elizabeth Bowen (1899–1973) delivered her "Blaysfield Address" to the American Academy of Arts and Letters (Victoria Glendinning, *Elizabeth Bowen* [New York: Knopf], 263). Burke was elected a member of the Academy in 1946; Williams was elected a member in 1958.

216. This note is from Williams to Burke; he made no other mark on the page except his signature on the right hand margin.

217. R. W. B. Lewis may originally have met Burke at Bennington College. He cited Burke's *Grammar of Motives* in his *The American Adam* two years later (Chicago: University of Chicago Press, 1955), 98.

218. Cranberry Lake is situated four miles from Burke's house in Andover, New Jersey.

219. Dr. William E. Williams Jr. often drove his father up to Burke's place after his strokes.

220. Williams was recovering from his latest stroke.

221. Norman Holmes Pearson (1909–75), 1938 editor of *The Oxford Anthology of American Literature* (in which he included eleven of Williams's poems) and professor at Yale (1941). As a collector for the American Collection at Yale, Pearson remained associated with Williams over the years, once asking him for a play that a colleague of his might use at the drama department. In an editorial capacity, he submitted a selected list of Williams's poems he felt should be included in *The Selected Poems*, published in 1949 (Witemeyer, *William Carlos Williams* 147). The recordings to which Williams refers here may be those eight poems and one selection from *Paterson* that were recorded at Kenneth Burke's house, 21 June 1951 (Wallace, *Bibliography*, 261–62).

222. Don Francisco de Quevedo, *A Dog and the Fever*, trans. William Carlos Williams and Raquel Helene Williams (Connecticut: Shoe String Press, 1954). Williams undertook the translation in order to give his mother a meaningful project (Williams, *Autobiography*, 350–51).

223. Milton Hindus, ed. *Leaves of Grass; One Hundred Years After* (Stanford, Calif.: Stanford University Press, 1955). Williams's essay included in that volume was "An Essay on *Leaves of Grass*" (22–31); Burke's contribution was "Policy Made Personal: Whitman's Verse and Prose—Salient Traits" (74–108).

224. Originally, John C. Thirlwall, professor of English at CCNY, was to write Williams's biography, but when the poet saw Thirlwall's first draft of his introduction to the *Selected Letters*, he realized it was not to be. Prior to that realization, Thirlwall had worked with Williams for at least a decade in preparation for such a project and thus had access to all the manuscripts stashed away in the poet's attic study (Mariani, *A New World Naked*, 685).

225. Allen Tate (1899–1979). The struggle between Tate and Burke ranged all the way back to his publication of *Counter-Statement* in the early thirties and ultimately centered on the dispute of the relationship of a work of art to its reader. Tate, predictably, argued for the autonomy of art; whereas Burke held to the idea that art was designed with intention of persuading the auditor (Selzer, *Kenneth Burke*, 155–58).

226. Jeremy Bentham (1748–1832), English philosopher, political theorist, and founder of utilitarianism. In Burke's *A Rhetoric of Motives*, he attacks Bentham's view of rhetoric as mere metaphoric deception.

227. This is a reference to the first passage of *Paterson, Book One*.

228. Sophocles, "The Women of Trachis," trans. Ezra Pound, *Hudson Review* 6 (winter 1954): 487–523.

229. Five audio recordings were made by Williams in 1954; the first was a reissue of a 1949 recording; the second was made for NBC radio program, "Anthology" (March); the third was again for NBC, two days later; the forth was a recording made at the University of Puerto Rico (March); and the fifth, the most likely candidate for this reference, was done by International Broadcasting Services for the Voice of America (June) (Wallace, *Bibliography*, 262–64).

230. William Carlos Williams, "Painting in the American Grain," *Art News* 4 (June 1954): 20–23.

231. William Carlos Williams, "Of Ashphodel," *Poetry* 86 (April 1955): 99–107.

232. Williams is referring to the new edition of Whitman's poems. See Williams to Burke, 17 June 1954.

233. These are Burke's preliminary explorations toward composing an essay on Whitman for the article referred to in Williams to Burke, 17 June 1954.

234. William Carlos Williams, "Comment: Wallace Stevens," *Poetry* 87, no. 4 (1956): 234–39.

235. See Burke to Williams, 31 October 1953.

236. See Burke to Williams, 19 July 1954.

237. Williams undertook a three-week western tour, starting the second week in May. It was a grueling reading tour that took in schools at St. Louis, Seattle, Chicago, Santa Barbara, San Francisco, and more. Noteworthy, too, is that upon his return, the staff at Passaic General Hospital presented him with a new electric typewriter to help counteract his stroke-enfeebled hands (Mariani, *A New World Naked*, 688), a fact which explains the altered type style for the remainder of his letters.

238. Denise Levertov (1923–97). The poem to which Burke refers is "Something," *Collected Earlier Poems, 1940–1960* (New York: New Directions, 1979), 61–63. See also *The Letters of Denise Levertov and William Carlos Williams*, ed. Christopher MacGowan (New York: New Directions, 1998), 27. Levertov was successful in gaining a Guggenheim in 1962.

239. Kenneth Burke, *Book of Moments* (Los Altos, Calif.: Hermes, 1955).

240. Burke, *Book of Moments*, 75–77. The line to which Williams refers reads: "Far away I should be" (75).

241. Henry Allen Moe was a trustee for the Guggenheim Foundation.

242. See Burke to Williams, 18 July 1955.

243. Burke, "The Monster" and "Atlantis," *Book of Moments*, 74, 61.

244. Burke, "Rhapsody under The Autumn Moon," *Book of Moments*, 75–77.

245. Burke, *Book of Moments*.

246. Edward Sapir, *Language: An Introduction to the Study of Speech* (New York: Harcourt, Brace and Co., 1959). The passage to which Burke refers is on page 230.

247. Harold Rosenberg (1906–78). Distinguished art critic and member of League of American Writers with Malcolm Cowley, Burke, and others (Malcolm Cowley, *The Dream of the Golden Mountains* [New York: Viking Press, 1964], 298).

248. See Burke to Williams, 5 September 1955.

249. See Williams to Burke, 19 July 1955.

250. Kenneth Burke, "Rhapsody under The Autumn Moon," *Book of Moments* (Los Altos, Calif.: Hermes, 1955), 75–77.

251. The short story to which Williams refers here is "The Farmers' Daughters" (Mariani, *A New World Naked*, 691).

252. Hannah Josephson (1901–76), wife of Matthew Josephson. Libbie enclosed the following letter from Hannah:

The American Academy of Arts and Letters

633 West 155th Street, New York

Sherman

Sept. 1, 1955

Dear Lib,

Here is the dope: Louis Untermeyer can get Decca Records, as a favor to him, to do the Williams Record on two sides, (ten-inch) 10 minutes each side, at $20.00 per side for the acetate and $2.00 a piece for the pressings, minimum of 10 records, total about $60. to $70., depending on the number of records made. Audio-video, at 730 Fifth Avenue, (Mr. Merson is the man to speak or write to) will do the acetate at $17.50 per side, (ten-inch) 10 minutes each side, and $1.85 a piece for the pressings, minimum of 11 copies, the same price up to 25 copies, and less, I believe for a larger number. That would amount to $54.25 for 11 copies, as you see, one or two of which would have to be sent to the Library of Congress for copyright. A twelve-inch record would be higher.

What could the Academy do toward paying for this? I am not authorized to do more than purchase what records I need, and I could justifiably say I need two records for the exhibition, in case I want to play both sides for the exhibition. But who would put up the other $45.00? You need an organization to sell even a small number of recordings. I have tried unsuccessfully to sell the idea to Caedmon, and Decca, Untermeyer tells me, does not want it. I shall write to the National Council of Teachers of English one of these days, and ask if they would try to market it, but of course they would want all the poems to be classroom material, and I just wonder about *Apres le Bain.*

Let me know if you have any further ideas.

Love,

Hannah

253. Anthony "Butchie" Burke, Burke's first son.

254. On 6 June 1954, Williams recorded eighteen poems for Caedmon Publishers. It is difficult to determine whether or not these eighteen are the subject of Hannah Josephson's correspondence.

255. William Carlos Williams, *Journey to Love* (New York: Random House, 1955).

256. Williams, "Asphodel, That Greeny Flower," *Journey to Love.*

257. Ibid.

258. Williams, "The Sparrow," *Journey to Love,* 10–15.

259. Williams, "A Negro Woman," *Journey to Love*, 5–7.

260. The refrain of Spenser's to which Burke refers is "Sweete Themmes runne softly, till I end my Song."

261. Marianne Moore, "Things Others Never Notice," *Predilections* (New York: Viking, 1955), 136–39.

262. David McDowell was an editor at Random House.

263. See Burke to Williams, 7 November 1955.

264. Winfield Townley Scott (1910–68). In early June 1955, on the return leg of their Western tour, the Williams visited Scott at his Sante Fe home (Mariani, *A New World Naked*, 688).

265. Williams gave a reading at the university and they stayed with the Abbotts (Mariani, *A New World Naked*, 691).

266. The play to which he refers is *The Cure*, "an allegory of Williams's own questionable recovery" (Mariani, *A New World Naked*, 649).

267. Williams, "The Birth of Venus," *Later Poems*, 187.

268. Williams, "The Sparrow," *Journey to Love*, 10–15.

269. Eleanor "Happy" Duva Leacock, Burke's daughter, was a professor of anthropology at the City College of New York.

270. After Williams's health began to deteriorate, he stopped driving.

271. "Scene-act and agent-act ratios," the first components in his chapter "Container and the Thing Contained" are part of Burke's study of motives called Dramatism. *A Grammar of Motives*, 3–20.

272. John Daniel Wild (1902–72) authored such philosophical works as *Introduction to Realistic Philosophy* (1948), *Plato's Modern Enemies and the Theory of Natural Law* (1953), *Challenge to Existentialism* (1955), and *Human Freedom and Social Order* (1959).

273. Williams was awarded a $5,000 fellowship from the American Academy of Poets in February 1957.

274. During 1957 and 1958, Burke was a fellow for the Center for Advanced Study in the Behavioral Sciences at Stanford University.

275. *The Selected Letters of William Carlos Williams,* ed. John C. Thirlwall (New York: McDowell, 1957).

276. Williams's 14 April 1924 letter to Burke is on page 105 of *The Selected Letters of William Carlos Williams.*

277. Burke, *The Philosophy of Literary Form* (New York: Vintage, 1957). Vintage Books were published by Alfred A. Knopf and Random House.

278. "Better Half": Libbie Burke. She was the principal typist of his manuscripts.

279. "The Center" is the Center for Advanced Study in the Behavioral Sciences. His talk was derived from the first portion of *A Grammar of Motives*, "Introduction: The Five Key Terms of Dramatism," xv–xxiii.

280. Kenneth Burke, "Apostrophe Before Desisting," *Collected Poems* (Berkeley: University of California Press, 1968), 243–44.

281. On 11 October 1958, Williams suffered the first stroke since the big one he had had in August 1952.

282. *4 Other Countries* was the title of Louis Zukofky's booklet (Mariani, *A New World Naked*, 744).

283. See Burke to Williams, 18 October 1958.

284. This is Burke's response to Williams's having had a stroke. See Williams to Burke, 24 October 1958.

285. See Williams to Burke, 24 October 1958.

286. Yvor Winters and Robert Frost. The first week of November 1958, Johns Hopkins hosted the poetry festival (Mariani, *A New World Naked*, 743).

287. This was a Williams short story that was first published in *Blast* magazine in 1933 (Mariani, *A New World Naked*, 345).

288. This is a reference to the depression Williams suffered after his latest stroke (Mariani, *A New World Naked*, 744).

289. "McD" is a reference to the publisher of his book: William Carlos Williams, *Yes, Mrs. Williams* (New York: McDowell, Obolensky, 1959).

290. William Carlos Williams, *Many Loves*, 432. The play, directed by Julian Beck, opened at the Living Theater in New York, 13 January 1959, and it ran for nearly a year.

291. Burke did compose a poem with such a title that does conclude with a wry diagnosis not unlike Williams's own: "The Momentary, Migratory Symptom," *Book of Moments* (Los Altos, Calif.: Hermes, 1955), 6.

292. John C. Thirlwall.

293. Louis Zukofsky. "A / Round of Fiddles" are the first two lines of Zukofsky's "A 1–7."

294. Carl Friedrich Von Marcus (1802–62), German physician; and Major Douglas, English economist, whose "Social Credit" theory of the early 1930s attracted the attention and advocacy of Ezra Pound (Mariani, *A New World Naked*, 348).

295. I have sinned, I have sinned.

296. In February, Williams and Flossie spent a month with Burke and Libbie in Englewood, Florida. See Burke to Florence Williams, 5 March 1963.

297. Williams, "Song," *Selected Poems*, 170.

298. After his latest stroke, Williams had not recovered the full use of his right hand.

299. Burke served as a lecturer at Penn State in 1960.

300. This is a reference to a list of questions that Burke sent Bill in preparation for the long article he had promised to compose on the poet's works. See Burke to Williams, 8 April 1960.

301. Williams, "Song," *Selected Poems*, 170.

302. See Burke to Williams, 16 April 1960.

303. Williams remained mute with regard to a list of questions Burke had sent him. See Burke to Williams, 8 April 1960.

304. Burke's comment may have been provoked by the fact that Lowell had nominated Jarrell for membership in the National Institute of Arts and Letters in 1960. Mary Jarrell, ed., *Randall Jarrell's Letters* (Boston: Houghton Mifflin, 1985), 443.

305. See Burke to Williams, 31 May 1960.

306. Marsden Hartley (1877–1943), American painter and long-time friend to Williams. "He was one of the most frustrated men I knew. Marsden was happiest toward the end of his life among the Down East fishermen of the Maine coast. A tragic figure. I really loved the man, but we didn't always get along together, except at a distance" (Williams, *Autobiography*, 171).

307. M. L. Rosenthal, "Salvo for William Carlos Williams," *Nation*, 31 May 1958, 497–502. Included in this celebration of Williams's 75th anniversary is an open letter from Louis Zukofsky (500) and a poem from Richard Eberhart: "To Bill Williams" (501). The index to which Burke refers includes two entries of his own works: "Civil Defense," 24 September 1960; "The Poet, on his Grand Climacteric," 11 March 1961.

308. Kenneth Burke, *Towards a Better Life*. The following reference to Carlyle occurs in his *A Rhetoric of Motives*, 120.

309. See Burke to Williams, 16 April 1960.

310. Of "Prologue in Heaven," Burke writes Malcolm Cowley on 23 June: "Today, in a way, I guess I finished a book, though I'm not sure that I'll use this last section in the book. It's a dialogue between The Lord and Satan, in which both of them talk suspiciously alike, because both of them talk suspiciously like one K. Burke, in a mood of weighty academic levity" (Jay, *Selected Correspondence*, 335). Burke was debating whether or not to include this essay as the last section of *The Rhetoric of Religion*, published in 1961.

311. William Carlos Williams, "The Polar Bear," *Pictures from Brueghel* (New York: New Directions, 1962), 16.

312. Williams, *Many Loves*; *The Cure*, included in this volume, was started "in 1952 when Williams was recuperating from a superficial stroke" (436).

313. Williams, *Yes, Mrs. Williams*.

314. The tape to which Libbie refers here was recorded, as her later comment verifies, on 21 June 1951 at Andover; the recording contained eight poems and one selection from *Paterson* (Wallace, *Bibliography*, 261).

315. Peggy and Malcolm Cowley were frequent visitors to the Burkes' Andover retreat.

316. See Burke to Williams, 8 August 1960.

317. In July, Williams and Thirlwall went to Indiana University to hear Mary Ellen Solt's presentation on Williams's variable foot (Mariani, *A New World Naked*, 758).

318. William Carlos Williams, *The Build Up* (New York: Random House, 1952).

319. The home of Flossie's family, the Hermans, was in Monroe, New York, forty miles from Rutherford.

320. In February 1951, *A Dream of Love* was staged by the National Arts Club (Mariani, *A New World Naked*, 761).

321. Williams, *Brueghel*.

322. Kenneth Burke, "Commentary on 'Timon of Athens,'" Laurel Shakespeare Edition of *Timon of Athens*, ed. Francis Fergusson (New York: Dell, 1963), 115–24.

323. This image occurs again in Burke's memorial article on Williams: "William Carlos Williams, 1883–1963," *New York Review of Books* 1 (special issue of spring and summer

books): 45–47 [also in *Language as Symbolic Action* (Berkeley: University of California Press, 1966)].

324. Yes, the world is stupid. But no, you have not sent me a book.

325. Burke taught at the University of Chicago in the late thirties, late sixties, and late seventies (Jay, *Selected Correspondence*, 411). "Burke served as a lecturer in the Department of English during the summer quarter of 1938. He taught English 306, 'The Psychology of Poetic Form,' and Literature 352, 'Samuel Taylor Coleridge.' Burke was solicited for the position by Richard P. McKeon and arrived in Chicago in early June (summer quarter began on June 20th; Burke arrived a few days earlier). The summer quarter ended on August 26, 1938." Ben Stone, Reference Assistant, University of Chicago Library, letter to the editor, 25 October 2000.

326. Burke, *Language as Symbolic Action*.

327. Robert Lowell, "William Carlos Williams," *Hudson Review* (winter 1961–62): 530–37. [The volume also contains four poems by Williams, 527–29.]

328. Kenneth Burke, "On a Photo of Myself," *Collected Poems, 1915–67* (Berkeley: University of California Press, 1968), 206.

329. Williams, *Brueghel*.

330. Williams, "Desert Music," *Brueghel*, 117.

331. Burke has discovered a passage from Williams's poem "Calypsos" in *Brueghel* that refers to a rooster with two hens behind a museum (57).

332. Williams, "The Corn Harvest," *Brueghel*, 9.

333. The "precious wobbly signature" is Williams's heroic attempt to overcome the disability of his latest strokes.

Bibliography

Ackroyd, Peter. *T. S. Eliot: A Life*. New York: Simon and Schuster, 1984.

Bak, Hans. *Malcolm Cowley: The Formative Years*. Athens: University of Georgia Press, 1993.

Blakesley, David. "Taking Burke On(line): The Kenneth Burke Bibliography and Archival Project." 2002. http://linnell.english.purdue.edu/burke

———. "William Carlos Williams's Influence on Kenneth Burke." Paper presented at the Modern Language Association conference, Toronto, December 1997.

Bremen, Brian. *William Carlos Williams and the Diagnostics of Culture*. New York: Oxford University Press, 1993.

Burke, Kenneth. *Attitudes toward History*. 2 vols. New York: New Republic, 1937.

———. *Book of Moments*. Los Altos, Calif.: Hermes, 1955.

———. *The Complete White Oxen*. Berkeley: University of California Press, 1968.

———. *Counter-Statement*. 1931. Reprint, Chicago: University of Chicago Press, 1953.

———. "David Wassermann." *Little Review* 8 (autumn 1921): 24–37.

———. *A Grammar of Motives*. New York: Prentice-Hall, 1945.

———. "Heaven's First Law." Review of *Sour Grapes*, by William Carlos Williams. *Dial* 72 (February 1922): 197–200.

———. *Language as Symbolic Action*. Berkeley: University of California Press, 1966.

———. "The Method of William Carlos Williams." *Dial* 82 (February 1927): 94–98.

———. *Permanence and Change: An Anatomy of Purpose*. New York: New Republic, 1935.

———. *The Philosophy of Literary Form: Studies in Symbolic Action*. Baton Rouge: Louisiana State University Press, 1941.

———. Review of *The Influence of Puritanism,* by John Steven Flynn. *Literary Review* (1 February 1921): 2.

———. *A Rhetoric of Motives*. New York: Prentice-Hall, 1950.

———. *Towards a Better Life: Being a Series of Epistles, or Declamations*. New York: Harcourt, Brace, 1932.

Cowley, Malcolm. *The Dream of the Golden Mountains*. New York: Viking, 1964.

———. *Exile's Return*. New York: Viking, 1934.

Foss, Sonja K., Karen A. Foss, and Robert Trapp. "Kenneth Burke." in *Contemporary Perspectives on Rhetoric*, 153–88. Prospect Heights, Ill.: Waveland Press, 1985.

Frank, Armin. *Kenneth Burke*. New York: Twayne, 1969.

Glendinning, Victoria. *Elizabeth Bowen*. New York: Knopf, 1978.

Harris, Wendell V. "The Critics Who Made Us: Kenneth Burke." *Sewannee Review* (summer 1988): 452–63.

Hindus, Milton, ed. *Leaves of Grass; One Hundred Years After*. Stanford, Calif.: Stanford University Press, 1955.

Irmscher, William F. "Kenneth Burke." In *Traditions of Inquiry*, edited by John C. Brereton. New York: Oxford University Press, 1985: 105–35.

Jarrell, Mary, ed. *Randall Jarrell's Letters*. Boston: Houghton Mifflin Co., 1985.

Jay, Paul. "Kenneth Burke." *Dictionary of Literary Biography: Modern American Critics 1920–1955*, vol. 63, edited by Gregory S. Jay, 67–86. Detroit: Gale Research Company, 1978.

————. *The Selected Correspondence of Kenneth Burke and Malcolm Cowley, 1915–1981*. New York: Viking Press, 1988.

Josephson, Matthew. *Life among the Surrealists: A Memoir*. New York: Holt, Rinehart, and Winston, 1962.

Kazin, Alfred. *On Native Grounds*. New York: Reynal and Hitchcock, 1942.

Kenner, Hugh. "The Rhythm of Ideas." *Sagetrieb* 3, no. 2 (fall 1984): 37–42.

Kreymborg, Alfred. *Troubadour, An Autobiography*. New York: Boni and Liveright, 1925.

Lowell, Robert. "William Carlos Williams." *Hudson Review* (winter 1961–62): 530–37.

Mackail, John William. *Virgil and His Meaning to the World of Today*. Boston: Marshal Jones, 1922.

Mariani, Paul. *A Usable Past: Essays on Modern & Contemporary Poetry*. Amherst: University of Massachussets Press, 1984.

————. *William Carlos Williams: A New World Naked*. New York: Norton & Co., 1981.

McAlmon, Robert. *Being Geniuses Together, 1920–1930*. New York: Doubleday & Co., 1968.

————. "Essentials." *Little Review* 7 (1920): 69–71.

————. *Robert McAlmon and the Lost Generation: A Self-Portrait*. Edited by Robert E. Knoll. Lincoln: University of Nebraska Press, 1962.

McLeod, J. R. *Theodore Roethke: A Biography*. Kent, Ohio: Kent State University Press, 1973.

Oliphant, David and Thomas Zigal, eds. *William Carlos Williams and Others* Austin: University of Texas Press, 1985.

Reich, Wilhelm. *Die Funktion des Orgasmus*. New York: Orgone Institute Press, 1942.

Selzer, Jack. *Kenneth Burke in Greenwich Village: Conversing with the Moderns, 1915–1931*. Madison: University of Wisconsin Press, 1996.

Shi, David E. *Matthew Josephson, Bourgeois Bohemian*. New Haven: Yale University Press, 1981.

Simons, Herbert W., and Trevor Melia. *The Legacy of Kenneth Burke*. Madison: University of Wisconsin Press, 1989.

Thirlwall, J. C., ed. *The Selected Letters of William Carlos Williams*. New York: McDowell, 1957.

Wallace, Mitchell. *A Bibliography of William Carlos Williams*. Middletown, Conn.: Wesleyan University Press, 1968.

Warnock, Tilly. "Kenneth Burke." In *Encyclopedia of Rhetoric and Composition*, edited by Theresa Enos. New York: Garland Publishing, 1996: 90–92.

Weaver, Michael. *William Carlos Williams: The American Background*. Cambridge: Cambridge University Press, 1971.

Williams, William Carlos. *The Autobiography of William Carlos Williams*. New York: New Directions, 1967.

———. *The Clouds, Aigeltinger, Russia, &*. Cummington, Mass.: Wells College & Cummington Press, 1948.

———. *The Collected Earlier Poems*. New York: Objectivist Press, 1934.

———. *The Collected Later Poems*. Norfolk, Conn.: New Directions, 1963.

———. *I Wanted to Write a Poem: The Autobiography of the Works of a Poet*. Reported and edited by Edith Heal. Boston: Beacon, 1958.

———. "Improvisations." *The Little Review* 6, no. 2 (June 1919): 52–59.

———. *Kora in Hell: Improvisations*. Boston: Four Seas, 1920.

———. *Many Loves and Other Plays*. Edited by J. C. Thirlwall. New York: New Directions, 1961.

———. *Paterson*. New York: New Directions, 1963.

———. *Pictures From Brueghel*. New York: New Directions, 1962.

———. *Selected Essays of William Carlos Williams*. New York: Random House, 1954.

———. *Sour Grapes: A Book of Poems*. Boston: Four Seas, 1921.

———. *The Wedge*. Cummington, Mass.: Cummington Press, 1944.

Witemeyer, Hugh, ed. *William Carlos Williams and James Laughlin: Selected Letters*. New York: Norton & Co., 1989.

Index